Women Musicians of Uzbekistan

NEW PERSPECTIVES ON GENDER IN MUSIC

Editorial Advisors
Susan C. Cook
Beverley Diamond

A list of books in the series appears at the end of this book.

Women Musicians of Uzbekistan

From Courtyard to Conservatory

TANYA MERCHANT

University of Illinois Press
URBANA, CHICAGO, AND SPRINGFIELD

Publication of this book was supported by the AMS 75 PAYS Endowment of the American Musicological Society, funded in part by the National Endowment for the Humanities and the Andrew W. Mellon Foundation, as well as by the University of California, Santa Cruz Arts Research Institute and the University of California, Santa Cruz Arts Dean's Fund for Excellence.

© 2015 by the Board of Trustees
of the University of Illinois
All rights reserved
Manufactured in the United States of America
1 2 3 4 5 C P 5 4 3 2 1
∞ This book is printed on acid-free paper.

Library of Congress Cataloging-in-Publication Data
Merchant, Tanya, author.
Women musicians of Uzbekistan : from courtyard to conservatory / Tanya Merchant.
 pages   cm. — (New perspectives on gender in music)
Includes bibliographical references and index.
ISBN 978-0-252-03953-9 (cloth : alk. paper)
ISBN 978-0-252-08106-4 (pbk. : alk. paper)
ISBN 978-0-252-09763-8 (e-book)
1. Women musicians—Uzbekistan. 2. Feminism and music—Uzbekistan. 3. Music—Social aspects—Uzbekistan. 4. Music—Uzbekistan—20th century—History and criticism. 5. Music—Uzbekistan—21st century—History and criticism. 6. Uzbekistan—Social life and customs.
I. Title.
ML345.U9M47   2015
780.82′09587—dc23   2014046922

Contents

Preface   vii

Acknowledgments   xi

Introduction: The Stories Women Tell about Their Music   1

1. Beyond the Canon: Feminizing the National Project through Traditional Music   42
2. Ancient Treasures, Modernized: Women's Dutar Ensembles and Arranged Folk Music   78
3. Like Tereshkova in the Cosmos: Women at the Forefront of Western Art Music   109
4. "Greetings to the Uzbek People!": Popular Music in Public and Private Settings   131
5. Marrying Past, Present, and Future: The Essential Work of Wedding Music   156

Conclusion: Women's Musical Communities Performing the Nation   170

Notes   185

Glossary   191

Works Cited   193

Index   205

Preface

In writing about Central Asia, issues of language are as complex and changeable as is the geography. First, the two source languages for the foreign terms that I gloss in this book are Uzbek and Russian. It can be confusing to navigate the code-switching, so for clarification, when a term comes from the Uzbek language, the gloss is left unmarked. Russian terms presented in text have their translations preceded by "Russian:". This is done to represent the postindependence norm of speaking and publishing in the Uzbek language, even though a significant amount of communication continues in the Russian language, especially when discussing Soviet history. My transliteration of Russian is based on the Library of Congress's system, but modified to avoid confusing diacritics so that words read as closely as possible to the way they sound.

In this book, I do my best to use the Latin script versions of Uzbek words that became standard when the Uzbek government switched from Cyrillic to Latin script in 1995. The majority of Uzbek terms are based on that Latin script, which uses apostrophes to delineate the pronunciation of two letters further back in the throat. *G'* is often described as a *Persian G* and sounds gargled in the back of the throat; *O'* is the pronunciation of *O* further in the throat placing it between long *O* and long *U* in English. It is also worth noting that the unmarked *O* is pronounced flatter and more like "ah" than the long *O* in American English. Levin (1996) and others often transliterated this *O* from the Cyrillic as *Â*, which is no longer necessary given the new Latin script conventions.

The only exceptions to my employment of accepted Uzbek spellings in Latin script occur when I am quoting others' texts or when a certain spelling is well known and often used in common English (for instance, the city of Bukhara, which is spelled Buhoro in Uzbek Latin script, and the word Uzbek, which is spelled *O'zbek* by current Uzbek conventions), or when my consultants refer to places or institutions by their Soviet-era names (which could be in either the Russian or Uzbek language and sometimes have different spelling conventions). One of the most notable exceptions to the current standard Uzbek spellings is the dutar, the instrument that provided much of my access into Uzbek musical spaces. In ethnomusicological literature, the standard spelling *dutar* (transliterated from its Russian-language spelling) is well established by Slobin (1971), Levin (1996), Sultanova (2005), and others. Using current Uzbek spelling rules, the instrument is spelled *dutor*, but I concede to the existing standard.

It is also worth noting that respectful address in the Uzbek language requires the use of suffixes that express one's relation to the person addressed in terms of familial relationship. I use them in this volume when discussing women that I know well. My private music teachers generally preferred this style of address to the more formal terms *domla* (teacher) or *ustoz* (master), and it was generally the way their students addressed them, although they would often use the term *ustoz* when discussing primary teachers in the third person. For example, my dutar teacher Malika Ziyaeva is referred to in my work as Malika *opa*, which literally means "Malika older sister." It would not be seemly to refer to Malika opa with only her first name, and using her last name would lend undue formality to our relationship. I use the appropriate Uzbek convention and refer to her and others with the familial term *opa* throughout this work. Terms such as *opa* (older sister), *aka* (older brother), *amaki* (maternal uncle), and *qaynona* (mother-in-law) are commonly tagged onto people's first names to express both respect and to locate one's place in the age hierarchy (as a result, there are sometimes discussions about which of the familial referents is most appropriate). Such familial labels are also often used without names attached in these contexts, providing a specific challenge for documentation.

Another complex and difficult issue when dealing with Central Asia is the changing geography as it intersects with ever-evolving conventions in alphabets, spelling, and place names. One important example is the name of the region in the tsarist and pre-tsarist era: *Turkiston* is the current spelling in the Uzbek language's official Latin script of a term often spelled *Turkestan* or *Turkistan*. The term refers to the region comprising what are now five separate nations: Kazakhstan, Kyrgyzstan, Tajikistan, Turkmenistan, and Uzbekistan. This is the region first conquered by the Russian empire during the tsarist era in the 1860s and called Russian Turkestan. After the Bolshevik revolution of 1917, it became the Turkestan Autonomous Region, with separate autonomous regions corresponding with the city-states of Bukhara and Khiva. The larger region was divided into separate Soviet republics in the 1920s and 1930s with geography similar to what now exists. For a thorough discussion of the politics of dividing the region during the early Soviet era, see Khalid (2006).

The code-switching inherent in a city with such a long history of belonging to various empires and engaging multiple cultures and languages is also filtered through my changing experience as a fieldworker. Many of the landmarks in Tashkent were renamed in the independence era, but are often referred to with their Soviet-era name in conversation (Adams [2010, 32] provides a helpful list of both sets of place names). My linguistic development added further complications. During my first trip to Uzbekistan, most of my interactions with people occurred in Russian, as I was only beginning to learn Uzbek at the time. The colonial implications were not lost on me, especially since I was warned before setting out that my primary teacher Malika opa did not like to speak Russian. Gradually, with the help of Malika opa, my other teachers, and my hosts, Uzbek replaced Russian as my primary field language—although Russian continued to have utility with the significant Russian (and non-Uzbek-speaking) population in the city. The result is that my early field research—especially that accomplished in 2002 and 2003—is much more framed with the linguistic boundaries set up by Russian than my later work.

Acknowledgments

I would like to acknowledge the many generous and talented Uzbek musicians and scholars who share their art, knowledge, and time with me as I continue my work on Central Asian music. My gratitude especially goes to the mentors and teachers who have spent time grappling with the challenge of instructing me on the dutar: Malika Ziyaeva, Ro'zibi Hodjayeva, Razia Sultanova, and Temur Mahmudov, as well as Komila Aminova, whose tireless efforts to teach me to sing maqom improved both my voice and my dutar playing. The music that these teachers guide me through continues to frame my understanding of Central Asian culture. Other musicians who have helped shape my work are too many to list, and I apologize for leaving important colleagues out. However, my thanks go to Firuza Abdurahimova, Faizila Shukurova, Viloyat Akilova, Gulshod Ataboeva, Dilbara Abdurahmanova, Ofeliya Yusupova, Gulzoda Hudoinazarova, Rustam S. Abdullayev, Farangiz Ziyaeva, Mehrihon Muminova, and Ilyos Arabov for adding their voices to my project, and to Soibjon Begmatov, Husniddin Atoev, and Bekzod Safarov for their conversations and input as well.

Funding for my research between 2002 and 2014 has come from grants provided by the American Councils for International Education, UCLA's Graduate Division, the Social Science Research Council, Fulbright-Hays, UCSC's Committee on Research, and UCSC's Arts Research Institute (ARI). ARI, the American Musicological Society's 75 PAYS Endowment, and the UCSC Arts Dean's Fund for Excellence provided subvention grants in support of this book's publication.

I would also like to acknowledge the help of my graduate research assistants who worked on aspects of my project: Lisa Beebe, Daniel Brown, and Huascar Garcia. Scholars who have read portions of my work and offered helpful perspectives include Helen Rees, Benjamin Carson, J. C. Ross, Christine Moellenberndt, and Daniel Jaffe. Andrew Hale of the Anahita Photo Archive and Denise Cicuto provided additional photographs, which I greatly appreciate. I am also thankful for the continued support of Bruce and Martha Merchant and Alen, Sadija, and John Sulejman Plicanic. You all have my gratitude for helping to strengthen this project.

Introduction

The Stories Women Tell about Their Music

Most ethnomusicologists have a unique story about how they first encountered the music they focus on. Mine begins on a train. In autumn 2000, I was traveling from London to Glasgow for the "Shostakovich Twenty-Five Years On" conference. Just ten days prior, a tragic train derailment in Hatfield had brought rail travel to a standstill and raised major questions about the safety of the British rail system after years of privatization. Before boarding, I heard that the six-hour itinerary that I had purchased was going to take fifteen hours. Concerned that I would miss the keynote speech but glad that I had packed a sizable lunch, I boarded the train and found someone I recognized in my car: Uzbek ethnomusicologist Razia Sultanova. She had recently attended a research colloquium at Goldsmiths, University of London, where I was studying and where we had been introduced. Glad for a familiar face, I asked if the seat next to hers was occupied and sat down. As the train crawled slowly toward Glasgow, we proceeded to get to know each other. Razia was open and charismatic, and she encouraged me to speak Russian with her. As a result, we conversed about our educational backgrounds and the journeys that had brought us to London.

Razia, originally from Uzbekistan (see the map in figure I.1), came to London after her graduate studies in Moscow and spending a long time in Paris; her husband Hamid had taken a position as the head of the BBC Uzbek Service. She reminisced about her studies, first as a pianist and later as a musicologist, but mostly we chatted about our childhoods, our upbringings, and our musical pursuits. As the discussion about our homes and families continued, it became clear that Razia found me a very odd example of an American. We shared our sack lunches and she expressed pleasant surprise

Figure I.1. Map of Central Asia. From the Perry-Casteneda Map Collection at the University of Texas. http://www.lib.utexas.edu/maps/commonwealth/caucasus_cntrl_asia_pol_00.jpg

at finding out that I had made the bread for the sandwiches and also at the knitting project I pulled out of my bag. She called me a "traditional girl," a label that I had never thought to place on myself, but she employed it with such pride and affection that I did not mind. I would later learn that the moniker *traditional* carries great cultural weight and pride of place in the Uzbek context. By the time we finished our journey, rushing to catch the end of Richard Taruskin's keynote speech, Razia and I had become fast friends in two languages.

After the conference, we ran into each other a few more times at the university; she always took the time to chat with me (usually in Russian) and to ask after my family and my work.[1] When Razia heard that I was not traveling home for the winter holidays, she invited me to celebrate New Year's Eve at her house with her family and friends. As a result, two months after our first encounter, I boarded another train to her house in a northern suburb of London, not realizing what a warm, festive, and life-changing event I was heading toward.

Razia's New Year's Eve party was like nothing I had ever experienced. When I arrived, there were more than a dozen people gathered in the living room.

After welcoming me, the guests resumed eating, drinking, and chatting in multiple languages. Soon a violinist, a friend of Razia's from Turkey, began playing a few of his favorite tunes, and later Razia encouraged her daughter to play a piece on the piano. The expectation for each person who had musical training or ability to participate and provide entertainment was not entirely clear to me until Razia requested that I sing them an "American folk song." I was shy about my voice and not sure exactly what Razia requested when she mentioned a "folk song," but I managed to call up a couple of verses of "Oh! Susanna" that seemed to satisfy everyone (and made me feel decidedly awkward). The obligatory participation and enthusiastic acceptance of even my amateur rendition of a simple tune revealed that I was in a musical context very different from what I was accustomed to. As the evening continued, there was more eating and conversation, and more people contributed songs and music according to their ability, usually at a request to share something from their homeland.

At the end of the evening, Razia brought out her *dutar* (a two-stringed lute) and began to play. The mellow sound of the silk strings was instantly captivating; it fascinated me that only two strings could provide such a wide variety of timbres and such melodic complexity. My enthusiasm must have been obvious as I asked Razia about the instrument and her training; she quickly agreed to show me how to play it and sat me down in the middle of the party to show me the basics. Later, after most people had gone home and her husband and children were tidying up, Razia gave me a more intensive lesson. The first thing that she had me do was to attempt the basic strumming motion, a wide stroke initiated in the forearm, striking both strings simultaneously with all five fingers of the right hand—first down, then up, down, up, down, up, over and over on the open strings. As I was doing my best to imitate the motions that Razia demonstrated and as she encouraged me to play louder and louder with larger arm motions, her husband Hamid came into the living room and gave us a quizzical look. Razia immediately shushed him and gestured for him to move along, saying that he would not understand because this was "just how women do things."

My spontaneous first lesson taught me much more than the basic strumming stroke used to play the dutar; it also gave me a hint of the rich relationship that dutar music has with women's culture and history in Uzbekistan. This interaction provided the foundation for many of the issues I continue to grapple with in my musical experiences in Central Asia. The issues of gender performance and national identity as they are personalized and individualized and then themselves performed and reiterated were central to my first interactions with Razia. Indeed, just as Razia found my love of scratch cooking and handicraft to be so atypical of Americans, it is also worth acknowledging that Razia is an exceptional Uzbek, one who was engaged with a variety of discourses as she presented herself and her music to a foreigner in Britain (this practice of engaging with exceptional individuals as common ethnomusicological practice is treated in Stock 2001). Although I was unaware of the trajectory my future research would take, these initial interactions featured many of the issues that I would confront while researching musical practices in Tashkent, Uzbekistan. Certainly the performance of national identity was different for both of us than it might have been within the frameworks of our home countries. Razia (and later many others) emphasized the importance of dutar playing as a female practice (even though men also play). Early on, it seemed as though women's dutar playing would represent the sole focus of my study in Uzbekistan because it was such a potent symbol of both woman and nation. However, much as Razia's own musical background was diverse—including her schooling in Western art music and subsequent study of the dutar and Uzbek folk and traditional music—I found that the performance of national identity, of femininity, and of a sense of tradition that engaged the modern world was not limited to the dutar but encompassed a wide range of professional musical activities. In fact, women are very important to the musical project of nationalism, not just as symbols but also as agents, actors, and innovators. They are the drivers of much of the musical activity that supports Uzbekistan's new national project and they engage in a variety of strategies of identity to make a place for themselves in these musical styles, musical worlds, and, ultimately, in Uzbekistan.

History: Music, Culture, and Society

Prerevolutionary Turkistan

My first interactions with Razia and subsequent studies with her hinted that I was participating in a practice that had long taken place in households in Central Asia: women got together to play quiet music appropriate for indoor private get-togethers. Once I arrived in Uzbekistan to study these practices further, my Uzbek teachers reinforced the idea that women have a long history of playing music in the region, specifically on the dutar.

I was certainly not the first traveler to Central Asia to discover this; foreigners have been traversing this region for centuries, and some of them discuss musical practices, although only a few mention women's musical practices. British and American travelers in the region in the nineteenth and early twentieth centuries were overwhelmingly male and had little opportunity to observe women's lives, a fact that they often exotically emphasized. Most travelers' accounts in the nineteenth and early twentieth centuries focus on spectacles that included the *vachcha* (dancing boys), who are always mentioned in conjunction with the moral taboo on women dancing in public.[2] US diplomat Eugene Schuyler's 1877 account provides a representative example.

> [I]n Central Asia Mohammedan prudery prohibits the public dancing of women; but as the desire of being amused and of witnessing a graceful spectacle is the same all the world over, here boys and youths specially trained take the place of the dancing-girls of other countries. The moral tone of the society of Central Asia is scarcely improved by the change. (Schuyler 1877, 132–33)

This account plays not only with the notion of contrasting moralities, mentioning the moral code that kept women from public displays such as dancing, but also imposing a judgmental tone about the morality of presenting boys dancing in feminine guises.

British civil servant and travel writer Francis Henry Skrine's 1899 tale (written in collaboration with linguist Edward Denison Ross) takes an equally negative and moralizing tone, making the strange claim that there is a lack of music and entertainment in home life in the city of Bukhara.

> The craving for amusement so deeply implanted in human nature finds an outlet in the performances of the *bachas*,—lads of between eight and fifteen with long flowing locks, who dance, posture, and sing with a *brio* which excites frenzy in Bokharan spectators. They supply the place of our opera-singers, ballet-girls, and actresses. (Skrine and Ross 1899, 369)

Other travelers did not make the mistake of assuming that there was little music played in private settings in urban Central Asia, but they often maintained the disapproving tone that was so typical of European and American travel writers at the time. Russian diplomat Nikolay Murav'ev's 1824 account includes a typically judgmental remark when describing the musical taste of the people of Khiva, a city in what is now northwestern Uzbekistan: "Music—the Khivans love music, that is to say, they are ignorant of both time and harmony, but they love a great noise and call it music" (Murav'ev [1824] 1871, 163).

Today the trope of describing women's lack of participation in public life in shocking and titillating terms remains present in media coverage of Central Asia (especially Afghanistan). Such rhetorical stances are even present in otherwise sensitive academic accounts of Central Asian women, such as historian Douglas Northrop's description of traditional urban Uzbek houses that lack windows opening to the street (he fails to mention the ample ventilation and sunlight provided by the inner courtyard and the many windows that open into that area) (Northrop 2004). Northrop goes to great lengths to present a balanced, multifarious account of women's lives and perspectives in the early Soviet period, but nonetheless manages to emphasize the seclusion of women that has become such a powerful image in Western discourse. Indeed, the stories that we continue to hear about Central Asia today often focus on oppressive conditions for women in Afghanistan, their veiling practices, and their lack of educational opportunities (Shah 2001; Sirrs 2001; Bumiller 2010). American and European journalists and writers are deeply invested in the discourse of the dreary lives of oppressed Central Asian women who direly need intervention from outsiders.

Nevertheless, even in the early twentieth century there were some voices that complicated that story. British anthropologist Annette Meakin, who traveled the region extensively and was the first Englishwoman to ride the trans-Siberian railway, is an interesting case. In addition to her travel tales, she wrote *Woman in Transition*, advocating for rights and better opportunities for women. She still viewed women in Central Asia as highly oppressed, calling them "the most secluded of all women under the sun," but also quibbled with the idea of their dreary existence (Meakin 1907, 22). In her 1903 travel account, she specifically picked out Skrine's assertions that women made no music,[3] saying "I cannot . . . endorse Skrine's remark that 'music is unknown in the cheerless interior'" (Meakin 1903, 218). In this remark, she refuted Skrine and Ross's harsh 1899 account of urban home life in Central Asia, where they said that

> [c]ustom, in fact, moulds the Bokharan's inmost being, and the degraded position assigned to women by its teaching places him beyond the pale of civilization. Home-life in the Central Asian Khanates exists no more than it did in ancient Rome. The citizens' houses are ranges of dark and cheerless cells surrounding a central courtyard, and presenting blind walls to the street. The intense cold of the winter months is mocked rather than mitigated by charcoal braziers. Music is unknown in the cheerless interior, and tobacco was till lately tabooed by the arrogant priests. (Skrine and Ross 1899, 368–69)

Although Western men may have assumed that the dancing boys or vachchas largely took the place of women's music making, accounts such as Meakin's and documentation by photographers such as Samuel Martinovich Dudin (1863–1929) show us that women's music was thriving in prerevolutionary Turkistan. Figure I.2, a photograph of a young Sart girl with a dutar, was taken by Dudin during one of his many photographic excursions into Russian Central Asia between 1893 and 1915. *Sart* is a term commonly used in the pre-Soviet era to describe settled peoples in Central Asia; it is not specific

Figure I.2. Sart girl playing a dutar. Photo by S. M. Dudin, 1893–1915, Anahita Gallery, Santa Fe, NM.

to any one ethnicity, but rather is used in contrast to nomadic peoples. The category of Sart in population studies was divided into the Uzbek and Tajik categories in 1926 (Matley 1994, 106).

Dudin's work is unique because he features women, and he is said to have found his models from "'houses of entertainment' near the bazaar(s)" (Fitzgibbon 2010). As with the male writers in Central Asia at the time, Dudin had access primarily to working women, not those who stayed secluded in their courtyards. This is why Meakin's accounts are so important to gaining a well-rounded picture of prerevolutionary Turkistan, one that matches more closely present-day accounts told by women in the region. She describes the dutar playing of hostesses she visited as follows:

> Sart music is peculiar. I should never have recognised it as music but for the instruments by means of which it was produced. . . . The *dutar* comes [second] in importance [to the *karnai* long trumpet].[4] It is a kind of guitar, used chiefly to accompany the human voice, and resembles those found in other Eastern countries. Many of the Sart ladies play, and sing to, the *dutar* in their own houses, or dance while their husband, or brother, accompanies them upon it. I was glad to find that the women had at least this one *tamasha* [entertain-

ment/spectacle] available, for they are shut out from nearly every other kind of amusement. If, when we were visiting at a native house, our hostess considered herself anything of a musician, she was always ready to play or dance at our request. (Meakin 1903, 217–218)

In her account, we gain a clear picture of women in Central Asian cities actively making music within their homes, a tale that is backed up by many women musicians in the present day who wish to trace a lineage of women's music making.

The Uzbek Soviet Socialist Republic

Most of the travelers' tales available before the Bolshevik Revolution were written by European and American men. These tales show us the Russian colonial relationship with Turkistan and foreshadow some of the values that became part of Soviet policy in the region as well, even though the rhetoric of the Soviet Union was one that eschewed colonialism and sought to emancipate workers and peasants from all regions of the former Russian empire. Music played an important role in Soviet policy, which addressed various ethnic groups and sought to incorporate all Soviet republics into a cohesive national whole.

During Russian colonial rule, which began in Tashkent (the colonial capital) in 1865, Western instruments became more common in the areas of Tashkent and other cities (such as Samarqand) with a large Russian presence, as colonial forces brought instruments with them as they established themselves. European opinions of indigenous Sart music were quite unfavorable, calling most of what was heard "noise." In addition to the accounts cited previously, consider this description from 1877: "The [Sarts'] voices are bad, and in general their music is tasteless to an European ear, for the constant use of intervals, which to us are not only unmelodic, but impossible to be expressed by our system of notation, makes it seem to us false and discordant" (Schuyler 1877, 131). This type of attitude continued to some extent during the Soviet period, and spurred a movement to "improve" and modernize Central Asian music and culture.

Two prominent aspects of the push to modernize and create a society that conformed to Marxist-Leninist ideals were the emancipation of women and the recasting of cultural forms. Music played a prominent part in both enterprises. In the late 1920s, the *hujum* (assault) was a major movement instigated by the Soviet government to emancipate women, incorporate them into public life, and turn them into a productive labor force. The most important symbol of this movement was the throwing off of the *paranja* and *chachvon*, the long coat and horsehair veil commonly worn by Uzbek women in the late nineteenth and early twentieth centuries. The work of historians Douglas Northrop (2004) and Marianne Kamp (2006) provides detailed accounts of the Soviet government's approach to this project and women's reactions to it. The hujum and resulting movements also exist in living memory; many of my colleagues and consultants in Tashkent told stories of their mothers or grandmothers throwing off the veil.[5]

The project of modernizing Central Asian music, which included creating performing groups that played European-style symphonic music, was deeply entwined with the project to modernize the local people themselves. Such ensembles of musicians playing folk instruments in new styles began in 1918, before the republic of Turkistan was split into the five republics that we now know as the nations of Kazakhstan, Kyrgyzstan, Tajikistan, Turkmenistan, and Uzbekistan. These ensembles included touring groups, as well as unions of local workers, and their founding represented an important moment when "folk musicians became participants in great mass-political measures" (Vyzgo 1972, 81).

In 1924, the Soviet government split the republic of Turkistan into the five republics mentioned previously, and although there have been minor changes, the current geopolitical boundaries have their roots in this division (Martin 2001, 31). These geopolitical divisions have their roots in early Soviet fears about the power of a pan-Islamic movement (represented by the *Jadids*, a group of intellectuals who were seen as a threat to Soviet ideology and sovereignty, and many of whom, such as intellectual and music scholar Abdurauf Fitrat [1886–1938], were victims of the purges in the 1930s).[6] Levin also discusses the importance of the Jadids to the pan-Turkic movement in the framing of musical culture (especially regarding multicultural repertoires such as the *Shashmaqom*). He notes that after leading Jadids were eliminated as "enemies of the people" in the 1930s, the resulting vacuum allowed "Soviet cultural strategists to begin to build a new society in Uzbekistan" (Levin 2002, 191).

This project, with its major push from the 1930s through the Stalin era, resulted in many of the intellectual frameworks that continue to categorize music in the independence era and that focus professional musical activity around the Uzbek State Conservatory of Music and the state-run radio and television station. The 1930s were truly a formative moment for professional musical categories in Uzbekistan and mirrored the shift toward a more centralized (and standardized) approach to the presentation of culture in the various republics. Musicologist Marina Frolova-Walker notes that this is exemplified not only in the Russian influence on musical creation in the outlying republics, but also in the standardization of language into the Cyrillic script beginning in 1937 (Frolova-Walker 2007, 307).

Socialist realism, with its slogan "nationalist in form, socialist in content," was the major artistic watchword of the 1930s and beyond. Frolova-Walker notes that this was applied to music in specific ways that addressed folk music and ethnonational identity.

> Since Socialist Realism was effectively "realist in form, socialist in content," composers were able to substitute nationalism for realism without adding anything extraneous to Stalin's instructions. Once it was established that realist music implied folk music, composers were able to work with the same speed and confidence as other artists. (Frolova-Walker 2007, 313)

The result was an incorporation of transcribed folk music into a variety of genres, most of which comprise the focus of this book: arranged folk music performed by ensembles of reconstructed instruments; symphonies, ballets, and operas on local themes incorporating transcribed folk tunes, often composed by Russian composers or their local students; and even pop songs inflected with folk rhythms and melodies. These styles of music have changed significantly since the 1930s, but the categories themselves and the idea that national identity can be expressed through the incorporation of folk music into other genres has not.

Government policy on culture dictated that each Soviet republic was to have its own culture representative of the ethnic group or nation for which the republic was named. During this period, scholars were expected to represent various musical traditions within an ethnonational framework. (This began under Lenin in the 1920s, but took on a different and more standardized framework under Stalin in the 1930s [Frolova-Walker 2007, 301]). One of the clearest examples of this comes from renowned Soviet musicologist Viktor M. Beliaev, who wrote a book dividing Central Asian music into musics of the five Central Asian republics, each of which had its own chapter and its own clearly demarcated repertoires (1962). This project necessitated some interesting negotiations of multiethnic (and multireligious) musical repertoires, such as the Shashmaqom that is performed by Tajiks and Uzbeks and is considered a traditional repertoire for both Muslim and Jewish populations. In this case, two standard versions of the repertoire were published, one with texts in the Tajik language (Fayzullayev, Sakhibov, and Shakhobov 1957–67) and one with texts in the Uzbek language (Rajabi 1970–76).[7] Each repertoire is largely the same and comes from the same body of work with roots in the courts of Bukhara; it was only during the Soviet era that the Uzbek and Tajik

Shashmaqom were considered separate entities. In the postindependence era, people acknowledge their unity, even while the Fayzullayev et al. text remains the standard reference in Tajikistan and the Rajabi text is standard in Uzbekistan.[8]

This specific artistic and musical implementation of Soviet nationalities policy is somewhat unique within the Uzbek republic. Historian Kiril Tomoff frames this in terms of Uzbekistan's peripheral location far away from Moscow, leaving local officials free to more flexibly interpret the directives on anticosmopolitanism that occurred toward the end of the 1940s (Tomoff 2004, 213). Like Frolova-Walker, he emphasizes the importance placed on "Russian tutelage in musical progress" through the Stalin era (Tomoff 2004, 234). This embrace of nationalities policy regarding the performance of identity for the Uzbek republic continued even after Stalin's death. Ethnomusicologist Theodore Levin notes that even in Brezhnev's "'Period of Stagnation' . . . [i]n Uzbekistan, by contrast, artists largely remained compliant with the norms of Marxist-Leninist culture policy" (Levin 2002, 202). Certainly, musical forms created during the early Soviet period continued to have relevance in Uzbekistan, and professional musical activity stayed centralized in the conservatory and state-run media.

The 1930s saw musical changes and developments across the Soviet Union: scholars and musicians took up the project of modernizing and reconstructing the music of the workers, the peasants, and the non-Russian peoples. Acousticians (Russian: akkustvovedy) would take indigenous instruments into their laboratories and alter them to better suit Western-style symphonic performance.[9] Armenian acoustician Ashot Petrosiants is considered the father of Uzbek "reconstructed music" (Russian: rekonstrirovanaya muzyka), which he undertook in conjunction with renowned Uzbek instrument maker Usta Usmon Zufarov. The State Uzbek Orchestra of Folk Instruments (Russian: Gosudarstvennyi Orkestr Narodnykh Instrumentov Uzbekistana) was founded in 1938, and represented the first of many government-supported performing groups that used reconstructed instruments (Odilov 1995, 48–49; Kuznetsova and Sadiqov 1990, 124–25).

Although folk orchestras and arranged folk music receive further discussion in chapter 3, suffice to say, the push for institutionalization of Uzbek folk music had ramifications for girls' and women's lives because they were encouraged to enter music schools and study the newly modernized instruments, and many later became well-known and well-respected performers in this genre. But reconstructed folk music was not the only genre of music important in the Uzbek Soviet Socialist Republic, nor was it the only one in which women played an important role. As a result of projects such as the hujum of the 1920s, women were encouraged to enter educational institutions and the workforce. In the Soviet period, women became prominent figures in the performance and teaching of Western classical music, pop music/*estrada*,[10] and traditional musics. Although the hujum has been appropriately critiqued by area studies scholars such as Kamp (2006) and Northrop (2004), the successful women in this book are standing on the shoulders of those women who participated and entered public life in the early Soviet era.

The legacy of the hujum is felt in independent Uzbekistan and remembered by my consultants in deeply personal terms. Most successful women in the conservatory cite the Soviet educational system (and its goal to educate across the gender divide and the rural-urban divide) as a major factor in their ability to successfully pursue their musical career of choice. Many women like Firuza Abdurahimova and Dilbara Abdurahmanova remember their mothers or grandmothers fondly as trailblazing career women. Indeed, women have been an important force in the music education system since before the Tashkent Conservatory (now known as the Uzbek State Conservatory) was founded in 1937. This major institution originally offered courses of study only in Western art music, adding a department of arranged folk music in 1949; a department of traditional music opened in 1972 (Sobirova and Abdurahimova 1994, 36).

Music with roots in Central Asian courts that was historically performed by professional musicians in cities throughout the region is often called *mumtoz musiqasi* (classical music) or the larger umbrella term *an'anaviy musiqasi* (traditional music). *Mumtoz musiqasi* refers to the three maqom repertoires that originate from cities that currently lie within the boundaries of Uzbekistan and that relate to Arab *maqamat*, Persian *dastgah*, and Azerbaijani *mugham* (see Naroditskaya 2002 and Racy 2003 for further details about these other related traditions). These three Central Asian maqom repertoires (associated with the regions of Bukhara/Samarqand, Xorazm, and Tashkent/Ferghana) are fixed and standardized now, but the term *mumtoz* also refers to other professional musical pieces that are not specifically included within standard versions of the three maqom repertoires, such as the dance songs called *tanovar*.

These professional maqomists of the pre-Soviet era came from a variety of ethnic and religious backgrounds, and that tradition continued into the Soviet era, even as the repertoires were standardized along ethnic and linguistic lines. The maqom repertoires are mostly associated with both Tajik and Uzbek musicians and with both Jewish and Muslim musicians. The Shashmaqom especially continues to have a strong association with musicians in the Bukharan Jewish communities in Queens, New York; in Israel; and in the small community left in Uzbekistan (Levin 1996). This heterogeneous ownership of tradition emphasizes the historically cosmopolitan orientation of many Central Asian cities and khanates that predate Russian conquest. By necessity, musicians in the region have been polyglots for centuries. Furthermore, until the hujum, it was men who publicly performed the mumtoz repertoire, including the Shashmaqom, whereas women were known to be accomplished musicians and vocalists in private life. This convention has shaped narratives about maqom and traditional music: accounts of the masters of maqom traditions (such as the one provided in Matyoqubov 2004) include lists of important figures that comprise only men. During the late Soviet era, however, women joined the radio maqom ensemble, usually as vocalists, and gained renown and official acknowledgment as talented performers and tradition-bearers. Even still, women are markedly absent from genealogies of the Shashmaqom and other repertoires under the umbrella terms *an'anaviy* or *mumtoz*.

Music from these styles performed on nonreconstructed (or less-reconstructed) traditional instruments continued throughout the Soviet period, even if it did not enjoy as much government support as arranged folk music and Western art music. The best known of these repertoires is the Shashmaqom, or six maqoms (melodic modes), which has its roots in Bukhara in the fifteenth century. This was a court music played for the elite, an elite that ceased to exist during the Soviet period (Levin 1993, 56). Although its context changed greatly, the Shashmaqom played a prominent part in musical scholarship as well as performance during the Soviet period. Historically, women of respectable classes restricted their musical performance to the privacy of the *ichkari* (the interior/nonpublic life). This musical history was borne out in the stories that I heard from women during my time in Uzbekistan. Many women credit Soviet emancipatory projects with their current role in public musical life. This includes my dutar teacher and primary informant, honored artist of Uzbekistan Malika Ziyaeva, who became the first woman to perform instrumental music with the state radio maqom ensemble. The Soviet era gave rise to a significant number of powerful women performing a wide variety of styles. This legacy of emancipation, education, and innovation has allowed women musicians to continue as a powerful force in post-Soviet Uzbekistan.

The Post-Soviet Period

The 1991 transition from Soviet republic to independent nation marks the beginning of the era that is covered in this book. Although this book focuses on prominent women musicians and vocalists in post-Soviet Tashkent, it also engages with history because these women negotiate their place in present-day institutions by engaging with stories about the past and the place of women within those histories. Both ethnomusicologist Theodore Levin and sociologist Laura Adams emphasize that Uzbekistan was never home to a significant revolutionary movement or even a revolution (Levin 2002; Adams 2010). It "became independent by default," and as a result, many of the approaches to musical production and meaning have displayed a notable level of consistency (Levin 2002, 202).

Political and institutional changes in Uzbekistan have been fairly conservative. After his election in 1991, President Islom Karimov began the project of concentrating power in the executive branch, strengthening connections between central and local institutions and branches of the government (Luong 2002, 121). Many of the institutions, especially educational institutions, experienced significant continuity, and Karimov sponsored the construction of a new building to house the Uzbek State Conservatory of Music (completed in 2002). In 1995, the government officially switched from the Cyrillic script to the Latin script, a move described by many of my contacts as one that provided challenges for citizens at the time, but that would be helpful in the long term for international business and learning Western European languages. There has also been a "gradual transition to the market economy" (Karimov cited in Luong 2002, 120), and that trajectory can be seen in the opening up of selected privatized media, mostly radio, but also a few television channels; however, the government still maintains oversight of these privatized ventures.

In terms of musical and cultural production, the orientation toward national identity was accomplished largely through already familiar means. Although the conservatory had a shiny new building, its institutional structure remained largely the same as it had after the Eastern music department opened in the 1970s. After independence, some new departments were added, namely the estrada (pop music) department and the department of music journalism and criticism. As a whole, the institution remains faithful to its Soviet-era structure and its similarity to analogous European institutions. The same could be argued about the primary media outlet, the Uzbek State Television Radio Company. This institutional and structural continuity that is accompanied by a shift in content is well documented in sociologist Laura Adams's account of cultural elites and national spectacles in Uzbekistan (2010). She labels the situation in Uzbekistan "postcolonial civic nationalism," and goes on to explain that

> [o]n the one hand, the content of official culture in Uzbekistan was a reaction against Russian cultural imperialism, but, on the other hand, it was an

affirmation of both Soviet nation building and modernist internationalism in Uzbekistan. Soviet institutions, far from destroying traditional culture, acted to preserve traditional culture even as they transformed it. (Adams 2010, 103, 106)

Adams's analysis rings true with my own observations and interactions in the independence era, especially regarding those musical practices housed in government institutions. Even with an institutional structure that maintains legibility with its Soviet-era precursor, the changes in focus toward nationalism, traditional music, and specifically Uzbek content have fostered a sense of national pride in individual musicians, especially as they engage with musical repertoires that are construed as national in one way or another.

Despite the continued national project that includes centralization and government oversight, independent Uzbekistan has a varied and complex musical landscape that includes a great deal of mediated music from a variety of sources (for example, cassette-mongers in the bazaars throughout the country sell pop music from Arab, Turkish, Russian, and other former-Soviet sources, as well as Bollywood film music and music produced by the American and British music industries). Beyond that, many children whom I met in Tashkent take lessons on either Western instruments like the piano and violin, or reconstructed instruments like the Kashgar *rubob* (fretted plucked lute) and the *gijak* (spike fiddle). These lessons may occur at full-time music schools, like the Glière and Uspensky schools in Tashkent, at extracurricular music programs, or through private lessons. Additionally, music schools have begun to follow the lead of the conservatory and *kollejs*[11] and now offer courses in traditional music as well. The city of Tashkent affords its residents many opportunities to purchase, study, perform, listen to, and otherwise interact with a diverse range of music.

As in the Soviet era, the state conservatory of music continues to serve as an important locus of musical production; musicians with conservatory educations are taken seriously in a range of musical genres from pop to maqom. Academic discourse on Uzbek music is produced largely within the conservatory and the related Institute for the Study of the Arts (which has no performance focus); furthermore, most prestigious professional musicians maintain a presence at the conservatory as instructors, ensemble coaches, or administrators. This renders the conservatory a vital setting in which prestige is created, canons are formed, and both are maintained and defended. Prestige is connected with values such as virtuosity, musical literacy, and expressiveness that are found in many musical practices, but especially in Western art music, the music for which the conservatory system was created.

The conservatory (or music department within a larger university) as a location for ethnomusicological inquiry was initially established by works focusing on American institutions of higher education (Kingsbury 1988; Nettl 1995). In recent years, ethnomusicologists have continued that project by focusing on similar institutions in Finland (Hill 2009), China (Stock 1996), Kazakhstan (Rancier 2009a), and Uzbekistan (Merchant 2006). Similar to the processes described by Kingsbury and Rancier, the conservatory in Uzbekistan has an important impact on musicians' lives and the ways their music is perceived and publicized to wider audiences. The prestige engendered by a conservatory pedigree is exceedingly important to the women in this book, and the continued recruitment of female students by master teachers has resulted in women carrying the mantle of important disciplinary and generic legacies—the result of the Soviet project that brought women into higher education.

Beyond educational institutions, concerts in large halls like the Turkistan Concert Hall or the newly renamed Bunyodkor Concert Hall (Creative Workers' Hall; it was named the Friendship of Nations Hall [Halqlar Do'stligi/ Russian: Druzhba Narodov] for the large majority of my fieldwork period and is still referred to by that name by all of my consultants) include performances of Western art music, traditional music, arranged folk music, and estrada. The city of Tashkent continues to host a state-sponsored symphony orchestra, ballet, and opera, as well as the maqom ensemble and folk orchestra associated with the state radio and television station. Small clubs often host estrada singers, jazz combos, or karaoke setups. Karaoke versions of English-, Russian-, and Uzbek-language songs are also common at kiosks along streets that are popular destinations for strolling crowds.

In addition, wedding music is another important source for musical entertainment in present-day Tashkent. Especially in the summertime, professional musicians are hired on a regular basis to perform various musical functions for the elaborate wedding celebrations and other celebrations of life-cycle events (*to'ylar*). Musicians who perform for these events range from professionals who exist largely outside state-sponsored musical institutions to the well-known estrada stars such as Rayhon and Lola. A great number of both students and instructors at state music kollejs and the conservatory are wedding performers. They sing estrada or play traditional music like the Shashmaqom in order to supplement their income.

Although outside the scope of this work, professional musicians who function completely outside the institutions of the conservatory and state-run media play an important role in wedding music. Specifically, there are shawm (*surnay*) and long trumpet (*karnay*) players who hire themselves out to accompany wedding processions and perform at other celebrations. Karnay and surnay players (and often the percussionists who accompany them on *doyra* [frame drum] and *nagora* [a pair of kettle drums]) are not considered "high-class" musicians. Always male, they are professionals who often make their living by performing at various wedding/life-cycle celebrations (to'ylar) and other events, such as the opening of an official event, new building, or concert hall. There is one area of Tashkent, near the circus building and the Chorsu bazaar, where many musicians can be seen with their instruments on sidewalks or in shaded areas waiting to be hired, picked up, and taken to perform for events. Because of their relatively low status as musicians, karnay and surnay players of this type exist largely underneath the government radar, and thus their practice (as far as I am told) has continued relatively undisturbed throughout the Soviet and postindependence eras.

Although some wedding events are gender-segregated and do not involve female musicians, women participate in the great majority of the aforementioned musical practices. Indeed, women contribute significantly to the musical landscape in Tashkent at all levels of prestige, from hawking cassette tapes at bus stop kiosks to directing the Alisher Navoiy State Opera company (currently run by Dilbara Abdurahmanova).

Considering traditional music, which is historically rooted in both Uzbek and Tajik peoples and among both Muslim and Jewish performers, a necessary compromise between the international tensions over the ownership and history of the Shashmaqom plays out in a variety of ways. Perhaps the most visible example of this occurred in 2003, with the promulgation of the second round of UNESCO's "Masterpieces of the Oral and Intangible Heritage of Humanity," when the Shashmaqom was listed as belonging to both Uzbekistan and Tajikistan (UNESCO 2013). This prestigious designation is seen as an important international acknowledgment of the musical traditions that locals have valued for centuries, and it addresses the national divisions of the Shashmaqom and related repertoires with needed diplomacy. There is now a national division involved in the training of performers, with the well-established traditional music department at the Uzbek State Conservatory competing with the Maqom Academy founded in Dushanbe, Tajikistan, under the auspices of the Agha Khan Foundation, in addition to the state conservatory there. One well-known female dutarist to emerge from this development is Tajik performer Nodira Pirmatova, who was featured in a 2010 Smithsonian Folkways album as part of their Music of Central Asia series (Pirmatova 2010). Pirmatova joins the ranks of Uzbek vocalist Munojat Yulchieva and Soviet-era Jewish vocalist Barno Ishakova as women who gained significant renown outside the former Soviet Union performing

Uzbek/Tajik traditional music and maqom. Women musicians also feature heavily in Daukeyeva, Köchümkulova, and Levin's textbook on Central Asian music, a testament to their continued importance to the region's musical practices (2015). Although the majority of the canon is formed and performed by and around men, women have made their mark on it.

Defining *Maqom*

Before delving into women's traditional musical practices observed during my field trips, as discussed in chapter 2, it is important to elaborate on the definition of *maqom* as "mode" or "melodic mode" because it has a more specific reference in the discourse of music makers in Tashkent, usually referring to specific repertoires.

The definition of *maqom* and the *Shashmaqom* is related to more general definitions of *maqom* throughout Central Asia and the Middle East. For instance, A. J. Racy defines *maqam* succinctly as "melodic mode" in the Arab world (2003, 26, 227). Another variant on this gloss defines *maqam* as the "Arabic modal system" (Ayari and McAdams 2003, 160). Polish ethnomusicologist Slawomira Zeranska-Kominek and her colleagues provide a helpful standard definition of the term *maqom* that locates *Shashmaqom* within the larger term. They describe *maqom* as referring to

> a set of norms regulating sound material organization in the music of some of the Asian cultures. . . . In practice, the Uzbek and Tajik *maqams* (makoms) can be understood by means of the term *Shashmakom*. This word means "six makoms" and refers to six large cyclic forms containing more than 250 instrumental and vocal-instrumental works. (Zeranska-Kominek, Kostrubiec, and Wierzejewska 1982, 74)

As Zeranska-Kominek et al. note, the term *Shashmaqom* is not simply an Uzbek variant of the Arabic term *maqom* (often spelled *maqam* or *makam*). Most musicians will use the term *maqom* when talking about the various maqom repertoires in the region, as well as maqom in the Arab world and the Persian *dastgah* system.[12] In addition to regional variations in the spelling of the term (and the use of a completely different term, *dastgah*, in the Persian context), the prevalence of Cyrillic and Arabic scripts in the writing systems associated with these musical styles leads to variation as a result of transliteration into Latin script. Some of the more common spellings of the term include *makam* and *maqam*, as previously mentioned, as well as *mukam*, *makom*, *muqam*, and *mugham*. Within Uzbekistan, maqom repertoires are divided by region: Shashmaqom, Tashkent-Ferghana maqom, and Xorazm maqom all use modifiers that indicate a specific repertoire, not just the system of modes on which that repertoire is based. As indicated, *Shashmaqom* means "six modes," but references a specific repertoire associated primarily with the city of Bukhara (and, to a lesser extent, Samarqand).

The other two maqom repertoires in Uzbekistan have their regional references in the title, with the Xorazm maqom hailing from the city of Khiva and surrounding areas in the northwest, and the Tashkent-Ferghana maqom associated with the capital city and regional centers in the Ferghana valley to the east. It is also important to note that it is not just the melodic content that is referenced by these titles any longer because all three of these repertoires underwent standardization and codification during the Soviet era. Musicians can certainly identify the appropriate pitch collections, and will talk about *maqom dugox* (the fourth of the Shashmaqom) or *bayot* (the first of the Tashkent-Ferghana maqom). They always mention if they are discussing (or performing) a piece that is composed with the pitch collection bayot but is considered outside the repertoire that has been canonized for that specific maqom.

The regional and historical associations linked to the maqom repertoires are very important to scholars and practitioners alike. Theodore Levin notes that although many scholars (such as Karomatov) trace maqom practices back to the fifteenth and sixteenth centuries (especially the *Risole i Musiqi* [1572] by Changi), pinpointing the exact date of origin is difficult, especially because the term *maqom* first appears in anthologies of the late eighteenth century (Levin 1984, 9–10). Regardless, maqom in general, and Shashmaqom specifically, enjoys pride of place in the Uzbek musical canon, such that the phrase *an'anaviy musiqasi* (traditional music) is used as a synonym for maqom by some, and indeed, the traditional music department of the conservatory focuses its pedagogy on the three maqom repertoires found in Uzbekistan as well as related "classical" pieces.

As mentioned earlier, the focus on the Shashmaqom as a locus for national pride and as a centerpiece of Uzbek tradition has a long history. Local musicologist Alexander Djumaev notes that "after the 1920s the Bukharan *Shashmaqom* became a tool in the political national struggle between the new political and cultural elites in Soviet Uzbekistan and Tajikistan" (Djumaev 2005, 172). Indeed, the canonization, standardization, and institutionalization of the Shashmaqom and other related repertoires has its roots in the Russian colonial period, when scholars such as Abdurauf Fitrat, Jadid reformer and author on a wide range of subjects, and folklorist Viktor Uspensky began collecting material from musicians in the areas of Russian Turkistan that are now part of Uzbekistan, especially from the city of Bukhara, which was not yet annexed into the Soviet Union (Fitrat 1927; Uspensky 1924).[13]

Folk Dance's Separate Trajectory, Gestural Vocabulary, and Institutional Home

Dance has long been an accepted feminine pastime in Central Asia. It also underwent extensive institutionalization in the Soviet era and is currently featured in concerts of all kinds of music from maqom to arranged folk to pop. Although both men and women dance in a variety of contexts, the musical performance of femininity seems to require dance in almost every context, whereas masculinity does not require such overt gestures.

As with arranged folk music, professionally choreographed folkloric dance is currently employed in large-scale mediated festivals that conspicuously and purposefully present dancing women as performers of the nation (male dancers are much more rare in such spectacles and almost always appear as soloists rather than in large choreographed dance troupes). Similar to the process of arranging folk music and reconstructing instruments, dance underwent processes of modernization and standardization during the Soviet period that modified dance's gestural vocabulary to better fit the concert stage.

Beyond institutions on an individual and personal level, dance (especially for entertainment) is often included in the histories that women tell about their lives before Soviet emancipation movements. In discussions of women's private lives in the pre-Soviet past, dance and music are usually combined. Musicians often spend more time focusing on their foremothers who played frame drums and dutars and sang, but also inevitably mention the presence of dance as part of the entertainment that everyday music making provided for women secluded in the ichkari (inside/inner courtyard). It also is often combined with private, nonconcertized musical experiences, such as those at informal parties and weddings.

Despite dance's prevalence as an activity in Tashkent, my research with musicians and vocalists kept me mostly separated from dancers, and thus it is largely outside the scope of my research and this book. Dancers generally study in separate institutions (with similar institutional histories grounded in European Soviet modeling), including the Tashkent Choreographic Kollej (Russian: Tashkentskoe Khoreograficheskoe Uchilische) founded in 1933 and the much newer Tashkent High School of National Dance and Choreography (Russian: Tashkentskaya Gosudarstvennaya Vyshaya Shkola Narodnogo Tantsa i Khoreografii), founded in 1997. This institutional separation has an interesting parallel to the US system, where conservatories and university music departments are often separate from dance schools and departments. Indeed, music and dance are separate terms in both languages. However, in terms of Uzbek performance practice, it is rare to see either a traditional music group or an arranged folk ensemble perform without the appearance of dancers at some point. The exception to this seems to be when folk orchestras perform programs of European composers; Uzbek music, by contrast, seems to demand some dance accompaniment.

The important linkage of European pedagogical styles and techniques with what is seen as local/national traditional practice exists in the dance world as well as that of arranged folk music. Although outside the primary focus of this work, it is important to consider similar processes and histories as they exist in the dance world; certainly some of the most important forces in the arrangement of folklore focused on dance. The most famous early innovator was Tamara Khanum (Tamara Artyemova Petrosian, 1906–91), of Armenian ancestry but acknowledged as a key figure in Uzbek dance. Under the management of her husband Muxitdin Kari Yaqubov, she began touring internationally in the 1930s and is credited with popularizing Uzbek dance throughout other Soviet republics and abroad (Ergashev, Scherbakova, and Inoyatov 1973). Khanum features prominently in the history of women's participation in public musical activity; she is an important symbol because she is seen as both a traditional dancer and an innovator. Indeed, her formation of a concertized tradition put dance at the forefront of the Uzbek national imaginary (Adams 2010, 83; Doi 2002, 44–48). In this sense she epitomized the emancipatory priorities of the early Soviet projects like the hujum and the efforts to bring young women into higher-educational institutions, while also solidifying dance's later role in Uzbekistan's national project.

In addition to Khanum, Mukkaram Turgunbaeva (1913–1978) made a significant contribution to the national choreographic aesthetic. She founded Uzbekistan's flagship dance company, the Bahor (Spring) Ensemble, which credits many of the works in their repertoire to Turgunbaeva (Doi 2002, 62). The founding of the Bahor Ensemble in 1957 was an important milestone for the development of dance in Soviet Uzbekistan. Turgunbaeva, like many of her contemporaries, delineated between "folk" (Russian: narodnaya) and "classical" (Russian: klassicheskaya) dances, but often presented concertized representations of them in the same programs. Indeed, she was much praised for "developing the varying genres, such that mass performance was possible for such important material" (Karimova 1979, 14). For example, Turgunbaeva choreographed beloved classical dances (which are often also called *folk dances* because of rather ambiguous boundaries between styles and labels) such as the tanovar dances. Her choreographies for these pieces are now considered standards for those who study Uzbek classical dance (Doi 2002, 56–61). Like Khanum's, Turgunbaeva's home has been made into a museum, and she is regarded as one of the most important artists in Uzbek Soviet history, mainly because of her significant choreographic contributions, which brought interpretations of traditional and folk dance to the concert stage in ways that are now standard for both dance spectacles and maqom concerts.

The enthusiasm for presenting Uzbek dance for the purpose of inspiring workers and peasants continued after World War II and reflects the values of early Soviet emancipatory projects like the hujum. Renowned singer and dancer Gulshod Ataboeva spent time touring rural areas with dance troupes in the 1960s and 1970s. In a 2003 conversation, she described the challenging surroundings experienced during a tour of the autonomous region of Karakalpakistan, northwest of Uzbekistan. She expressed a great deal of pride in her company's perseverance, singing and dancing in adverse conditions and still maintaining good spirits and putting their hearts into it. This tour attracted people from outlying villages who would travel long hours to attend the dance troupe's spectacle. Ataboeva and her compatriots would perform for audiences of 200 to 500 without any kind of performance structure, in the sand with a tarp strung up and no electric lights—people would use the headlights on their cars aimed toward the group to light the performance. She mentioned that there was no kind of amplification or microphones, so noisy cars rumbling by would drown out the music briefly. She said that there was "so much sand on our legs and feet—sometimes it was impossible to dance!" And yet, despite "impossible" conditions, somehow they continued to perform for their huge and enthusiastic audiences (Ataboeva 2003). Ataboeva and others of this generation, including Viloyat Akilova, all remember the challenges of performing in less-than-ideal spaces with gleeful pride. This is an era remembered fondly more for its enthusiastic audiences and lofty goals than for its comforts.

The group dance numbers that Ataboeva and others describe were clearly the result of following models from Russian dance ensembles, such as those of Moiseyev and of the Beriozka Dance Company (Adams 2010, 109). Regardless of the history and what some critique as a colonial valorization of Russian models and denigration of Uzbek styles, it is important to note how meaningful many of these performers found such dances. Although it does represent a problematic relationship with Europe and the power of Russia within the Soviet Union, musicians and dancers both embraced this powerful, concertized approach to their music. It is important not to dismiss the value placed on it by enthusiastic participants and audience members alike.

In the post-Soviet era, dance continues to be an important cultural commodity and representation of national identity, one that is often presented alongside musical performance. Indeed, although dance spectacles are still highly choreographed and involve many of the innovations associated with the Soviet era, participants describe them with pride and often contrast their current approach with what they saw as the forced or contrived aspect of spectacles in the Soviet era (Adams 2010, 181–85). One important figure in post-Soviet Tashkent is renowned choreographer Viloyat Akilova (b. 1936), a member of the Akilov "dynasty" of dancers that goes back at least four generations. Like Ataboeva, she fondly remembers touring rural areas and collective farms. She would tour with her family's ensemble and began dancing at a young age, remembering how audiences so loved to see her dance even as a toddler that she would be the grand finale of the programs (Akilova 2009). In addition to her reminiscences of rural tours during her childhood, she described with pride her recent international tours and her new projects in the post-Soviet era. She continues to teach in the choreographic institute, to take her female dance troupe on international tours, and to choreograph the Jewish contribution to the International Celebration of Cultures held in Babur Park during each Independence Day (Akilova 2008). In 2008, she choreographed a *hora* for her group, which they performed in vivid blue dresses with gold menorahs embroidered on them. When asked about the choreography, which Viloyat opa referred to as "Ashkenazic," she remarked that she wanted to do something new for that celebration because she has presented so much music and dance of the Bukharan Jews (which is also her ethnicity), she felt that audiences at the international celebration would enjoy something out of the ordinary.

The exoticizing of Ashkenazic practices is worth noting here, and it presents a marked contrast to the strong history of Bukharan Jewish musicians and dancers, of which the Akilov family was a part for many generations. Bukharan musical practices are Akilova's mainstay for presentations in conjunction with the Jewish community's participation in multicultural events like the one described above. The Bukharan Jewish community has largely emigrated from Uzbekistan to Israel; Queens, New York; and elsewhere. Theodore Levin provides an excellent account of this new community in his book *The Hundred Thousand Fools of God* (1996), and examples of music from this community in Queens can be heard on the album he produced titled *Music of the Bukharan Jewish Ensemble Shashmaqam* (1991). Ethnomusicologist Evan Rapport's 2014 monograph, *Greeted with Smiles: Bukharian Jewish Music and Musicians of New York,* also focuses on the musical practices of this diasporic community. Akilova is one of the few members of the Bukharan Jewish community still permanently living in Tashkent and actively working to continue its musical practices there.

Dance continues to be an important part of women's everyday lives in Tashkent and is now a way to publically perform acceptable Uzbek femininity. Dance, in private and in public, is an important signifier of both national identity and femininity and contributes to the overall "gender reality" as it is constructed in Uzbekistan. Indeed, because dance is something that every woman is expected to do (not necessarily professionally and not necessarily well, but repeatedly at weddings and other celebrations), it is very much part of the "sustained social performances . . . that [create] the very notions of an essential sex, a true or abiding . . . femininity" (Butler 1988, 528). The types of gestures made by professional "traditional" or "classical" dancers in concerts featuring arranged folk music, and (surprisingly) at pop concerts, are often mimicked in the way women dance for pleasure at celebrations. As such, there is a performative link between the everyday practices of individuals and the explicitly national dance movements seen in concerts and spectacles.

Furthermore, although institutionally separated, arranged folk music and dance continue to support one another in the media and in major national spectacles held for various holidays and events (such as those described in Adams 2010). Though musicians and dancers play very different roles in spectacles, the nuances of femininity that they perform inform and reinforce one another, so that audiences expect a smiling and youthful nationalism from female performers of any ilk.

Fieldwork and Research Questions

After my time in London learning songs and dutar pieces from Razia Sultanova, I began graduate study at the University of California, Los Angeles (UCLA), and in 2002 obtained funding for summer research and language study. Following my discussions with Razia and others, I became interested in women's wedding practices and hoped to focus my research on wedding music, using participant observation at various celebrations throughout the capital city of Uzbekistan, Tashkent.[14] I also wanted to continue studying the dutar, but at the time I did not realize how central the study of that instrument would be to my research. At my request for help finding a teacher, Razia directed me to Malika Ziyaeva, whom she knew while she was studying piano at the Tashkent Conservatory—now known as the Uzbek State Conservatory—and with whom Razia studies dutar whenever she is in Tashkent. With Malika opa's contact information in hand, I proceeded to Tashkent and called her soon after I arrived.

My first lesson occurred in my host family's apartment in the center of the city, just across from the Monument Muzhestvo (which means *courage* or *chivalry*, a word in Russian that is similar to *masculinity*; see figure I.3), a statue commemorating the earthquake that ravaged the city in 1966.[15] Malika opa came in and exchanged the appropriate greetings and familiarities

Figure I.3. Monument Muzhestvo (Monument to Courage/Chivalry). Photo by author, 2008.

with my host family in Uzbek, then sat down to talk with me in Russian and start our first lesson. The first thing that Malika opa did in our lesson was to test my abilities on the dutar by having me play one of the melodies that I'd learned from Razia. She then had me mimic her playing of certain phrases, especially of rhythmic articulations called *strykhs* (in Russian and Uzbek) that are played by making specific strumming patterns with various fingers on the right hand. At one point she had me play a 3+3+2 pattern that involved accented downstrokes with the whole hand at the beginning of each group and then a series of upstrokes with the thumb and sometimes forefinger for the remaining beats.

After seeing that I was able to correctly mimic that pattern with no trouble, Malika opa declared that she was willing to teach me. She asked me which repertoire I would like to focus on; my choices included folk music, composed music, and maqom. I said that I was especially interested in maqom, which Malika opa replied would be very challenging. She did not begin our studies with maqom, but rather with a melody called "Nolizh," which comes from another part of the classical or mumtoz repertoire, which would allow me to gain skills similar to those required to play maqom. After a challenging lesson using mostly imitative rote learning, Malika opa settled down to discuss the price of our lessons and concluded the lesson, promising to meet with me twice a week. She admonished me to practice hard.

The focus of my lessons with Malika opa provided the catalyst for me to meet another teacher who would introduce me to other aspects of dutar playing and of women's music in Tashkent. My host mother wanted to connect me with wedding musicians, and set out to find another teacher for me to study with, one who also performed at weddings. Through her network of family and friends, she connected me with Ro'zibi (Ro'za) Hodjayeva, who would become my other primary source of information in Tashkent. A few days after my first lesson with Malika opa, I met Ro'za opa for the first time, visiting her at the state radio station where she rehearsed with the state-sponsored folk orchestra in residence at the radio station. We sat in chairs just outside the passport control section of the radio station,[16] and she said that she would be happy to teach me lessons for a small fee and would also be happy to have me accompany her as she played and sang at wedding ceremonies. From our first meeting, it was clear that Ro'za opa engaged with different repertoires and pedagogical styles. I had found two very different and accomplished women, each with her own approach to her chosen music.

The learning experiences that I had with my two teachers varied greatly as a result of the musical styles that they engaged with. Whereas the maqom ensemble that Malika opa played in falls under the category of *mumtoz* or *an'anaviy musiqasi* (classical or traditional music), the music that Ro'za opa performed on the dutar was most often labeled *narodnaya muzyka* (folk music) in Russian or *halq cholg'u musiqasi* (literally "people's performed music" or arranged folk music) in Uzbek. As a result, my first lesson with Ro'za opa was quite different from my experience with Malika opa: Ro'za opa happily spoke Russian with me, and after asking me to play a piece for her to show her my basic skill level, she started drilling me on scales. Our lessons still used primarily imitative learning methods, but Ro'za opa also brought printed music for me to follow, and she instructed me using Russian terms that had familiar equivalents for me in English: scale (*gamma*), octave (*oktava*), and so on. It was clear in our first lesson that she was comfortable teaching in a way that was similar to the way I had learned music while studying bassoon in a conservatory setting during my undergraduate education. Although Malika opa and Ro'za opa were both faculty members in the Uzbek State Conservatory, it was Ro'za opa's musical style from the halq cholg'u (arranged folk) department that was the most familiar to me. Ro'za was adamant that she also played the "traditional" dutar and was comfortable teaching it, but it was clear from the beginning of my fieldwork that there were at least two very distinct styles of learning, performing, and understanding the dutar available to musicians in Tashkent.

Studying the dutar and attending weddings in Tashkent caused me to come into contact with the other important musical styles that shape the soundscape of the city: Western art music and popular music. All four musical styles now have dedicated departments within the flagship institution for the study of musical performance in Tashkent, the Uzbek State Conservatory. Although my practical study of the dutar lent itself to a focus on "traditional" and "arranged folk" music, it was impossible to ignore the prominent place that both Western art music and popular music (that is, the mediated pop tunes heard on the radio and at weddings, often referred to as *estrada*) hold within the diverse musical activities in the city of Tashkent.

I continually studied dutar with Malika opa and Ro'za opa throughout my five trips to the field. I also engaged in a variety of activities, including attending concerts, rehearsals, and competitions; listening to the radio and watching music videos with my hosts and friends; and participating in academic conferences in Tashkent. The material for this book was collected during five trips to Uzbekistan between 2002 and 2009, as well as Malika opa's visit to the United States in 2014. The primary methodology for my fieldwork has been participant observation that focuses on learning music as an effective way to gain understanding of musical meaning and cultural practices that would not be evident to mere observers.[17] As a result, my lessons on the dutar and vocal technique with teachers including Malika Ziyaeva, Ro'zibi Hodjayeva, Komila Aminova, and Timur Maxmudov were vital to helping me understand the nuances of musical style in Uzbekistan and also to understanding the powerful ways that music is used within Uzbek society.

During my first trip in the summer of 2002, in addition to lessons and dutar ensemble rehearsals, I accompanied Ro'za opa as she performed at wedding ceremonies around the city of Tashkent. My second trip to Tashkent occurred in fall 2003, which gave me my first opportunity to observe classes, rehearsals, and music competitions in the Uzbek State Conservatory and at the Hamza Kollej.[18] During this period I also attended rehearsals of the freshman maqom ensemble in the conservatory and other lessons as students prepared for the biannual Yunus Rajabi Maqom Competition. I returned to Tashkent for the 2004–5 academic year, where I continued studying dutar and voice; attended concerts, festivals, and weddings; and observed classes and rehearsals at the conservatory, various kollejs, and music schools throughout the city. I also attended the jury exams in the traditional music departments of the conservatory and the Hamza Kollej and traveled to regional music competitions in the cities of Urgench and Karshi (see figure I.1, a map of Central Asia, which includes the city of Urgench). In addition, I spent two one-month periods in Tashkent in the summers of 2008 and 2009. During these periods, in order to learn more about the diversity of women's musical practices in Tashkent, I observed rehearsals of the Women's Dutar Ensemble (Dutor Qizlar Ensembli) affiliated with the state radio station and conducted interviews with important women in the Tashkent music scene, including Dilbara Abdurahmanova, director of the Alisher Navoiy State Opera; Firuza Abdurahimova, director of the Sogdiana Folk Orchestra; and renowned pianist Ofeliya Yusupova.

My conversations and lessons with women musicians led me to the conclusion that their situation is much more complex than I originally thought when I first came to Tashkent to study dutar and wedding music. During the course of my research, when I tried to create a cohesive image of the musical culture that I experienced, a few themes and questions surfaced repeatedly. Musical diversity was accompanied by a diversity of stories that I heard about how women came to perform specific genres and to ascribe a variety of meanings to music. The questions that arose as a result included: How do women in Tashkent come to perform the music that they specialize in? How does that relate to the meanings that they ascribe to it and the histories that they tell about it? How do Soviet projects of modernization and reconstruction maintain relevance in a post-Soviet state? How are the notions of nationalism and femininity related and incorporated into the musical practices and histories that are important in the current music culture of Tashkent?

Moreover, what exactly is traditional music in this context? What role do institutions play in shaping the musical lives of musicians? How much agency do women have in choosing and changing the music that they engage with? Certainly, other ethnomusicologists have addressed some of these questions. Virginia Danielson's important work on Umm Kulthūm as a national figure in Egypt addresses her responsibility to uphold national pride and to present an appropriate femininity, as well as the important meaning ascribed to her voice and her songs (Danielson 1997). Anthropologist/ethnomusicologist Tullia Magrini surveys the issue of women's agency despite musical marginalization throughout the Mediterranean (2003). She notes especially that women have been challenging ideas about their representation as silent, passive, and secluded since before recent changes in women's social roles and status (Magrini 2003, 13, 22). Within the context of Tashkent, women continue to narrate histories of seclusion and public silence at the same time that they are respected actors and agents of musical representation and change.

Tashkent as a Cosmopolitan Locus of Musical Activity

As one might predict from the variety of musical activity described, Tashkent is a burgeoning and cosmopolitan city, with many citizens who are deeply invested in participating in the global arena. Tashkent is Central Asia's largest urban center, with a population of around two and a half million in 2009 (Stronski 2010, 257), and an ethnic makeup estimated as 80 percent Uzbek, 5.5 percent Russian, 5 percent Tajik, and 9.5 percent other groups in 1996 (CIA World Fact Book 2011).[19] It was the fourth most populous city in the Soviet Union, and the third largest in terms of territory (Lubin 1989, 619). Its origins are harder to trace, but geographer Ian Murray Matley adduces evidence to suggest that it was probably founded during the first or second century BC. Before Russian conquest, Tashkent was a secondary trade center, less important than the more famous Silk Road cities of Bukhara, Samarqand, and Ququon. Tashkent's role as the center of the Russian colonial government of Turkistan, and its important location along early railways, led to its growth and importance in the tsarist and Soviet eras (Matley 1994, 101–2).

Tashkent has a long history as the colonial center of Russian Turkistan and as a major cultural and scientific center throughout the Soviet period. As a result of an earthquake in 1966, a great deal of the architecture dates from the late Soviet period, as opposed to the Silk Road–era architecture that is a major feature of other well-known cities in Uzbekistan such as Bukhara, Samarqand, and Khiva. As noted by Levin (1996), Stronski (2010), and others, the post-Soviet era has ushered in a new architectural vision of modernity, one that includes smoked-glass high rises, and a remaking and renaming of a great many Soviet landmarks. The result is a vivid pastiche of adobe buildings, Soviet-era buildings (some of which were built with a nostalgic nod to European classicism, while others have a more boxy and utilitarian feel), and flashy exteriors made of metals and smoked glass, as well as ornate mosques built to resemble historical counterparts from Silk Road cities that were sponsored by Turkish and Iranian organizations. There is a palpable mix of the nostalgic construction of the historical past along with an aspirational modernity that aims to participate in global markets. The streets are filled with pedestrians, bicyclists, people driving carts pulled by donkeys and horses, Soviet-era Zhigulis and Volgas and South Korean cars like the Nexia that have become popular in the independence era, and the occasional herd of fat-tailed sheep chomping on grass in the median. Although many continue to appreciate the secular legacy of the Soviet era, newly constructed mosques funded by organizations from the Persian Gulf states and Iran have reshaped Tashkent's skyline as much as the smoked-glass high rises funded by business interests from Japan, South Korea, and other areas. There is a clearly visible religiosity in Tashkent, but it is one that is gendered as somewhat masculine, as women largely continue their practice of praying and worshiping in the home rather than attending mosque or worshiping in public.

People in Tashkent are aware of global politics, often feel connected with Russia and other former Soviet states, and consume a variety of media via cassettes and CDs sold in the bazaars (where most of the local shopping and commerce occurs). They listen to state-sponsored and private radio and television channels; some also access the BBC and other international channels via satellite television. Cellular phones have become increasingly widespread and provide a more reliable service than the landlines. During my first trip to Tashkent in 2002, home Internet use was exceedingly rare among my contacts, a few of whom went online via Internet cafés. By 2009, during my most recent trip, many more of them had home Internet access, and even more Internet cafés had sprung up. The Internet was controlled by the state, which did not allow access to certain sites that it found suspicious, like that of the George Soros Foundation. However, life for many in Tashkent is as immersed in modernity as it is rooted in tradition. Those two tropes are constantly swirling around one another, supporting one another in their contrast as well as their confluence.

Musical Metaphors at Play in Tashkent's Soundscape

Beyond competing and combining notions of traditionality and modernity, the notion of what music is and how it can and should function varies a great deal in Tashkent's many musical circles. Tashkent is a complex locus for musical activity, with its multinational and multiethnic population, as well as its historical ties to various nodes in the global political sphere. In his 2003 article, ethnomusicologist Timothy Rice examines multifarious musical experiences by locating them along three axes: time, place, and musical metaphor. He explains the use of the term *musical metaphor* as drawn from the ways that people discuss their beliefs about "the fundamental nature of music" by stating "music is x" (Rice 2003, 163). In this case, x can be a range of ideas, including "art," "commodity," "social behavior," or "entertainment," to name a few of the more common answers (Rice 2003, 161). In any complex system, such as a cosmopolitan city, myriad musical metaphors exist to explain and support diverse musical practices and cultural beliefs.

One of the overarching metaphors important across genres, classes, and institutional affiliations was music as national identity. Whether employed in representing a sense of forward-looking modern state (as in arranged folk music) or one of a historic nation rooted in ancient tradition (as in traditional music), all manner of Uzbek music was employed to perform the nation. Indeed, the use of this metaphor was surprising in both its ubiquity and its range. While often serving the national project, the primary metaphors at play in my musical interactions in Tashkent centered on prestige, professionalism, and popularity, thus boiling down to the metaphor "music as art."

Music's value as a prestigious art object (or process, which underscores the inherently performative nature of music rather than its utility as a commodity) not only makes it a natural candidate for buttressing national sentiment, but also gives rise to certain kinds of music making. Since most musicians I worked with were connected with the conservatory, it is understandable that the music-as-art metaphor so important to conservatory systems everywhere would be of primary importance in this project as well. It also highlights the important role of the concert stage for elevating the prestige of one's music and one's nationalism. However, nation and art were not the only important metaphors that highlighted my musical interactions. Music as living history, music as commodity, and music as entertainment also figured prominently in discussions of Tashkent's musical practices, especially pop music and wedding music.

One aspect of the music-as-entertainment metaphor that was surprisingly absent in my musical and conversational interactions was music's profitable and prestigious use as tourist entertainment. Current anthropological and ethnomusicological literature examines tourism and travel as an important way to understand music's participation in export culture. For example, anthropologist James Clifford includes discussion of music and sound in his analysis of a museum exhibit (1997, 148), ethnomusicologist Helen Rees discusses the rising importance of tourist concerts for *dongjing* musical associations in the Yunnan region of China (2000), and ethnomusicologist Timothy Cooley highlights the importance of performing for tourist audiences in his work with musicians in the Tatra region of Poland (2005).

I found no analogue for such activities in my work with women musicians in Tashkent. Tourism is a growing industry in Uzbekistan, one that is often centered in the historically important Silk Road cities, such as Bukhara, Samaroand, and Khiva. Tashkent, as the capital and the main hub for international travel, serves as the arrival point for most tourists, but there is little focus on tourist entertainment in the city. Although there are beautiful hotels with international clientele and many fine cultural activities for tourists to engage in, those cultural activities generally serve the people of Tashkent primarily—musical activities in the capital may embrace tourists in the audience, but are not generally presented as tourist shows. Rather, concerts are presented as widely televised large national spectacles in outdoor settings like Independence Square (such as those described in Adams 2010, 101–52). As a result, there is definitely a sense of the performance of group identity enmeshed in these national spectacles and even in concerts aimed at smaller, more specific audiences (such as maqom enthusiasts or opera buffs). In national holiday concerts, various regions in Uzbekistan are often presented as having separate group identities that all serve the larger Uzbek nation, but the undercurrents of nationalism remain explicit (Adams 2010, 176–79). However, in all of these concerts, the intended audience is Uzbekistan's citizenry. This may change as Uzbekistan attracts more tourists and other international travelers, but for now, music as entertainment is engaged primarily in the service of the nation and its people.

One aspect of the ubiquitous connection between music and nationalism that is often difficult for American and European scholars to accept is the seemingly unanimous support for the national narrative by individuals and groups. Music as resistance is a markedly absent metaphor in Tashkent. The situation in Central Asia as a whole, and in Uzbekistan specifically, is one that does not give rise to acts of resistance, musical or otherwise. Ethnomusicologist Megan Rancier expresses consternation at the lack of musical change or resistance to the institutional status quo in post-Soviet Kazakhstan, but also notes that "there is no financial benefit to doing so, since all of the jobs associated with traditional music are within the institutional framework" (2009b, 6). Adams also underscores the prevalent acceptance and even enthusiasm for established institutionalized norms in her work on large Uzbek spectacles, stating, "The vast majority [of Uzbekistan's intelligentsia] tolerated or even enjoyed [the top-down, ideology-oriented way of producing culture] because it provided them with opportunities to feel they were influencing the public and the future of the nation" (2010, 2). Certainly, all the professional musicians I encountered voiced their pride in participating in such a nationally important musical project (regardless of musical style). Furthermore, they find a great deal of fulfillment in their participation in state-run musical institutions such as the Uzbek State Conservatory, the Alisher Navoiy State Opera and Ballet, and the various musical ensembles associated with the Uzbek State TeleRadio Company. Such institutions allow them to make the music they find most meaningful and to make a living doing so. As a result, resistance is not a pervasive musical metaphor in this context. Tensions and conflicts that arise are usually expressed as frustrations with individuals or with a specific situation, rather than skepticism about the institution or system as a whole. Throughout this work, the nuances of musicians' experience of the nation come to the forefront; the nation and its musical institutions are a unifying common factor in musicians' lives.

Language, Labeling, and Code-Switching

One of the most noticeable markers of cosmopolitanism in the city of Tashkent is the diversity of languages in common usage. Many of the people I met spoke at least two languages, with fluency in three, four, or five languages not unusual. Speaking multiple languages is not necessarily a marker of significant class difference or education level, although Russian certainly retains its association with European identity as well as with modernity and international renown. This is complicated in the independence era with a new focus on learning English, which is often pushed as an important language for international business and scholarship. Other languages commonly spoken by those who are seeking business opportunities abroad include Turkish, Japanese, and Korean. Korean is an especially interesting case, because of the *koryo saram*, a diasporic Korean community that has existed in Central Asia since the nineteenth century (Gelb 1995, 392–97). This provides an interesting connection, as South Korea is currently one of Uzbekistan's main trade partners. Beyond those languages, which are sometimes used to represent education levels or international aspirations, Tajik and Uzbek are commonly spoken in the home, as is Arabic for those who are engaged in religious studies. This largely multilingual populace is a legacy of centuries of ethnic cohabitation in cities, as well as the strong emphasis on Russian language during the colonial and Soviet periods.

Indeed, one of the most confusing aspects of doing research in the first decade of the twenty-first century in Tashkent is that most places, streets, and institutions have multiple names, often in multiple scripts. During my entire fieldwork period, Latin script was in official use, but most people over the age of twenty persisted in using the Cyrillic alphabet and referring to things by their Soviet-era names. To my knowledge, this kind of confusion about labeling continues today. Discussions of music, especially of writings and institutions from the Soviet era, involve a great deal of code-switching between Russian and Uzbek (and sometimes Tajik) that is now further complicated by translation into English. Most institutions, departments, concert halls, and publications have transitioned from Soviet-era Russian-language titles to Uzbek-language ones, although people usually use them interchangeably. The Tashkent State Conservatory (Russian: Tashkentshkaya Gossudarstvenaya Kontservatoriya), founded in 1936, is now known as the Uzbek State Conservatory (O'zbek Davlat Konservatoriyasi). The Department of Eastern Music (Russian: Fakul'tet' Vostochnoy Muzyky) that Faizulla Karomatov founded in the 1970s to promote the pedagogy of maqom and other traditional/classical music is now known in Uzbek as the Department of Traditional Music (An'anaviy Musiqasi Fakulteti), whereas the arranged folk music department, once known in Russian as the Folk Music Department (Russian: Fakul'tet' Narodnoy Muzyky) is now known as the Department of Folk Instruments (Halq Cholg'u Fakulteti; folk performance practice). Such terms are often used interchangeably within a conversation, especially the Russian *narodnyy* and the Uzbek *halq cholg'u*. However, in the practice of mixing languages in conversational speech, the choice of either one can mark a conversation as referring to Soviet history; it can also function to position oneself in a more "modern" or "traditional" stance. Of course, polyglots may simply choose words that come most immediately to mind, or may code-switch because they learned a concept in the context of speaking a different language. In fact, the term *Eastern music* is not in use the way that the Russian term *narodnyy* continues to refer to the other department. Almost all discussions of Uzbek traditional music, even in the Russian language, tend to now use terms for "tradition" instead of the more general moniker of "Eastern."

Theoretical Perspectives

My experiences and questions in the field led me to engage with theoretical perspectives that could help unpack the complex and plural experiences of the women musicians I worked with. The "nation" (*millat*) and "tradition" (*an'ana*) were words on the lips of most of my friends, colleagues, and even passing strangers. As a result, issues of nationalism naturally came to the forefront, but not simply because of the expected top-down propaganda. The idea of the Uzbek nation with a rich and long heritage is something that the Uzbek women I spoke with were deeply invested in. The nation that they describe is not monolithic and often depends greatly on the actions of women, at least from the stories and perspectives that they shared with me. As a result, it is natural to engage with scholarship that addresses issues of nationalism and gender.

Works by historians and area studies scholars such as Benedict Anderson (1991, 2001), Rogers Brubaker (1996), and Ronald Grigor Suny (2001) help to clarify complex situations like the one that I found myself in during my fieldwork in Uzbekistan, where nationalism was so often discussed in a variety of ways, depending on context and social role. The idea that national identity is constituted through "the stories people tell about themselves" (Suny 2001, 866) allows for the very personal and individual relationship that people have with their national identities; it also allows for plural national identities that maintain at least an illusion of a cohesive whole. Such stories hold a great deal of meaning for the individuals who both receive and retell them; this process of reinscribing national narratives is part of how, as Brubaker notes, "the political fiction of the nation becomes momentarily yet powerfully realized in practice" (1996, 16). These stories and moments of practicing or performing the nation are crucial in the creation of a true sense of the nation as "imagined community" (Anderson 1991), and music has a vital role to play in that practice. It provides a multisensory experience of a national community as it is internalized and interpreted by individuals. Laura Adams's sociological analysis of nationalism's specific manifestation in Uzbekistan is also helpful, especially when read within Anderson's and Suny's larger frameworks. She posits nationalism in Uzbekistan as "constitutive of power rather than an instrument of power; national identity constitutes its subjects, both institutions and individuals (Adams 2010, 12). This constitutive power is especially important as this work seeks to understand individual musical interpretations of gendered national identity across a range of musical genres. Music in this case is a way to individuate larger and broader tropes about femininity and national identity.

In Tashkent, I encountered a variety of self-presentations that were all ascribed national status, both by individuals with whom I worked and by the media that sought to present the Uzbek nation as one simultaneously engaged in the modern project of industrial and technological progress and firmly rooted in a rich tradition with a long history. Such claims for national identity by both individuals and institutions are the discursive markers of Anderson's "imagined community" as it manifests in present-day Uzbekistan (1991). These nationalist sentiments that provide important markers of self-identity for my contacts exist in a seemingly unproblematic fashion within larger cosmopolitan and transnational awareness, positing an important nationalism that is modern and also in conversation at a global level with international tours, Internet access, and linguistic code-switching and mixing of languages. This constant mixing of the national and transnational seems to support what philosopher Pheng Cheah describes as "nationalism as given culture in a cosmopolitical force field" (1997, 160). As a result, cosmopolitan aspects of self-identity layer with prominent national ones in the Uzbek context.

Ethnomusicologists have also produced a great deal of scholarship on issues of nationalism and the construction of tradition in support of them. For example, Chris Goertzen's examination of fiddle practices and musical revival in Norway provide a helpful study about an instrument's powerful place in the symbolic vocabulary of a nation (1997). His work strongly resonates with my exploration of different approaches to dutar performance in independent Uzbekistan. Deborah Wong's exploration of national themes at play with the alteration of Thai *wai khruu* ritual court music for inclusion into state-sponsored educational institutions is also helpful, in that she emphasizes that change and institutionalization do not necessarily give rise to fakelore (2001, 208–10). Donna Buchanan's study of musical and rhetorical continuities in Bulgarian society as it underwent its transition out of communism is especially useful, especially regarding arranged folk music and the Koutev Ensemble in particular (2006, 231–55). As in other postcommunist nations, in Uzbekistan, such negotiations around the location of national/traditional music in state institutions are complex and long-standing. The institutionalization of traditional music is not new to independent Uzbekistan, nor is its utility for buttressing nationalism. These processes have a long history in the Soviet era, even as they find new roles in the current era.

Ethnomusicological work focused specifically on Central Asia helps contextualize the musical and national situation in present-day Uzbekistan. Works by Alexander Djumaev (1993, 2005), Rachel Harris (2002, 2008), Theodore Levin (1993), and Razia Sultanova (2005) inform my discussion of music's connection to the gendered performance of national identity. All these scholars note the importance of nation-building projects in Central Asia. Harris's analysis underscores the ways Uyghur musicians' musical choices become a rare opportunity for resistance to dominant narratives, something that is exceedingly rare in the Uzbek context (Harris 2002). Levin, Djumaev, and Sultanova all discuss the importance of the post-Soviet national project, and indeed they highlight many continuities between Soviet and post-Soviet musical realities. Levin especially is highly critical of the institutionalization of Uzbek and Tajik musical traditions that has continued through the twentieth and twenty-first centuries; he dubs the traditional musical production enacted in the conservatory "frozen music" (Levin 1996, 47). Although his point about the standardization and institutionalization of music in Uzbekistan is salient, my work seeks to take this institutionalization seriously and examine the ways individual narratives incorporate, manipulate, and transform institutional and national narratives about music. Women have become especially powerful in Uzbek musical institutions and are working to shape musical production and performance there; this work is important to consider.

Furthermore, literature and media scholar Svetlana Boym's work on nostalgia, place, and history (1994, 2001) aids in understanding how histories are dynamic, how nostalgia can be "prospective" (2001), and how such nostalgic histories can provide information about the present and the desired future. In the context of twenty-first-century Uzbekistan, the nostalgia for a variety of pasts (some of which may never have existed) invokes Boym's notion that time can be visited like space (2001, xv). In the Uzbek context, time is also constructed as something that can be heard musically, and different musical practices—for example, Shashmaqom on the one hand, and arranged folk music on the other—represent different aspects of the musicocultural past.

Gender, Feminist Theory, and Nationalism

Gender is an important factor when considering the machinations of the national project, especially as it is negotiated in individuals' lives. In this context, third-wave and postcolonial feminist scholars provide important insights into the ways women are implicated in larger identity projects.[20] Anthropologists who work on gender issues, such as Anne McClintock (1997) and Lila Abu-Lughod (1998), and postcolonial feminist theorists like Chandra Mohanty (1991, 1997, 1998) have done a great deal to problematize the often ethnocentric and misogynist way that national projects are framed in Western discussions. Examples of the plurality of women's voices and experiences are especially helpful in the case of Central Asia, where so much of the foreign media is focused on narratives of seclusion and oppression in the region.[21] McClintock's work on the important role that women play in the performance of national narratives is especially helpful when considering the Uzbek context (1997).

Recent feminist scholarship that takes on the gendered quality of nationalism is especially helpful when considering Uzbek women's musical participation in the nation. Feminist and political theorist Zillah Eisenstein elaborates on the notion of gendered nationalism and its homogenizing force by explaining,

> A nation always has "a" gender and "a" race although that gender is usually not spoken. . . . "The" imagined female body represents the nation and silences patriarchy simultaneously. . . . The language of male privilege (sexism) speaks through the metaphors of love. It embraces the feminine as mother, nurturer, caregiver. It is a symbolic motherhood; women are the mothers of *all* children of the nation. In nationalism the fictive power of motherhood stands against the varied realities of women's experiences in society. (Eisenstein 2000, 41)

The power of the nationalized maternal image in the face of "varied realities" is a useful point when considering how individuals interact with larger group identities like that of the nation.

Women's bodies themselves have evocative symbolic power when presenting the national project in Uzbekistan. Women's domestic role as home and hearth keeper is a commonplace image, as billboards and television advertisements declare: O'zbekistan—Ona Yurtim! (Uzbekistan, my motherland!). Although there are many ways one can be a woman in Uzbek society, marriage and motherhood have a primacy within the concept of womanhood. The dividing line between girlhood and womanhood is marriage, such that the rare never-married women in her thirties or forties is referred to as a "girl" (*qiz*).

Notions of womanhood within a national symbolic vocabulary illustrate scholarly assertions that women's bodies are conscripted to uplift national projects. Sociologist and gender studies scholar Oluwakemi Balogun states: "Women's bodies are often the symbolic sites wherein debates about the trajectory of a nation take form" (2012, 357). Balogun continues McClintock's (1997) project of linking women, nationalism, and the politics of dress by asserting, "Bodily practices and markers of appearance such as dress, make up use, accent, and grooming are vehicles of collective identity, and women's bodies are often the terrain where national identities are produced, maintained, and resisted" (Balogun 2012, 368). Although resistance is not a significant feature of the gendered politics of dress and bodily comportment on the streets of Tashkent, Balogun's assertion rings true—women's bodies are the prime locus for the production and maintenance of the nation. Women's musical bodies, especially those engaged in playing markedly Uzbek instruments while adorned in national fabric, take up the task of embodying and performing the Uzbek nation.

Discussing (male) gendered representations of the nation (and the accompanying erasure of women) in representations of postapartheid South Africa, media studies scholar Jeanne Prinsloo remarks, "Citizenship remains frequently gendered in both its duties and entitlements. . . . [T]he patriarchal nature of the nation tends to propose confining identities or scripts for women" (1999, 45). Once again, presentations of the national feminine center on motherhood and the woman's place in the home. Historian and African American studies scholar Paula Giddings states, "[M]otherhood, with its notions of domesticity—and confinement—holds a sacred place in [nationalist] ideology" (2011, vi). Although marriage and motherhood are largely uncontested norms in Uzbekistan, I do not believe that any of my interlocutors would frame the current situation as "confining." Indeed, the legacy of Soviet-era emancipatory projects and their continuation in the independence era is something that Malika opa, Firuza opa, and others spoke of with great pride. However, Giddings's use of the term *confinement* is apt in this case because the enclosure of women in the pre-Soviet era and their subsequent emancipation is a powerful narrative. This is perhaps why women would argue so strongly that the current situation is not confining—the modern nation is experienced as a place of possibility for women, even as domesticity is also required.

Following on these ideas, Mohanty's point that women often become the "ground" on which national projects are enacted links well with an examination of national identity from a performative perspective (1998). Throughout this study, I look at music's importance to the project of constructing gendered national identity. In doing so, I find feminist philosopher Judith Butler's treatment of gender as being enacted "through identificatory and performative practices . . . [that are] . . . not as clear or as univocal as we are sometimes led to believe" (Butler 2004, 212) to be very important in understanding the various subject positions that women take when describing their musical lives.

The remarkable women I talked to, played music with, and learned from had a great deal to say about nationalism and their role in it. When dutar student Mehrihon Muminova mentioned that "they say to us that it is more necessary for women to uphold nationalism" (Muminova 2005), she confirmed assertions that feminist scholars make when discussing other national contexts: "[W]omen serve as the visible markers of national homogeneity" (McClintock 1997, 97) and "[women] become the ground on which discourses of morality and nationalism are written" (Mohanty 1998, 495). Indeed, the musical and visual culture of Uzbekistan further confirms the important and complicated role that femininity plays in its national project. Mehrihon's words are symbolized clearly by a new statue in Tashkent's Independence Square that depicts a woman holding a newborn underneath the national seal and a reproduction of the globe with the national boundaries of Uzbekistan emblazoned on it (figure I.4).[22]

Figure I.4. The Independence and Humanitarianism Monument in Tashkent's Independence Square (Mustaqillik Maydoni). Photo by author, 2008.

Women musicians in Tashkent perform a variety of roles and construct differing identities, many of which reinscribe the notion of Uzbekistan as a modern nation with rich traditional roots. Gender studies scholar Deniz Kandiyoti's concept of the importance of "indigenous pedigree" within modern contexts and the complex ways that women's work is coopted to that end is useful when thinking of the relationship between representations of women and nationalism (1998, 271). Kandiyoti's and McClintock's thoughts on gender and nationalism inform my discussion of musical practices as they link to the larger discourses of gender, nationalism, and cosmopolitanism that are so relevant to the Uzbek context.[23] In this context, the rhetoric of femininity works in tandem with ideas about music to support Uzbekistan's national project, rendering women vital as both symbols and agents constructing a multifaceted national identity that embraces tradition and modernity simultaneously.

Chapter Summaries

The musical style that does the most work to construct a cohesive pre-Soviet past is traditional (an'anaviy) music. This genre, the subject of chapter 1, encompasses the three maqom traditions with roots in cities that currently exist within the borders of Uzbekistan: Xorazm maqom, Shashmaqom, and Tashkent-Ferghana maqom. This chapter includes accounts from musicians who primarily identify themselves as playing an'anaviy (traditional) music. Often called "classical" (mumtoz) music when referring to pieces within or related to maqom repertoires, traditional music is usually associated with male professional musicians, although many women stake a claim on the history of the genre by positing the possibility that women performed maqom within the private sphere (ichkari); I have been unable to verify this, although it is not inconceivable. Malika opa and her colleagues Komila Aminova and Munojat Yulchieva, as well as their students, provide a variety of perspectives on traditional music in this chapter.

Chapter 2 examines women's role in the arranged folk music of the post-Soviet era. After the previous chapter's account of dutar players, Ro'za opa and her students provide a contrasting perspective. Their rhetoric focuses much more on musical literacy, virtuosity, and international standards. These priorities stem from the emancipatory impetus, during the Soviet period, to include women in the ethnonational project of creating folk orchestras. Accounts from important figures such as Firuza Abdurahimova, director and conductor of the Sogdiana Folk Orchestra, and Faizila Shukurova, the first female player of the hammer dulcimer (*chang*) in Uzbekistan, round out the chapter with discussions of how their Soviet-era education and experience shaped further innovations during the independence era.

Western art music is important to Tashkent's soundscape, and women play an important role in this as well. Chapter 3 focuses on the way women perform post-Soviet nationalism using the canon of European classical music. Their performances support a construction of national identity that began in the Soviet era and continues today. The chapter features interviews with Dilbara Abdurahmanova, the first female director of the Alisher Navoiy State Opera, and prominent pianist and former conservatory director Ofeliya Yusupova.

By far the most pervasive musical style heard in Tashkent, popular music (estrada) provides audiences with a glamorous construction of Uzbek femininity. Chapter 4 examines estrada as it blasts from tape and CD vendors in the bazaars, is sung karaoke-style by wedding musicians, and is performed to sold-out audiences in the Bunyodkor Concert Hall (Creative Workers' Concert Hall, formerly known as the Friendship of Nations Concert Hall) located in the center of the city. I examine the ways that women interact with popular music as performers and consumers, and analyze concert footage, recorded songs, and music videos (*kliplar*) by Rayhon G'anieva, Yulduz Usmanova, Sevara Nazarkhan, and Gulzoda Hudoinazarova.

A large variety of these musical practices converge in wedding music. Chapter 5 thus shows how musicians cross the genre divisions set out in previous chapters. Most of the women interviewed for this book interacted with all four genres at some point, and most have strong opinions about each type of practice. The diversity of styles of music present in events associated with Uzbek weddings and the ubiquity of weddings means that they act as unifiers for Tashkenters across disciplinary divides.

Finally, in my Conclusion, I analyze this border-crossing process further, applying educational theorist Etienne Wenger's ideas about learning as engaged by a community of practice to musical activity—specifically to the musical activities of professional women musicians both inside and outside institutions (1998). By contrasting practices within and beyond the conservatory and by putting the rhetoric surrounding each of these musical styles into conversation, the diverse nature of women's musical contribution to the Uzbek national project comes into sharper focus.

1 Beyond the Canon

Feminizing the National Project through Traditional Music

When viewers tune in to the Yoshlar (Young People's) television channel at 7:45 P.M., a daily broadcast of traditional music appears, offering the *Oltin Meros* (Golden Legacy) segment. The camera starts shooting through geometric latticework with gauzy curtains as lights rise on a semicircle of chairs. Seated there is a group of men in dark suit pants with white button-down shirts and ties. Each of the men holds an instrument, either a chordophone (plucked: dutar, rubob, or tanbur; bowed: gijak; or hammered: chang) or a frame drum (doyra). Separate from them, in the center of the screen, stands a woman in a brightly colored, modestly cut gown made of national fabric (usually *atlas* [patterned silk] or *adras* [patterned cotton]) with a square *duppi* hat covering her braided hair (see figure 1.1 for an example of this type of fabric [adras] worn by Malika opa).

The men begin solemnly with an introduction to a piece of maqom. It starts from the deepest and softest registers of the instruments and they perform it in a heterophonic fashion, with each instrumentalist adapting the melody to the strengths and needs of his own instrument. The brief introduction states the opening phrase of the piece, called the *daromad*; it establishes the pitch center and allows the instruments to begin to highlight the variations of articulation and ornamentation best fitting each instrument that will provide both interest and support for the vocal line. Now the woman begins to sing, starting the piece softly in the lower reaches of her range, often repeating the opening, and gradually progressing through the piece with increasing volume and intensity as the melody reaches higher pitches. The instrumentalists focus on her, following the vocal line by continuing a heterophonic accompaniment, occasionally repeating phrases without the vocalist to allow her to breathe and prepare for increasingly strenuous vo-

Figure 1.1. Malika Ziyaeva with her dutar in Santa Cruz, CA. Photo by Denise Cicuto, 2014.

cal feats. Having begun the piece with her face quiet and her hands clasped softly, the vocalist now begins to gesture, occasionally waving her hand to emphasize the execution of pulsating vibrato-like ornaments called *nola*. The expression on her neatly made up face becomes more serious, then almost strained, as the melody ascends toward the very upper edges of her range.

After building for a few minutes, the piece climaxes at the highest point of pitch and volume with great force from both the vocalist and the instrumentalists, who add more and more forceful timbres and pulsating vibrato ornamentation to create a moment of supreme intensity. After reaching the climax, the pitch, volume, and ornamental density begin to wane, with a few repetitions of earlier, lower phrases that meander down and often repeat a phrase or two of the daromad as the performance of the piece concludes after eight to twelve minutes of buildup and denouement. The vocalist then nods a short bow with her hand over her heart, and the lights dim as the camera pans out through the latticework. Thus ends tonight's *Oltin Meros*; the programming moves on to *Esmerelda*, the Mexican soap opera so popular with Uzbek audiences.[1]

Aside from the final transition to dubbed soap operas, spectators in Uzbekistan can regularly witness this kind of performance—women singing and/or dancing while men play instruments—in concert halls, at the conservatory and music schools, and in prerecorded videos. They can hear similar performances on radio stations and the tapes and CDs available in the bazaars. The inclusion of female instrumentalists in traditional musical performances is much less common. Furthermore, the dutar—the traditional instrument most associated with women—in traditional or classical contexts, although present, is less ubiquitous than its near constant use as an important symbol in spectacles involving arranged folk music and dance. Women have a much-vaunted history with the dutar, but much less of a history performing maqom in public. Even today, most of the presentations of maqom ensembles involve almost all-male instrumentalists. Women dutarists are certainly present in some performances because there are now many women studying dutar in traditional music departments as well as arranged folk music departments. Malika opa was a trailblazer in this respect, being the first female instrumentalist in the state radio maqom ensemble. (Both men and women play the dutar in Uzbek and Tajik contexts. Despite the associations with femininity, playing the dutar does not seem to be considered an effeminate behavior for men; it simply underscores women's femininity.)

The image of a female traditional performer is remarkably standard: usually a vocalist or a dancer, though also sometimes a performer on the dutar, she is almost always garbed in colorful national fabrics with matching or complementary hat and braided long hair. This type of costuming often contrasts with the men performing instruments in the accompanying ensembles; they usually wear Western-style suits, often displaying national garb only in their headpieces, which are frequently traditional duppis. This situation creates a visual emphasis on the larger role that women play in performing national identity, noted by Anne McClintock as "the intense emotive politics of dress" (1997, 97). Yet such deeply expressive images go with musical sounds that are most often associated with male musicians, who do not carry the same expectations when engaging in the performance of maqom or related repertoires. Indeed, male vocalists who also perform maqom are much more commonly garbed in Western suits like their instrumentalist counterparts.

Perhaps it is the strong historical association with male performers in public that lessens the expectation of explicit national referents through male costume and hairstyle. The performances of maqom in small groups have a decidedly male history that is often traced back to the fifteenth century by scholars, especially focusing on the legacy provided by well-known performers in the nineteenth century.[2] Women seem to have been able to join in this historically male practice of public performance by accentuating their role as performers of national identity. Women's creation of space for themselves within the largely male tradition and history of maqom and classical (mumtoz) music is notable because their performance of musical femininity is often linked with a vision of traditional womanhood.

This chapter begins with an examination of the established canon of traditional music in Uzbek institutions, a canon that is populated almost completely by men. After tracing the history of this canon construction, it discusses traditional music and maqom's links to nationalism in the city of Tashkent, especially as it is seen as a heritage tradition that outsiders cannot access. After the lineage of great men credited with creating maqom, the roles of performer and teacher are open to both genders. The chapter centers on the personal narratives of two of my teachers, both of whom were among the first students to study maqom in the conservatory, and who went on to establish successful performance careers. It closes with a discussion of dutar ensembles as an area of contested gender identity that is very much context dependent.

Traditional Music: A History and Canon Dominated by Men

Maqom performance, especially in public, has long been the domain of men. In addition, the collecting, transcribing, standardizing, and writing of its history has been a largely male enterprise. This is certainly not unique to the Uzbek situation; second-wave feminist scholars (such as Denise Riley [1988], Robin Morgan [1970], and Gerda Lerner [1979]) often reacted specifically against what was perceived as a male framing and narrating of history. In Uzbekistan, women performers do include women's stories in their telling of maqom and its histories; despite this, it remains a history populated mostly by men. Yet feminist perspectives on canon formation, which are then applied to the most commonly told version of maqom history as it traverses the pre-Soviet, Soviet, and independence eras, can help illuminate the process of constructing the traditional music canon in Uzbekistan. Examining the canonization of Central Asian maqom practices from the perspective of feminist theory brings up a few questions: Are the processes of canonization and institutionalization working in similar ways for Central Asian maqom as they have for Western art music in Europe and North America? Are the issues surrounding the erasure of women from the narrative as salient here, where women often posit a sort of parallel musical history separate from the canonized performances by men? Finally, in what ways are women contributing both to the canon and to the lived practice of professional traditional music, and how does that inform the connection between that musical style and larger discourses of nationalism and authenticity?

Feminist Approaches to History (and Canons)

Scholars and activists associated with second-wave feminism from the late 1960s to the 1980s were focused on bringing about equality for women through their inclusion in areas that were considered male-dominated at the time, such as the workplace in North America and Western Europe, and in narratives and pedagogies of history.[3] One of the results of their project was the coining of the neologism *herstory* in the late 1960s; its first appearance is credited to Robin Morgan (1970, xxxvi). The use of this term does seem to posit separate histories for men and women; however, a range of feminist historians endeavored at the time to write inclusive histories that focused on women not as a way of erasing men from history or of replacing history with herstory, but in order to narrate a history of people of both genders. Historian Joan Wallach Scott describes this process.

> Inspired by the feminist movement of the 1960s . . . historians set out to establish not only women's presence, but their active participations in the events that were seen to constitute history. If women's subordination—past and present—was secured at least in part by their invisibility, then emancipation might be advanced by making them visible in narratives of social struggle and political achievement. (Scott 1996, 2)

Although the goal of this book is not movement toward anyone's emancipation, telling inclusive stories about important musical events allows for further diversity and deeper understanding of women's role in current Central Asian society. It is also worth noting that the project of writing women's histories did not begin with the second wave of feminism; historian Gerda Lerner cites quite a few nineteenth- and early twentieth-century works (which can be considered part of the first wave of feminism, the suffrage movement) that sought to create lists of important women in American history (1979, 4).

Women in Tashkent open the possibility for a female canon of traditional music most often by discussing their ancestors who played music or sang. One may have a beloved aunt, a grandmother, or other foremother who is remembered for her exceptional musical talent that filled the house with music and joy. This type of storytelling is vital to the project of personal inclusion in a musical legacy, even if the ancestor was not alive to act as a role model for the woman telling the story. For example, Ro'zibi Hodjayeva's musical grandmother did not live long enough to pass her knowledge on to Ro'za opa, although her treasured memory is a source of inspiration (Hodjayeva 2008). The knowledge of a musical foremother in the family creates the sense of lineage that is so important in the construction of tradition.

Musicologist Marcia Citron notes this in her discussion of women and the canon in Western art music.

> The presence of a past can go a long way toward assuaging creative anxiety. But which past does the female creator relate to: some neutral or universal past, a male past, or a female past? Perhaps she might want to relate to more than one tradition. But if one of them is a female tradition the problem is that there is still no fully formed female tradition to relate to. Music by women is performed occasionally but still has not acquired the status of a meaningful tradition. (Citron [1993] 2000, 67)

Indeed, the long lists of men codified in books and who have their portraits hanging in the halls of Uzbek conservatories are being subtly subverted by the suggestion that women have also had a place in bearing the tradition of maqom. There are currently no books available seeking to place women within the canon of revered creators and performers of maqom as there have been codifying the contributions of women composers in Western art music (Pendle 1991; Bowers and Tick 1986). However, within the stories that women tell about themselves, the opportunity to locate women in the music history of maqom arises.

Just as feminist scholars sought to ensure women's place in the historical canon, Uzbek women seek to view the canon of traditional music as including women (at least as a possibility). The canon has a great deal of power for the musicians who perform traditional music. Indeed, the fact that such repertoires are written down is also of primary importance. As ethnomusicologist Philip Bohlman says, "Texts are essential to the canonizing process because they replace the timeliness of music as an oral phenomenon with the timelessness of music as a textual ontology. To enter the canon of great works, a piece of music must 'last,' and how better to make it last than to transform it into a text?" (Bohlman 1992, 202). The standardizing processes that occurred during the Soviet era greatly contributed to the kinds of cultural capital that present-day musicians are able to draw upon, as they now have a clear text to depend on (Rajabi's volumes), as well as a cohesive historical narrative.

The most common version of maqom's history encountered during my time in Uzbekistan was one that hearkens back to music in the courts of Silk Road cities, especially Bukhara, Samarqand, Khiva, and various cities in the Ferghana Valley. When told by musicians, such stories often tend to reference a vague ancient history rather than listing specific dates or even centuries, and often mention important scholars such as Ibn Sino, or Avicenna as he is often known as in the English language (980–1037), and Al Farabi (870–950), both of whom discuss music in their works (Leaman 2004, 105–6). Musicians take care to note the panethnic and even panreligious roots of this music that was played in multiethnic cities by Tajiks and Uzbeks and by Muslims and Jews. However, there seems to be little conflict in talking about maqom as a treasure of the Uzbek people while also noting the many groups who created it and continue to perform it.[4]

Musicologists and other scholars tend to trace the history of performance practice back to the eighteenth and nineteenth centuries, while supporting the idea of older related practices via mention of musical instruments and concepts from manuscripts. For example, Faizulla Karomatov, renowned Uzbek musicologist and founder of the traditional music department in the Uzbek State Conservatory, traces maqom practices back to the musical system brought to the region by the Arabs in the ninth century. He bases this on mention of instruments such as the *'ud* (fretless lute), rubob (fretted lute), and tanbur (fretted lute) in writings about music by famous authors like Al Farabi and Alisher Navoiy (1441–1501), and he discusses the foundation of this traditional musical repertoire that was passed from master to student via oral tradition (Karomatov 1972, 3–4). This master-apprentice relationship (*ustoz-shog'ird*) has been strongly emphasized as a key component of maqom pedagogy and transmission, and has even received the attention of UNESCO, which hosted a concert/master class in Tashkent in 2005 celebrating the ustoz-shog'ird system. Repertoire and playing technique is seen as having a genealogy that stretches back through pre-Soviet history, through ustoz-shog'ird transmission (Matyoqubov 2004).

Defining Tradition—Institutional and Everyday Meanings

When describing something as *traditional music* (an'anaviy musiqasi), a variety of meanings can arise, depending on context. Much like in English usage, the term is vague and problematic. Which tradition is one referring to? Does it mean that music is necessarily old or necessarily passed on via oral methods? Is it referring to village music or art music or both? Depending on context, the answer to all of these questions could be yes. Certainly the folk music celebrated in the UNESCO-sponsored "Musical Spring" festival in the Boysun region of southern Uzbekistan is generally more rooted in village life than music with the same moniker as played in the state conservatory. UNESCO included the "cultural space of the Boysun district" on its Representative List of the Intangible Cultural Heritage of Humanity in 2001 and is clearly invested in the preservation and continued practice of folk music in the region (2013). Even though the UNESCO-sponsored festival focuses on themes that emphasize folk tradition, there is a great deal of choreography and spectacle within the performances that bring up larger issues of modernization, arrangement, and invention, such as those discussed by Hobsbawm (1983) and Lau (1996) in different contexts.

Clearly the concept of tradition is fraught with competing ideas and ideals. Traditions must be treated as dynamic processes that have important stakes for individuals, institutions, and nation-states. Furthermore, traditions and the performance of them are often deeply gendered and coopted into national and international institutional agendas: women are often used to represent tradition via media and within institutional frameworks. These are thoroughly modern processes, even though the notion of tradition is so often used as a foil to modernity in academic and public discourse. Tradition is at once deeply personal, thoroughly institutionalized, and uncontrollably mediated. Individuals often view the line between what is traditional and what is modern in widely varying frameworks.

For the purpose of this book, the label *traditional* as regards music is used as it is enshrined in the Uzbek State Conservatory. Because the women in this book all pass through the conservatory and are often speaking from within its borders both physically and conceptually, it is helpful to define and employ the term in this usage. The result is that traditional music is generally a frame for maqom and related Central Asian classical repertoires. This expands to encompass some beloved folk songs and dances, but not all, and generally refers to the maqom art music traditions that trace their roots to the major Central Asian trade cities such as Bukhara and Khiva. It tends to exclude rural folksong and dance, though in other contexts both would fall under the word's umbrella. Often people discussing rural vernacular musical practices within the frame of the conservatory label such musics *folklore* (Russian: folklor'); this is also helpful, since generally musicologists who work on rural Central Asian musics in local institutions describe themselves as studying "musical folklore." As a result, within professional contexts like the conservatory or the state radio and television station, an'anaviy music is professional music, which is contrasted with vernacular folklore.

The term *traditional* is also used to indicate explicit contrast with musics that were treated by Ashot Petrosiants in his quest to create folk orchestras and equal-tempered reconstructed folk instruments. Interestingly, these instruments were given the term *halq* in Uzbek or *narodnyy* in Russian, which means "people's" or "folk." In other contexts, folk music and traditional music could be employed as synonyms, but in the context of the Uzbek State Conservatory, they are clearly delimited, defended, and very separate. This separation is one that is emphasized by conservatory musicians and disciplinary boundaries, but often does not translate to the general public, who would take a broader view eliding the terms, instruments, and repertoires.

These terms are deeply embedded in the history of non-European music in Central Asia. Specifically, this division of arranged folk versus traditional music bears the mark of Soviet institutionalization. These institutions continue their legacy in independent Uzbekistan, and indeed the divisions seem even more calcified as practitioners compete for resources in a framework where state support is compounded with private capital.

Pre-Soviet Histories

The rootedness of current (and twentieth-century) maqom practices in the precolonial courts of the region is one reason that maqom repertoires were suspect during parts of the Soviet period (Tomoff 2004). However, it is also one of the key aspects of how traditional music is reinforcing current narratives of nationalism. It is even more important that scholars writing the histories of the maqom were often Uzbeks (although scholars of Russian origin such as Viktor Uspensky and Viktor Beliaev, in addition to Tajik scholars such as Boboqul Fayzullayev, also did important work on the genre). Maqom has become an important piece of the histories that are used to support Uzbek nationalism (as well as Tajik nationalism, and in linking a pan-Turkic and pan-Islamic history of the region, which was a project of Jadid reformers in the early twentieth century). Both the Uzbek and Tajik narrations of the Shashmaqom acknowledge its multicultural nature and that the repertoire was shared by Muslims and Jews, though certainly the emphasis is always placed on the nation about which the history is told.

Regarding the codification of stories about Central Asian maqom repertoires, the first scholar who is generally cited as writing a history of maqom is Uzbek Jadid reformist Abdurauf Fitrat (1886–1938) (Fitrat [1927] 1993). As Partha Chatterjee notes, it is significant that a people write their own history, and colonized groups are loathe to accept histories written by colonizers (Chatterjee 1993, 77, 88). Leaving aside the debate as to whether Uzbekistan was a colonial state while it was a Soviet republic (Northrop 2004, 13; Suny 2000, 487–88), it is important that this history of maqom as a Central Asian (and specifically Uzbek) practice has been written by Uzbeks, even during the Soviet period.

When considering the politics of identity in regard to musical production, the perception of Uzbekistan's role in the Soviet Union as voluntary and participatory is also noteworthy. Although difficult to capture in recorded interviews, my consultants often took the time to correct me when I framed Central Asia as having had a colonial experience or asked if something was a relic of the Soviet period. Many people feel strongly that the Soviet experience was not one of Russian dominance, but rather of the fifteen member states participating in an equal and modern state. Although many will acknowledge a sense of coloniality for the tsarist period, they frame the Soviet era as markedly different from that, and as a period when people had agency and power, even if Moscow was still the center of the country to which all roads (and railroads) led.

One issue related to the standardization and canonization of the various maqom repertoires is the history of written versions of maqom. In the Xorazm region (northwestern Uzbekistan), there is a pre-Soviet history of codifying Xorazm maqom in the nineteenth century, which has received a great deal of attention by scholars and pedagogues. Musicologist Otanazar Matyoqubov has published about this notational system in both the English and Uzbek languages (Matyoqubov 1990; 2004, 76–78). The importance of this notation is also noted in the curriculum of the Uzbek State Conservatory. Uzbek State Conservatory dean and musicologist Soib Begmatov told his version of the historical notation system's origins during a 2005 lecture in his class "Uzbek Music before the 20th Century," attended by undergraduate students in both the traditional and arranged folk music departments (Begmatov 2005). Begmatov's version begins in the courts of renowned leader Shah Muhammad Rahim Khan in Khiva (1806–25). Rahim Khan had an occasion to attend a concert of European chamber music. Impressed by the use of notation he witnessed, he wanted the "maqomists" to play from notation as well. According to the story, the notation for the tanbur (a fretted plucked lute) arose from his desire. It displays a line for each fret on the tanbur, so that the graph notation is read fairly easily as tablature.

Of course, the conservatory in Tashkent is not the only place that emphasizes the canonic importance of this notation. In Urgench, the regional capital of the Xorazm region, the walls of the local music college are bedecked with photographs of this historical tablature, as well as images of those famous performers and codifiers associated with it. One plaque in particular stood out because it demonstrated the prominent place that written music has within this music culture that relies primarily on oral imitative methods for pedagogy: the notation was prominent in the center and all the images of masters of the tradition encircled it. Although the notation is central, the plaque also gives us a visual representation of the canon of great men of Xorazmian music, a group that has parallels in the traditions of the Bukharan Shashmaqom and the Tashkent-Ferghana maqom. The men on the plaque parallel the canon of great men often referenced in Western art music and displayed on the walls of our conservatories and concert halls as well.

Soviet-era Canonization: Codifying Maqom Repertoires

Although the Xorazmian tablature that Begmatov, Matyoqubov, and others describe was conceived of and created before Russian colonization and the creation of the Soviet state, the current narratives about traditional repertoires as well as the standardization of those repertoires stem from the institutionalization of music during that Soviet era. Indeed, much of the written history and theory that is transmitted to music students as well as to the general public about the Shashmaqom (and maqom in general) was written and published during the Soviet period. As mentioned earlier, Abdurauf Fitrat published the first work on the subject (1927); he is considered a native scholar, and his work was greatly venerated in the post-Soviet era. Arguably, he set the foundation of national music studies in Uzbekistan with his work on Uzbek musical history, where he posits Uzbek classical music as grounded in Turkic origins that integrated Persian and other local practices (Djumaev 2005, 171–72).

Another key scholar who straddled the colonial and Soviet eras was Viktor A. Uspensky (1879–1949), considered by most a Russian scholar who focused on Central Asian music, even though he grew up in Central Asia and in 1918 helped create the precursor to the Uzbek State Conservatory, the People's Conservatory in Tashkent. Levin's assessment is that although scholars are grateful for the contributions of Uspensky (and others, such as Viktor Beliaev), they view his work with some skepticism because he is inevitably marked by his Russian ethnicity (Levin 1996, 13). Despite this, Uspensky is lauded for creating the first version of the Shashmaqom—albeit just the instrumental-only sections—to be transcribed into Western notation. Additionally, Uspensky's version is bolstered by its use of renowned musicians for primary sources: Ata Giyaz-Abd-Gani and Ata Jalal-Eddin-Nazirov, who seems to be often referred to as Ota Jalol (1845–1928) in interviews and conversation (Uspensky 1924). Fitrat edited this volume (along with N. Mironova), so it bears the mark of his approval.

In line with the emphasis on ethnic identity as "national" identity for the separate Soviet republics, the panethnic and panreligious repertoires of the Shashmaqom also needed to be standardized and delimited in ethnic terms. As a result, both Tajik-language and Uzbek-language versions were created. The creators of these two now-standard versions of the Shashmaqom were Boboqul Fayzullayev (1897–1964) et al. for the Tajik version (1957–67), and Yunus Rajabi (1897–1976) for the Uzbek version (1970–76). Both versions have the benefit of being seen as representatives of their respective ethnicities/nations. Rajabi, especially, is venerated as a tradition-bearer, performer, and scholar (and the extent of that veneration is discussed later in this chapter).

Beyond Ota Jalol, Abdurauf Fitrat, and Yunus Rajabi, there does seem to be a canon of figures who are represented as forefathers of both traditional music in Uzbekistan and the scholarship on the topic. Most books published currently, whether collections of songs or other scholarly work, cite a string of great men whom the authors acknowledge as important predecessors to the current practitioners (Mahmudov 2006, Ziyaeva 2008, Hodjayeva 2009b, and G'anieva 2003 are all examples that engage in this practice of reciting the canon). Temur Mahmudov's list of canonic figures in his book of repertoires for music schools that offer traditional performance reads similarly to Malika opa's 2008 list—it starts with the generation of masters from the late nineteenth century: Ota Jalol, Hoja Abdulaziz Abdurasulov (1852–1936), and Mulla To'ychi Toshmuhamedov (1868–1943), then moves on to those active in the twentieth century during the Soviet era, citing Yunus Rajabi (1897–1976), Tuxtasin Jalilov (1896–1966), Komiljon Jabbarov (b. 1915), Faxriddin Sodiqov (1914–77), Muhammadjon Mirzaev (1908–99), and Orifxon Xatamov (b. 1924), and others as important composers and tradition-bearers (Mahmudov 2006, 3). Most of these people were or are well-known performers, and the constant reappearance in such lists reinscribes the notion of a cohesive canon that is transmitted from (male) master to (usually male) student in perpetuity, even if such processes are now framed within modern institutions such as conservatories and state television stations.

Post-Soviet Expansion

As Djumaev and Levin have noted, since 1991 there has been a renewed focus and a resurgence of works focusing on nationalism and the restoration of traditional musical contexts in Uzbekistan (Djumaev 2005, 179; Levin 1993, 57–58). This has further calcified the separations between the Uzbek and Tajik versions of the Shashmaqom, if only because national tensions have increased and contact between relatives, friends, and colleagues in the two nations has become much more challenging. For example, during the majority of my fieldwork period, flights between Uzbekistan and Tajikistan were halted, so that air travel between the two countries required a transfer in either Moscow or Istanbul. Border crossings for residents in the Ferghana Valley (an area now divided between the nations of Uzbekistan, Tajikistan, and Kyrgyzstan) were most commonly accomplished through checkpoints on foot. This was a significant hassle for people who just a decade earlier had had relative freedom of movement between what were then republics of the larger Soviet Union.

This resurgence of enthusiasm for national works that render maqom and traditional music a natural fit for publicizing Uzbek traditions engages with existing material and standards created during the Soviet period. Indeed, the codification and institutionalization of the Shashmaqom have lent it credibility. Thus, traditional music has become a focal point not just in the conservatory and elite musical circles. After the fall of the Soviet Union, the Uzbek Ministry of Sport and Culture, as well as the Ministry of Education, sought to rework curricula at all levels, including those for music classes in nonspecialist schools around the country. The resulting curriculum includes units on traditional music and maqom, especially in the sixth-grade music textbook, which dedicates one of its four units to classical music (mumtoz musiqasi), another term used for maqom and related genres that functions similarly to the term *traditional music* (an'anaviy musiqasi) but does not have the extra connotation that might allow it to be confused with folkloric music. This unit on classical music gives us a great deal of information on how the canon of the Shashmaqom and of traditional music is disseminated to nonspecialist audiences. In the opening paragraphs of the chapter, the text reads, "Dear children! Classical music is our legacy; all the musical works are like a treasury of melodies created for future generations" (Begmatov et al. 2001, 6). This denotation of legacy/heritage gives the musical repertoire significantly more weight than the repertoires of European classical music/Western art music, opera, ballet, arranged folk music, estrada/popular music, and world music, all of which are treated in the fifth- and sixth-grade curricula but not given the kudos of being a legacy and a melodic treasure trove to be handed down to future generations.

In addition to high praise and the weight of legacy, this unit on traditional music gives us information on how the canon is delimited for the public. The text draws a distinction between vocal music and purely instrumental music, and among traditional musical repertoires from four regions: Bukhara/Samarqand, Xorazm, Surxondaryo/Qashqadaryo (in the south, an area that has traditional/classical melodies, but no maqom tradition associated with it), and Ferghana/Tashkent (Begmatov et al. 2001, 6–7). The photographs in this unit show primarily men playing instruments, some in traditional striped robes (*chopon*) and many in Western suits and ties. The repertoire includes pieces from all three maqom repertoires, including "Soqinomai Savti Kalon" (a vocal piece from maqom Rost) and "Tasnifi Buzruq" (an instrumental piece from maqom Buzruq).

Women's Roles Performing the Great Works

Although the terminology is often the same, the type of "tradition" that Uzbek women are associated with is significantly different from the tradition that is referred to when maqom and related genres are called *traditional music*. Women's traditions as remembered historically largely focus on the internal lives of their households in the ichkari or the inside, as opposed to the public sphere (*tashkari*) that was the realm of men. Thus we hear tales of women performing the dutar from both Uzbek women and travelers like Annette Meakin, and the media images of women enacting traditions focus often on activities that are centered in the home—food preparation, child care, and playing instruments such as the jaw harp.[5]

The stories about the maqom tradition that are codified and canonized center on men as performers, creators, and transcribers. Despite women participating in maqom performance at a variety of skill levels, the canon of Shashmaqom and of traditional music is decidedly male-centered. However, the legacy of the Soviet hujum left its mark on the practice of maqom performance, with numerous lauded female performers. The importance of the Soviet system's emphasis on women having places in higher education and in public life is often acknowledged by female performers as a precursor for personal success.

During my fieldwork, it was clear that the most acceptable way for women to participate in the performance of the traditional canon was as singers and dancers. Dutarists could be either men or women, and their gender identity was not challenged, but aside from the circle of performers that included Malika opa and her students, the majority of dutarists represented in the media and in concert halls were men, unless the representation was of dancers using dutars as props. Other instruments are also now options for women to perform in arranged folk contexts, including the hammer dulcimer (chang) and a metal-stringed, fretted lute (Kashgar rubob); these instruments would seem to be the next opening for women who want to perform traditional music, but while I was observing traditional ensembles, those instruments were still performed almost entirely by men. When women participate in maqom ensembles, they thus engage with modern discourses of tradition to carve out a place for themselves in a performance practice that excluded them until the twentieth century.

Malika Opa's Career Teaching and Performing Maqom

Although women have recently become renowned vocalists and, in the case of my teacher Malika Ziyaeva (b. 1956), renowned instrumentalists, the histories, images, and anecdotes told about maqom are still about men. Indeed, it is most often male researchers working with male instrumentalists who describe histories and genealogies that stem from male master teacher to male student for generations. What are the strategies and narratives that women currently use to place themselves within traditional musical contexts? It is worth beginning with a single woman's history playing maqom: Malika opa's.

Malika opa's story of coming to play maqom starts like that of many of the musically talented young girls of her generation (some of whose stories are covered in chapter 3). She grew up in a small village near Ferghana City in eastern Uzbekistan, and began studying the Kashgar rubob (plucked lute) at a local music school. The music that she was taught had been standardized by the Soviet educational system, and Malika opa was proud of her musical literacy, her fluency in reading Western notation, and her knowledge of solfège and harmony. This high-quality musical education that was established during the Soviet period and continues today is something that musicians of many backgrounds with training in diverse repertoires take pride in.

The story of Malika opa's early musical education is one that she liked to tell often, saying that she began on the Kashgar rubob playing tunes like the "Andijon Polka" (a folk tune that was often arranged and performed during the Soviet era). As she listened to the radio with her family during this time, she did not understand why the music that she was learning at music school did not sound like the music that she heard "Yunus aka" (Yunus Rajabi) and his ensemble perform on the radio (Ziyaeva 2005b). Even though she often cited her confusion about the music that she was learning as opposed to what she heard from the radio maqom ensemble, Malika opa was deeply proud of her education and of the opportunities that she had as a young adult. At one point she mentions this explicitly: "Whatever people may say about the Soviet Union, it allowed me, a girl from the village, to get a free education" (Ziyaeva 2005b).

Malika opa also said she originally found the notion of "traditional" music confusing because the arranged "folk" music she was learning in music school (which was labeled "folk" music in Russian: narodnaya muzyka) was so different from the "traditional" music that she heard on the radio (Ziyaeva 2005b). She excelled in her musical studies and won a place in the third class of the new Eastern Music Department founded by musicologist Faizulla Karomatov while composer Muxtor Ashrafiy was the director of the Tashkent conservatory. Malika opa began her studies there in 1973. Upon graduation in 1979, she was given a post in the radio maqom ensemble that she grew up listening to, which she modestly credits to fortunate timing because Orif Qosimov, one of the long-standing dutarists in the ensemble, retired just as she finished at the conservatory. Malika opa worked at the maqom ensemble from 1979 to 2003, and she remembers her time in the ensemble fondly, describing strenuous and well-received tours throughout the Soviet Union and beyond. She also often emphasizes the discipline and mastery of the repertoire that twenty-four years of almost daily rehearsal, recording, and performing provided.

Although many performers refer to the published volumes of maqom transcriptions by Rajabi and others, Malika opa is always clear that maqom is transmitted via oral methods and that she would not be able to teach and perform as she does if she had not spent all that rehearsal time, week after week, playing maqom. To add to an already demanding rehearsal and performance schedule, she took an additional position at the Uzbek State Conservatory in 1991, making the 1990s a hectic and productive decade. After retiring from her position in the radio ensemble, Malika opa took up additional teaching duties at the Xamza Music Kollej (Xamza music high school), where she continues to teach, as well as at the kollej that is associated with the conservatory. Teaching at the kollej level allows her a great deal of continuity with her students, as she takes many of the most talented ones through master's degrees.

But Malika opa's groundbreaking career trajectory was not as effortless as her summary from July 2009 might make it seem. In that same interview, she also explained that it was very important for her to have her family's blessing to move to the capital city for her career. She mentioned the importance of her grandmother giving permission for her to study at the conservatory and of her mother supporting Malika opa's desire to stay in Tashkent and work in the maqom ensemble. Her mother did support her decision, but only with the stipulation that she marry before starting her job. As Malika opa put it, "My mom said, 'I'm going to marry you off. If you say that you'll get married, then I will agree to your work'" (Ziyaeva 2009). Fortunately, Malika opa had a suitor she favored from her time at the conservatory, so she and Nurddin Ziyaev married in the summer, and she began work in the fall of 1979.

This emphasis on the importance of marriage and children to women continues to have great weight for many Uzbek families, even for those families who support their daughters and sisters in career ambitions. Marriage stands firm as the primary rite of passage that people engage in to make the shift from childhood to adulthood. It is marked by a change in terminology: marriage is when women shift from being referred to as a girl (*qiz*) to a woman (*ayol*), regardless of the age at which marriage takes place. Historically, it also marks the time when women move out of their family homes and into their husband's home. Even if married couples find an apartment in a different city, as Malika opa and Nurddin aka did when they married, women still find themselves under the sphere of influence of their husband's family, especially their mother-in-law. It was very important to Malika opa that she marry another person involved in the arts (Nurddin aka teaches voice at a local kollej), and that she would not be pressured to give up her career by her husband or his family.

This issue of the double burden of career and family, which may not be supported by one's husband and mother-in-law, continues to be a serious concern for women in traditional music, especially because many of them hold values that are deemed more conservative and traditional. Even as Malika opa broke through the gender barrier in the radio maqom ensemble, she often expressed worry and concern about her talented female students who would develop so much ability and then, if they married into a family that did not support their musical ambitions, would end up teaching part time at a music school or not working at all. While I was in Tashkent, Malika opa worked especially hard to promote the careers of her star students, both of whom were men, and often explained it in terms of the two of them needing a strong career in order to support a family. As a result, the issues of women making careers in traditional music in Uzbekistan continue to be complicated and restricted not only by the gender roles expected within ensembles or associated with instruments, but also by those roles that each woman is expected to embody within social and familial frameworks.

The expectation that women will have children was one of the largest obstacles put up by those who opposed Malika opa's appointment to the maqom ensemble in 1979. She addressed this in her discussion of her appointment to the maqom ensemble, saying, "People said that [the director of the maqom ensemble] shouldn't give me the job, since I'd be giving birth all the time, but at the time it was the Soviet period and at the time there was a law that doesn't exist anymore. It was called Young People's Specialization, and stated that after successfully completing higher education, the government gives you a place to work" (Ziyaeva 2009). Despite vocal opposition to hiring a woman into the ensemble—because of maternity leave(s)—the Soviet policy of placing graduates in available positions, combined with Orif Qosimov's retirement and Malika's position as the only dutarist graduating from the fledgling maqom department at the conservatory, resulted in her successful twenty-four-year career with the ensemble.

When I asked if it was difficult to work in an all-male ensemble, she noted that she was always careful to comport herself in a respectable and professional manner: dressing modestly, acting demurely, and practicing diligently. She replied, "This is why I always wore long sleeves, always dressed very modestly, wore [the traditional hat known as] duppi, and was always very serious and didn't gossip" (Ziyaeva 2009). With her high-profile position as the only female instrumentalist in the radio maqom ensemble, Malika opa needed to represent the best of women in both a traditional and a Soviet context. Like many of the women I spoke with in Tashkent, the generation of women who entered high-profile musical careers in the mid- to late twentieth century knew that they were held to a different standard and strove to meet the double burden of home life and career success with modesty and professionalism.

Ziyaeva takes great pride in the dissemination of dutar music outside of Uzbekistan, and it figures prominently in her account of her career. She often refers to it as "advertising Uzbek culture" and describes it as an important way to reach international understanding that is often impossible with words (Ziyaeva 2014). Malika opa discusses a variety of her professional activities in terms of her goals for creating cultural understanding through music, activities such as her many tours of Europe as part of the state maqom ensemble and in a smaller group accompanying vocalist Munojat Yulchieva and Shavkat Mirzaev (Yulchieva's teacher [ustoz]), as well as Malika opa's creation of the Shukrona (Gratitude) Ensemble and her help preparing me to found the University of California, Santa Cruz's (UCSC) Eurasian Ensemble (a student ensemble that focuses on Uzbek music; see figure 1.1, a photo of Malika opa during her 2014 visit to California). The concerts, teaching, and ensemble creation unite for Ziyaeva in terms of the continuation of the legacy (*meros*) that she learned from her teacher, Faxriddin Sodiqov, as well as an opportunity to share Central Asian musical culture with the world and with younger generations. This notion of legacy connects the student-teacher relationship with the broader performer-audience relationship and feeds them all into a larger national narrative about the importance of musical continuity and the preservation of tradition through musical performance. In this way, broad categories like nation and tradition become personal and individual. For Malika opa, the dutar encompasses it all.

The Primacy of the Voice: Lessons with Komila Aminova

Maqom is based on vocal lines and techniques. The various maqom repertoires include both accompanied song and instrumental pieces; even without a vocal line, the techniques and expressive idioms mimic vocal performance style. Malika opa emphasized this to me repeatedly in our lessons, often asking me to sing along with the melody that I was learning. She would explain the pulsating vibrato techniques (known as *nola*), the sense of legato in phrases, the pitch-bending pulls (called *qashish* by Malika opa), and even the trills in terms of sounds that one could sing. I struggled with some of the techniques that Malika wanted me to produce on the dutar, often because I found the vocal techniques unfamiliar and strange.

Figure 1.2. Komila Aminova (left) and Malika Ziyaeva in her apartment in Tashkent. Photo by author, 2008.

After my struggle with these issues during my first two trips to the field, in 2004 Malika opa decided that I needed to take voice lessons from a teacher in the traditional music department. She arranged for me to meet her close friend Komila Aminova (b. 1952), with whom she performed in the state radio maqom ensemble for many years (see figure 1.2, a photo of Malika opa and Komila opa together). Beginning in January 2005, I went to the conservatory every other week and sat at the piano with Komila opa in her studio. Our lessons proceeded from vocal warm-ups into the traditional/classical (mumtoz) repertoire that she and Malika opa agreed would help me to develop a more nuanced understanding of the expressive vocabulary so important to traditional music.

Much of what Komila opa taught me were the mumtoz pieces that are named for the maqoms in the Shashmaqom and Tashkent-Ferghana maqom repertoires. They are composed pieces that often sound rather improvisatory and are not included in the standard repertoire of each maqom, but are considered very closely related. In his book *The Hundred Thousand Fools of God*, Theodore Levin discusses Turgun Alimatov's version of one of these pieces, "Segah" (Segox). Levin includes significant discussion of his repeated recording sessions with Alimatov that resulted in his surprise at the consistency of Alimatov's versions; one of those recordings is included in the book's accompanying compact disc (1996, 53–56, track 4). Alimatov's performance of the piece is as an instrumental solo, but these compositions do have texts associated with them. Komila opa worked with me during 2005 on "Chorgox I" and "Bayot I" from the Tashkent-Ferghana maqom and "Dugox" and "Segox" from the Shashmaqom. Our work on these pieces was to provide me with a better understanding of and ability to produce the pulsating vocal ornaments (nola), so that I could perform the vocal sections of maqom pieces without embarrassing myself. Komila opa repeatedly told me that nola is a very Uzbek thing, and that it was an important way for pieces to succeed in expressing their emotional qualities. In her opinion, these mumtoz pieces would provide me the best entry into more authentic and expressive nola performance.

As we worked on pieces, she would play the melody on the piano, usually articulating the melody to be sung in a staccato fashion in octaves, filling in at the end of phrases with fourths and fifths, creating a sense of open chords. This approach confused me because the performance style of this music is not harmonic, and because the piano lacks the flexibility of pitch that most of the instruments featured in the traditional music department have. Komila opa explained carefully that the pitch variation in Uzbek music exists largely in the nola and other ornaments, not in the skeletal melody that she played. As a result, in the framework of a pitch reference, the piano was completely appropriate. Throughout our lessons at the piano, Komila opa exhorted me to stop singing through my nose and to sing with lots of air, loudly and from my stomach. "Ovozni chiking!," she would say, meaning "let your voice up/out." This was the clearest way to explain the difference between the head voice that I had learned to use in my school choir and the throat voice that she wanted me to extend into my highest vocal range. Only with that throat voice could singers achieve the intensity required for an appropriately expressive *ouge* or climax of the piece, which occurs at the highest point of both volume and range. This difference in vocal technique and timbre is one of the primary ways that Uzbek vocalists of traditional music distinguish themselves from the vocalists who study and perform Western art music in Tashkent.

Indeed, the difference in vocal quality is one of the reasons that certain vocalists studied in the Eastern Music Department during the latter part of the Soviet period, and why vocalists continue to flock to the Traditional Music Department today. Levin notes a famous story of the renowned Uzbek singer Munojat Yulchieva (mentioned previously) auditioning for the vocal department at the conservatory that taught opera and Western art music, and how she met her future teacher Shavkat Mirzaev when crying after finishing that disappointing audition. Mirzaev immediately invited her to audition for the Eastern Music Department, an audition that was well received and launched a very successful vocal career for Yulchieva (Levin 1996, 77–78).

Komila opa has a remarkably similar story of her entrance to the Tashkent Conservatory in 1974, when she was accepted as the first female vocalist in the Eastern Music Department. Like Yulchieva, who joined the department years after her and whom Komila opa tutored for a while during Yulchieva's first years at the conservatory, Komila opa first auditioned for the vocal section of the European Art Music Department. Born in a village near Ququn, she spoke very little Russian and was upset because she could not understand much of what was said (in Russian) at her audition. She realized that she could not study there because she would not understand, and left the audition crying. A member of the vocal faculty who heard her audition later approached her and told her about the Eastern Music Department. Komila auditioned there and was accepted, studying with Faxriddin Sodiqov and O'lmas Rassulov. During her time as a student at the conservatory, there were no female instructors in the Eastern Music Department; later a female voice teacher was brought in (Aminova 2008).

Like Malika, after the conservatory Komila opa joined the maqom ensemble at the state radio station as a vocalist. The radio maqom ensemble is quite a prestigious place to work, and it provided Komila opa with constant practice and repetition, leading to a mastery of both technique and repertoire that she now carefully passes on to her students. Even when using the piano as an accompanying instrument, picking out the rhythm and skeletal melodies in her teaching, she makes it clear that the voice is the primary vehicle for Central Asian maqom. The expressive vocabulary for all the instruments grows out of vocal technique, and it is that expression that makes the music sound truly Central Asian.

This kind of mastery and commitment to technique and musicality is amazing, considering Komila opa's tales of her modest, traditional village background: "An artist [professional vocalist] was something I didn't want to be; it was something bad to become," she declared during a 2008 conversation (Aminova 2008). In this quote, she is alluding to the associations that link loose morality with female musical performers, which I found still commonly discussed in Tashkent. That association was at odds with Soviet projects for the emancipation of women, and Komila was pulled between the two priorities. In the end, her passion for singing prevailed. She won local vocal competitions starting in the eighth grade, but when officials came and suggested that she audition for the conservatory, she did not want to because of the traditionally negative image of professional vocalists. Her father, however, encouraged her; he said that it would keep her from having to pick cotton on the collective farms. Komila opa, like Malika opa, mentions the importance of the opportunities that the Soviet era provided for women, and they try to give the same opportunities to their female students. Higher education was and is an important way for women to avoid both menial labor and early marriage.

Male Masters of the Tradition

Performance practice informs the formation of canons, but there is not always a one-to-one relationship between the performance of a repertoire and the stories and histories that are told about it. As with other repertoires that underwent canonization, maqom often omits from its history the women and other groups that do not fit the desired narrative. The process of canonizing traditional music in Uzbekistan depended a great deal on performers who became living representations of ancient history and on musicologists who narrated these histories, creating a cogent cast of men to populate the canon. Of all of the people working on traditional music as performers and scholars, Yunus Rajabi is the best possible example of a canonized and canonizing man.

Yunus Rajabi: The Great Modern Forefather of the Shashmaqom

Yunus Rajabi occupies a pivotal place both in the canon of great men in Uzbek traditional music and in the creation of this canon. He is considered an icon for the musical performance of national identity; he was both an active performer of traditional music and a major proponent of its codification through his musicological endeavors. As such, Rajabi is a name and an image known to represent maqom and Uzbek traditional music for both specialists and nonspecialists. He is, to my knowledge, the only musicologist to have a metropolitan transit station named in his honor. There is also a biannual national maqom competition named in his honor. Articles about Rajabi and his dynastic musical legacy (his son and grandsons are musicians and musicologists) appear in unlikely places such as the women's magazine *Jannat Makon* (The heavenly hearth). Rajabi's son Hasan is the curator of Rajabi's house museum and is a well-regarded musician and scholar himself, and often serves on the juries of traditional music competitions, including the biannual maqom competition.

Hasan Rajabi is much invested in the preservation and propagation of his father's (golden) legacy. Such recognition was well earned, since Rajabi founded the maqom ensemble at the state radio in the 1940s, which continued even during times when maqom was considered suspect by the regime.

Interestingly, he is also credited as one of the fathers of the arranged folk music genre because he began an ensemble with instruments that were reconstructed in order to produce a bass line. Thus Rajabi gives credibility to both that which is considered traditional and that which is modernized.

Another important role that Rajabi played in becoming the primary Uzbek musical icon was in collecting and transcribing the Shashmaqom and other traditional tunes. He published two large sets in his lifetime, six volumes of *Shashmaqom* (edited by musicologist Faizulla Karomatov) and eight volumes of *Uzbek Halq Musiqasi* (Uzbek folk music). This is especially important because the collection and codification of these works in Western notation was being carried out by an Uzbek expert rather than a Russian one. Indeed, it is also worth noting that Rajabi codified a specifically Uzbek version of the Shashmaqom, which is seen as a counterpart to the Fayzullayev et al. transcriptions of a Tajik version of the Shashmaqom that were published prior to Rajabi's. Theodore Levin provides an informative account of the process of canonizing separate Uzbek and Tajik versions of the Shashmaqom, beginning in the 1920s with Uspensky's textless publication of transcriptions of the Shashmaqom (Levin 1996, 47–59, 90–92).

These standardized transcriptions are centerpieces of traditional music pedagogy in Uzbek musical institutions, where maqom and related repertoires are taught via oral imitative methods, but students are required to demonstrate their abilities to read Western notation and use solfège. As a result, the Rajabi transcriptions are often described as an incredible act of preservation and a valuable memory aid because people no longer have to memorize the entire body of work. Malika opa says about the Shashmaqom collection:

> Not everyone can play it, even with this score. This is the biggest challenge [of maqom performance]. Here you have to fix it, every piece. For example, if you play music written by professional composers, they write the music down very exactly, but in maqom there are *nimparda* [halftone] . . . but [Rajabi and Karomatov] really worked hard. The [transcriptions] are a grammar, a skeleton. I also forget and can't remember the entirety [of the Shashmaqom]. So, it is a gift, that I have the music in my head. If it isn't in one's head, then there's nothing doing, right? This comes from twenty-five years' experience practicing in the maqom ensemble . . . the notes are just a graphic. (Ziyaeva 2004)

In this comment, Malika opa displays the extreme reverence that musicians have for Rajabi and the collections that have become so standard; however, it is clear that they also place a great deal of emphasis on practice, experience, and oral learning methods. The transcriptions provide important mnemonic devices, but performers are expected to play beyond what was transcribed and even to alter the notes that are written to match what they know to be the best way to perform the piece (either from experience or to match the manner in which their teachers played). Even with such caveats, the Rajabi transcriptions have allowed the Shashmaqom to be venerated as intangible national heritage,[6] as well as a tangible relic.

Male Pedagogues in the Ustoz-Shog'ird (Master-Apprentice) System

The master-apprentice (ustoz-shog'ird) system is one way that maqom repertoires are marked as different from other institutionalized genres such as European art music, arranged folk music, and estrada (popular music). It underscores the tradition that brought about the maqom repertoires, and it connects current practices with a past that is associated with the region before contact with Europeans. Although we know that women played dutar and music in private, the public master-apprentice system was not available to women until the twentieth century after the hujum; indeed, the patriarchal system still privileges men in traditional performing spaces, especially those that feature instrumentalists.

The preservation of this traditional method for musical transmission has been given high priority by Uzbek government institutions and international organizations alike. The further promotion of the master-apprentice system has become an important aspect of maqom performance and pedagogy, so much so that UNESCO has invested resources in preserving it. Thus, UNESCO has sponsored Shashmaqom Master Classes, which held their opening concert in the Uzbek State Conservatory in Tashkent on June 6, 2005. The program mentioned the master-apprentice system and encouraged masters to continue dissemination of their repertoire via this system. The concert program even included a list of prominent masters: Turgun Alimatov, Ikram Ibragimov, Hasan Rajabi, Shavkat Mirzaev, Munojat Yulchieva, Rifatilla Kasimov, Mahmud Tajiboev, Salohiddin Azaboyev, and others, who are all associated with the conservatory, the state radio, or both. Indeed, the ustoz-shog'ird system is seen as being part of the conservatory system now, as it is the main locus of maqom pedagogy in Uzbekistan (unlike Tajikistan, which has a Maqom Academy run outside state institutions, sponsored by the Agha Khan Foundation, which I visited in 2005).

Of the masters offering classes in 2005, Munojat Yulchieva (b. 1960) is the only woman on the list.[7] As the most famous traditional vocalist of her generation, it is not a coincidence that of the dozen names on the list, the only woman is a vocalist and is listed in conjunction with her teacher, Shavkat Mirzaev, as opposed to the others, who are given their own space in the list. As a result, the historical emphasis on male musical tradition-bearers continues in present-day contexts, although there are beginning to be efforts to include women like Yulchieva.

Munojat Yulchieva: Canonization through the Student-Teacher Relationship

Yulichieva's inclusion on that list of otherwise male maqom masters is no accident. She is one of the most internationally famous Uzbek figures; she toured extensively in Europe and is featured on quite a few recordings, including two that are dedicated solely to her work, one by Ocora (1994) and another curated by Razia Sultanova for the WDR World Network record label (1997). She is well known and deeply respected at home in Uzbekistan, throughout the former Soviet Union, and around the world. She provides the most famous representation of the professional canon of Uzbek traditional music. Even traditional music stars emulated by recent vocalists, such as Barno Ishakova (1927–2001), do not carry the symbolic importance that Yulchieva does. She is seen as carrying on her mentor Mirzaev's legacy. Other women, such as Malika opa and Komila opa, also do this for their mentors, but have not received the public attention that Yulchieva enjoys. Certainly Yulchieva's fame contributes to her inclusion in canonic representations, such as that in the UNESCO Masterclass.

Yulchieva's trajectory to mastery and canonization in traditional music follows a well-established path. Her origin story in traditional music is well known and often repeated, and she is inextricably linked with Mirzaev, seen as the one carrying on his art and bringing it to future generations. Her history is specifically told when describing the rise and importance of the Eastern/traditional music department, especially because it emphasizes the continuation of the master-apprentice (ustoz-shog'ird) system within the department's teacher-student relationships. Levin labels it "a mentor-protégée fairy tale" (Levin 1996, 77), but it resonates with many students' experiences forging a relationship with a master teacher at the conservatory. It also represents one of the ways that women are gaining access to canonizing processes—through mentoring relationships with male master musicians.

The importance of the master-apprentice/student-teacher relationship in traditional music cannot be understated and it is one of the aspects of traditional music that everyone, from conservatory deans to UNESCO event organizers, is interested in preserving. Combined with the emphasis, since the hujum, on including women in higher education, this means that many women are now in the position of public tradition-bearer and representative of their teachers' legacies. Both Malika opa and Komila opa were important students of Faxriddin Sodiqov and are seen as masters now in their own right, as Yulchieva is seen as continuing Mirzaev's legacy. The importance of these relationships is constantly emphasized in official and casual discourse—for instance, in Malika opa's comment to me about the system during a dutar lesson: "Traditional music depends on the relationship between master and apprentice [ustoz and shog'ird]" (Ziyaeva 2005c).

The fruitful quality of many of these mentoring relationships begun in the Soviet-era Eastern Music Department is resulting in women now in the position to act as masters in their own right. In this case it is the relationship (not the institution) that is foregrounded in providing Yulchieva with credibility. In an interview with Levin, she was asked, "Did you learn to sing like that at the Conservatory?" She responded by emphasizing the student-teacher relationship: "I learned from my teacher, Shâwqat-aka" (Levin 1996, 79). In this sense, the project begun with the hujum to bring women into professional life in music and other fields is only just starting to bear fruit because women are now seen as the natural choices to carry on their male teachers' work.

Furthermore, it is important to note that even though many women are in the position of tradition-bearer and legacy holder, they are not necessarily treating musical performance or repertoire as "frozen" (Levin 1996, 46–48) wherein they simply become a mouthpiece for their teachers or blindly follow the standardized versions of Rajabi and others. Malika opa described her relationship to the great men of the canon as one of gratitude but not necessarily deference when it came to issues of musical interpretation: "Rajabi hurried to publish those volumes [1970–76], collecting everything when he was 70 and 80 before he died, and for that I am very grateful to him. However, there are differences in how we perform the maqom now, and that [difference] is not a mistake" (Ziyaeva 2005d). In this sense, Ziyaeva and Yulchieva are engaging in the important work of keeping repertoires alive beyond their standardized transcriptions. Although the canonizers and standardizers have been male, women contribute to the continuation of its legacy as living performance. Their ownership of that legacy stems from ties to previous masters and participation in established ensembles.

Maqom and Nationalism in Tashkent

Of all the diverse musics that sound in the city of Tashkent, maqom and its related repertoires have the most strictly policed boundaries in terms of ethnonational identity. With the prestige of ancient heritage and legacy described in the music textbook mentioned previously come high stakes for the maintenance of specific imagery—especially national imagery—associated with the repertoire. As a result, the prevailing opinion in the city is that Russians and others of European descent do not play maqom because they lack the capacity to truly appreciate it that comes from heritage and/or upbringing. Maqom is understood as something that exists in one's blood, and discussions of heritage are often intricate enough to resemble notions of blood quantum or blood memory in the United States and to call to mind its treatment of minority groups from the eighteenth to twentieth centuries (Spruhan 2006).

This notion of a national hereditary link to maqom repertoires was prevalent in those I spoke with, and arose often in discussion of my desire to study and play mumtoz music. Malika opa would occasionally ask questions about my heritage, insisting that my family must have originally come from somewhere other than the United States. After I described my family's roots in Ireland, England, Germany, and Holland, Malika opa responded (probably facetiously) that it was possible that I had Uzbek heritage on the Dutch side of my family because the Uzbeks were great traders and merchants, and Holland has famous port cities.

Despite my distinct lack of a tangible heritage link to Central Asia, Malika opa was willing to help me access the repertoire, which shows that she had a fairly complicated understanding of this national construction of appreciation for the repertoire (it also marks her as progressive—many musicians whom I met with early in my fieldwork encouraged me to study folk tunes, but assured me that maqom would be beyond my understanding because I was not Uzbek). Even though she was willing to teach a non-Central Asian about maqom, Malika still believed strongly that music and other traditions are carried via blood ties. In an interview she emphasized this, saying "the most small [basic] thing is in the blood, regardless. Traditions exist in the blood. It pulls in the blood. Whether you like it or not, tradition pulls you back to it regardless. It is as our fathers and grandfathers said, regardless, it is in the blood" (Ziyaeva 2005a).

This notion of musical talent as hereditary is certainly not unique to the Uzbek or Central Asian context, nor is the expression of this notion of musical talent being carried "in the blood." Indeed, ethnomusicologist A. J. Racy notes a similar assessment of musical talent for musicians in the Arab world (Racy 2003, 20). This does, however, separate it from the rhetoric of musical talent or capacity being something that results from labor or as a gift from the divine; both such tropes are also present in discussions of musical ability in Uzbekistan. The idea of blood-borne affinity is unique to maqom, as opposed to European art music, which is accessible to everyone regardless of heritage. This contrast reflects the value that maqom holds specifically for Central Asian people, as opposed to the universal beauty that is often ascribed to other musical traditions (most commonly Western art music). It also may represent a defense mechanism against outsiders who undervalue maqom's complexity and beauty. The connection between heritage and musical facility allows maqom to have significant value even if it is underappreciated by those Russians and Europeans who lack the requisite heritage to understand it.

These connections between maqom and Central Asian ethnicity also play out on institutional levels, with structures, pedagogies, and materials supporting the concept, even if it did not originate in institutions. Indeed, in the Uzbek State Conservatory students are allowed to take classes in either Russian or Uzbek languages; there are specific numbers allowed for each program in either a Russian-language or Uzbek-language academic track. This is true in the departments of Western art music, popular music, and musicology, but, notably, the departments of traditional and folk musics only have an Uzbek-language track. Less formally, I have never seen a Russian student in any of the traditional music classes that I attended at music schools, high schools (kollejs), institutes, or the conservatory, even though the conservatory requires all students to take a short course on Uzbek classical music, and I even attended one taught in Russian for a group of musicology students. Despite the presence of a required course, the prevailing attitude is that people of Russian ethnicity are not interested in maqom, and that the language divisions in courses stem from a natural phenomenon.

Because maqom is so deeply entwined with notions of history, heredity, and blood ties, it is a powerful choice for the promulgation of an Uzbek national identity. Malika opa expressed the value of dutar performance and of maqom in terms of their ancientness many times, perhaps most clearly in the introduction to her 2008 volume on the music of her mentor (ustoz) Faxriddin Sodiqov.[8] In that introduction she declares, "[T]hrough the dutar, our beloved instrument, our Uzbek people reflect all the ritual and ancient practices, as well as national traditions" (Ziyaeva 2008, 3). Here the connection between ancientness and national value is evidenced in the strength of her statement as well as the proximity of the two concepts.

This employment of ancientness in service to the nation is not unique to Malika opa's perspective. In the introduction to his volume of mumtoz pieces for instruction at music elementary schools, Uzbek musician and pedagogue Temur Mahmudov emphasizes the weighty importance of his project in terms of national pride, saying, "In this era [of independence], the imparting of a musical legacy and its appreciation to our [Uzbek] people occupies an importance place within our national spiritual ethic. It is also important for enlightened education, in terms of music's place as a lifelong art with a long history" (Mahmudov 2006, 3). Mahmudov clearly places maqom and mumtoz music in a special place that connects Uzbeks as a people with a coherent national spiritual ethic, and this is a connection that resonates deeply with many musicians in the city of Tashkent.

Students of traditional music also acknowledge maqom's role in supporting narratives of Uzbekistan's national history. Dutarist and then conservatory student Mehrihon Muminova discusses the link between women's practices and nationalism, emphasizing the idea that women have a large role to play in displaying national heritage. In doing so, she provides a list of things that represent nationalism to her, all of which are associated with women.

> They tell us that it is more necessary for women to carry nationalism. Perhaps not for other nations, but for us Uzbeks, we approach things differently. For example, atlas fabric is nationalism, duppi hats are nationalism. For example, performing our ancient style of playing music is nationalism, braiding our hair in little braids is nationalism. All of these are examples of nationalism. (Muminova 2005)

She goes on to discuss this issue of performance and maqom, discussing how important our teacher, Malika opa, is and what a rare gem she is for her dedication to both teaching and performance. Muminova expresses this value in familial terms, saying that "[Malika opa] looks after us like her own children. For example, in the course of lessons, for example with one melody, she gives it to us beat by beat, note by note . . . because of this, we are so glad we became her students" (Muminova 2005). Once again, the connection between nationalism and heritage is experienced for women as a connection between individual musicians, a very personal, often familial history with music. This linkage between nationalism, tradition, and a familial understanding of the student-teacher relationship demonstrates how complex it is for women to participate in traditional music as national symbols.

Maqom and the Shift in Cultural Capital after Independence

Upon entering the field, with the notion that Shashmaqom was a desirable and complex repertoire that I wanted to understand better, as mentioned earlier, I contacted Malika Ziyaeva for lessons. When Malika opa assented to guide me through a course of study that would help me perform maqom, she insisted that we could not start there, since maqom is extremely complex. She noted at that lesson that I had some "European" bad habits that needed to be broken before I could play maqom. Her teaching purposefully veered away from what she perceived as European methods involving practicing scales and arpeggios (which are used in Uzbekistan when learning other styles of music, such as arranged folk music and Western art music). Her teaching methods involved imitation and repetition of phrases and rhythmic isolations of specific important patterns articulated by a relaxed right hand.

By the end of my first trip to the field in 2002, I had started to learn some of the most approachable pieces in the Shashmaqom ("Tasnifi Dugox" and "Garduni Dugox," both from the instrumental portion of the fourth maqom). Despite her aversion to what she saw as European habits that impaired my expressive ability in maqom, Malika opa was quite happy with the fact that I was a conservatory-trained musician.[9] She often provided me with photocopies of the Rajabi transcriptions of the pieces that I studied from the Shashmaqom and handwritten transcriptions of other pieces. In lessons and conversations, Malika and others praised the Shashmaqom as a "pearl of Uzbek history," a great treasure, and a golden legacy, and the Rajabi transcriptions played an important part in establishing and preserving that legacy.

Traditional music in general and Shashmaqom in particular has risen in status with the national project engaged in by the Uzbek government since independence. Although the Shashmaqom is a shared Uzbek and Tajik tradition, it—along with the poetry of Alisher Navoiy ([1441–1501]; the first "Uzbek poet," he published his works in the Chagatay language, a precursor to Uzbek) and of Zulfiya Izrailova ([1915–96]; a renowned female poet who has a prize in her honor given to women who make significant achievements in their field)—has become one of the cornerstones of national arts publicity in Uzbekistan. No longer a suspect national practice as it was during parts of the Soviet period, it is now a celebrated art that allows citizens to feel tied to their ancient heritage. This shift is also supported by foreign scholars and institutions that focus a great deal of attention on Central Asian maqom practices, specifically the Shashmaqom. The result is an atmosphere of pride and historical and international relevance cultivated by musicians who perform maqom, which is mixed with a sense of having prevailed through a time when maqom practices were not appreciated as worthy of celebration, canonization, and promulgation by state outlets. A strong canon of performers who continued performance traditions during the challenges of some parts of the Soviet period has formed. People add to that canon the larger historical and national narratives that they tell about maqom; unsurprisingly, the characters in these narratives are almost always male.

Collective Participation:
Traditional Ensembles, Modern Contexts

In discussing the borders and boundaries of gender identity within the practice of traditional music making, I want to avoid the oppression/repression narrative so common in the travelers' tales of the nineteenth century referenced in the introduction, as well as the travelers' tales of the twenty-first century. Indeed, in a 2010 episode of the series *Anthony Bourdain: No Reservations* on the Travel Channel that was set in Uzbekistan, Bourdain pointed out the vibrant tea culture of the *chaykhana* in Tashkent and Samarqand, but then claimed that the women are oppressed, doing all the work and the child care while the men sit in teahouses relaxing all day. As many feminists have noted, patriarchal essentialisms hurt both those in power and those who are not. Indeed, life in Tashkent is far more complex than lazy men and overworked women, or veiled secluded women and men who oppress them. Even women dedicated to traditional values and traditional music take advantage of thoroughly modern opportunities for international success and public renown. That said, social roles in urban Uzbek life are remarkably well defined, and most people choose to conform to them for all the benefits and praise that such actions bring. This is especially true of any identity marker or activity that falls within the traditions that are constructed and framed within Uzbek modernity.

Women's role in traditional music is complex, especially when considering the various forces policing differing notions of social role, traditionality, authenticity, and appropriateness. As noted by scholars such as Anne McClintock (1997) and Chandra Mohanty (1997, 1998), women are often associated with traditional practices and are often tasked as being representative of home, hearth, nation, and tradition. This is certainly true in Uzbekistan, where women are much more often seen in national costumes, and various food culture practices are their domain as well.

However, this gets complicated regarding music; although women are acknowledged to have a history of playing certain musical instruments that are seen as traditional, the traditional role of women requires them to avoid the public eye. This means that although there is an acknowledged long history of women playing traditional musical instruments, the history that has been documented is a male one. This is especially true of the traditional genre of maqom and its related repertoires as it is manifested in larger ensembles.

Women's Roles in the Uzbek State Radio Maqom Ensemble

Women have a curious role in the performance of traditional music: they are far outnumbered but also seem to carry much more expectation in terms of traditional dress and bearing. Despite cultural and individual variations of expected feminine behavior in Tashkent, the clarity of the boundaries around traditional musical performance and the performance of traditional femininity provide a useful lens through which to examine how gender is especially meaningful in musical performance.

Both Malika opa and Komila opa remembered their time in the state radio ensemble fondly as a period when they refined the techniques learned in the

Eastern Music Department of the conservatory and mastered a large portion of the repertoire. They acknowledge the challenges that women face in such ensembles, and are cautious about encouraging their female students in the direction of professional performance if they are more oriented to a family life. As a result, many of Malika opa's female students find positions as dutar teachers rather than in large ensembles. However, although the instrumental portion of the ensemble has reverted to its all-male status, there are still female vocalists who meet the demands of the maqom ensemble's broad repertoire, rigorous rehearsal schedule, and international tours. These women benefited from the precedent set by Malika opa and Komila opa.

Women's Roles in An'anaviy All-Dutar Ensembles

Women comprise a much higher percentage of the performers in all-dutar ensembles that perform traditional music than they do in the multi-instrument ensembles most closely associated with classical and traditional repertoires. Many of these all-dutar ensembles stem from the performance studios that Malika opa and other instructors have at music schools, kollejs, the pedagogical institute, and the state conservatory. Most of these ensembles are populated either by all of the members of an instructor's studio or by the most accomplished students of that studio. I observed many rehearsals and performances of the ensembles that developed out of Malika opa's conservatory and kollej studios, and some of them had no male members whatsoever. However, when questioned about such things, Malika opa framed the single-gendered makeup of the ensemble as entirely coincidental. She simply did not have any male students at that institution for that year. In 2005, she founded the Shukrona (Gratitude) Ensemble with a group of her current and former students, which included both men and women. This insistence on the coincidental nature of all-female dutar ensembles in the genre of traditional music is in significant contrast with the all-female dutar ensembles in arranged folk music, which are labeled specifically as women's ensembles.

In addition to gendered performance, there is also the issue of repertoire because the dutar ensembles arose during the Soviet era. Much like the confusion that Malika opa felt as a child studying arranged folk music while listening to maqom on the radio, dutar ensembles traverse the range and repertoire of both traditional and arranged folk music, which often creates tension and sometimes confusion. As mentioned previously, the dutar has an established history with musicians of both genders. The creation of publicly performing groups of dutar players that engage in either unison or polyphonic textures has roots in the Soviet era, especially the association of these groups with not just a single instrument, but also a single gender: women. This norm is so established that when discussing my own performance group in the University of California, Santa Cruz, with a woman at a wedding in 2009, I was told that the fact that both men and women played dutar in the ensemble was "exotic." That said, many traditional dutar ensembles are not single-gendered. The fame achieved by prominent female ensembles seems to have colored the view of nonspecialists, who now associate dutar ensembles with women. In fact the association of dutar ensembles with women seems to be the result of the many arranged folk ensembles that are called "girls' dutar ensembles" (*dutarchi qizlar ensembli*). Those I discuss further in chapter 2, but it is worth noting the difference between public perception and actual practice.

There are also interesting overlaps between the dutar ensembles associated with either arranged folk music or traditional music, in terms of instrument usage in educational institutions. As with Malika's perceived dissonance between a school education in arranged folk music and state radio station ensembles performing different traditional music, all the dutar ensembles that I worked with in elementary schools were based on reconstructed instruments, and many of the ensembles from kollejs were as well. Those ensembles often play arranged folk music, but sometimes have a focus on the early maqom repertoire as well. Despite the prevalence of arranged folk music in educational institutions, the most publicly renowned dutar ensemble is the Uzbek State Young Women's Dutar Ensemble, which has been housed in the state radio and television station since the Soviet era. Its repertoire and associations are with traditional music. Additionally, Malika opa has founded dutar ensembles with her kollej students (who happened to be all female when I worked with them in 2004 to 2005) and with her conservatory students (mixed gender). She also leads an ensemble of current students and alumni, who often perform other instruments like the tanbur (plucked lute) and gijak (bowed lute).

The Uzbek State Young Women's Dutar Ensemble has its roots in the Uzbek SSR during the World War II era. According to dutarist Ro'zibi Hodjayeva, just before the start of the war, the Ferghana television channel broadcast a variety of traditional musical performances and began showing performances of an all-women dutar ensemble. These performances received a positive reaction, and the women's dutar ensembles became one of the types of groups that were sent to the front to entertain the troops in USO-style entertainment shows (Hodjayeva 2009b). Even with this specific history, Ro'za and others (both musicians and nonmusicians) refer to women's dutar ensembles as representing an important and ancient tradition. The story that goes with such accounts usually includes the details that women have played the dutar in the ichkari (the inside/private life) for centuries, and that women would often play for one another in gender-segregated celebrations, such as life-cycle celebrations (to'ys) that include weddings, circumcisions, and the celebration after a baby reaches forty days old. Some such celebrations still retain the gender segregation that is considered traditional, and women musicians often perform at them, which makes such histories quite plausible.

The strong association between the dutar and femininity has a link to a larger gendered understanding of musical instruments. Malika opa explained it in terms of the tanbur and dutar as a matched pair like husband and wife or "yin and yang." Aside from associations with women's musical practices, the dutar is clearly the feminine side of the pairing, with silk strings plucked by hand that create a much softer timbre than the metal-stringed tanbur, which is plucked with a metal plectrum. This gendering of instruments is not unique to Uzbek culture; neither is the idea that men can also play female-gendered instruments without complication. As ethnomusicologist Veronica Doubleday notes, "Another outcome of male dominance is that women rarely enjoy a gender-exclusive relationship with a musical instrument. A number of instruments are closely associated with female performance, but in most cases men also play them if they wish (Doubleday 2008, 19). Her argument about nonexclusivity is appropriate in this context as it is unheard of for a woman to play tanbur, the masculine side of the balanced maqom instrument pairing. Indeed, I never encountered a female tanburist or any story told about a woman who could play. Truly, the historical emphasis on the dutar as the only nonpercussion instrument that women played seems to continue to have strong suggestive power. Many women, including Malika opa, were encouraged to play the Kashgar rubob in the Soviet era, and indeed many women still do play that and occasionally the hammer dulcimer (chang). However, the dutar continues to be seen as the default option for girls who aspire to be traditional and arranged folk musicians.

Dutar ensembles, which straddle the genres of traditional and arranged folk music, are thus some of the more important ways that women locate themselves within Uzbek musical institutions. They represent a bridge between notions of tradition and modernity, as dutar ensembles are common in both traditional and arranged folk music departments and often share repertoire to a certain extent. Given its associations with femininity and the pre-Soviet past, dutar performance provides women an avenue for participation in the larger national project; the women's dutar ensembles that arose during the Soviet era do not seem to carry the mark of Soviet culture. They manage to reference the pre-Soviet past, with the notion that women played the dutar historically, while reaching to the modern with large ensembles that take on ambassadorial roles, introducing foreign audiences to music that links up with Uzbek traditionality. This may be a function of the strongly gendered nature of these ensembles—their association with women's ancient practices (imagined or otherwise) trumps any association with a given regime or ideology. In chapter 2, however, we see that dutar ensembles that employ reconstructed instruments engage with the discourses of femininity and nationalism differently, often while negotiating a space for the dutar in the framework of modernity.

Conclusions

Although women are not generally included in written accounts of the history of maqom and related repertoires, they are currently poised as important legacy keepers within the master-apprentice framework that continues to hold a key place in the larger narrative about traditional music's role in present-day Uzbekistan. Some of this is because the extension of this canonic transition from teacher to student to performers such as Munojat Yulchieva, Malika Ziyaeva, and Komila Aminova is recent enough that it is not codified into texts. Another aspect of this phenomenon may be the result of a similar kind of erasure to the one that Citron documents in Western art music ([1993] 2000). Namely, women continue important legacies but are not necessarily credited with their accomplishments in larger discourse or documented histories. This sense of exclusion from the canon is part of a larger emphasis on men's historical role performing traditional music in public, whereas women's private musical performances do not find places in the history books.

However, beyond asking the basic question stemming from the second wave of feminist theory—"Where are the women?"—it is important to consider what work women are presently engaging in regarding the performance and the discourse on (professional) traditional music, and how that work connects to larger narratives and projects. Certainly we can find evidence of women musical performers throughout the centuries, even if they are largely absent from the codified narrative of the maqom traditions. The work that female professional traditional musicians do in support of national narratives of an ancient Uzbek cultural legacy enlists performers beyond the most internationally famous, such as Munojat Yulchieva. Even dutar students in Malika opa's studio are engaged in the important work of interpreting national narratives into their own lives and musical performance. Women's performance of traditional music is one of the key ways that the performance of national narratives is individualized, personalized, and imbued with layers of meaning not necessarily provided by larger institutional messages. Mehrihon Muminova's account of how nationalism is created in a variety of arts and handicrafts was a spontaneous iteration of her own experience and worldview; certainly it was influenced by dominant tropes about national identity, but the list is clearly personal and individual. Traditional musical performance is a key actor in this process of feminizing national projects and internalizing them.

All-women dutar ensembles are especially important in showcasing the vital role that female musicians have in demonstrating the act of tradition-bearing through music. Rooted in these important narratives and oral histories of women playing within the ichkari, they allow women to occupy that important border, deeply rooted in pre-tsarist Turkistan, that is both traditional past and modern present. This youthful smiling performance of gendered nationalism is enacted through engagement with a variety of repertoires, not all of which are linked specifically to pre-Soviet folk music. Even dutar ensembles that feature equal-tempered, reconstructed instruments and polyphonically arranged tunes manage to access this important trope of traditional femininity in modern contexts.

2 Ancient Treasures, Modernized

Women's Dutar Ensembles and Arranged Folk Music

On a scorching summer day in 2002, in a new conservatory building recently opened in Tashkent, it is largely quiet during the vacation period. Nevertheless, the sounds of strumming and chattering female voices emanate from one classroom, as Ro'zibi Hodjayeva (known to her students as Ro'za opa) leads a rehearsal for the dutar ensemble of a local music school. About half a dozen girls, ages eight to thirteen, hold different sizes of the same instrument, including the tiny prima dutar, the mid-sized alto dutar (thought to be well suited to women's voices), and the largest—the tenor dutar—that is the equivalent size to the dutars played in traditional ensembles. The sounds coming from the classroom range from wobbly unisons to triadic harmonies that suggest Western chord progressions. Ro'za opa encourages her students to play together, to match one another's pitches and strumming gestures in order to achieve perfect simultaneity. Many of the pieces that the group rehearses are instrumental, but on a few occasions, they add their voices, singing along with the melody that they perform on the dutars. The girls are encouraged to learn their pieces from notation and then memorize them. In the course of their memorization, it seems as though oral imitative method is engaged to a great extent, even though the primary focus is on reading the music and performing the arrangements and compositions precisely as written.

One of the favorite pieces that the girls rehearse over and over is "Ayvon" (The patio). In this, the girls play the alto or tenor dutars, and those who have learned the vocal part sing along, all in unison. The piece, composed by Tuxtasin Jalilov (for whom the state folk orchestra in Tashkent is named), is written out in Western notation with letters above many notes to indicate which finger to strike the strings with and in which direction to strum. The text that they sing is sung from the perspective of someone who holds unrequited love for a neighbor.

"AYVON" (FIRST VERSE), TUXTASIN JALILOV, COMPOSER

Sizni Ayvon, bizni o'rgilay, ayvon emasmu
O'rtasida chinni o'rgilay, ravon emasmu
Kelasizu-ketasiz, bir suz demaysiz
Bu hammasi yurakka o'rgilay, armon emasmu

Your patio is not our patio, is it, my dear?
Here in the middle, the truth isn't eloquent, is it, my dear?
You come and you go, and don't say a word
All of it emphasizes the painful lack I feel in my heart, doesn't it, my dear?

Ro'za opa leads them through the song phrase by phrase, playing and singing with them, occasionally stopping to correct a student's finger position or strumming technique. She encourages her students to sing with full voices, but not to push too hard when the pitch makes a sudden jump of a fifth in the second phrase of the chorus, which causes them to increase the volume suddenly. The girls in her class pay her rapt attention and clearly understand and appreciate her willingness to come in during summer vacation to rehearse with them.

The arranged folk music that Ro'za opa and her students play represents a distinctly different practice from that of traditional music. Although there are many similarities, especially instruments that share the same name, category, and basic appearance, the music diverges from traditional practice in terms of sound, aesthetic, and texture. Further, those who play arranged folk music employ strategies to connect to national projects and ideas of femininity that diverge starkly from the strategies that traditional women musicians use when discussing the music that they play. This is linked to multiple factors, including the history of the genre of arranged folk music in the Soviet period, as well as the histories and narratives that women performers use when discussing their musical style, its importance, and their role in it.

However, despite such diverging strategies, pedagogies, and histories supporting the performance practice and rhetoric of both styles, within the discourse, unifying factors are identifiable. Beyond the organological roots that unify the two styles, performers are both encouraged to "play from the heart" (*yuraqdan cholish*) and to go beyond merely playing the notes. Although the aesthetics of what constitutes emotional and musical performance differs in both styles as much as the rhetorical strategies supporting them, the effort to communicate musical meaning and engage in emotional expression unifies the two genres.

This chapter focuses on women who are active in arranged folk music performance and examines the history of their role in the genre, as well as the discourses surrounding it. It begins with a discussion of the assumptions of youth and femininity associated with certain ensembles, then traces the history of such ensembles as they share history with similar ensembles from other former Soviet republics. After the historical outline, prominent women musicians provide three accounts of the Soviet period, including conductor and instrumentalist Faizila Shukurova, conductor Firuza Abdurahimova, and dutarist Ro'zibi Hodjayeva. Following both general and individual histories, specific themes arise as they unite Soviet and post-Soviet contexts. These themes include the valorization of European masters and their "academic" style, the relevance of folk dance, and arranged folk music's role in elementary education. Finally, the discussion ends by examining various ensembles' positioning in terms of national relevance in the postindependence era, an issue that remains primary in the musical discourse.

Gendering the Dutar: Young Women's Dutar Ensembles

One of the most common ensembles at both educational institutions and in the media is the young women's dutar ensemble, such as the one described above, which I first observed rehearsing in the summer of 2002 in a sweltering conservatory classroom. The name for this type of ensemble, *dutarchi qizlar ansembli,* is somewhat challenging to translate. The Uzbek word *qiz* is usually translated as *girl* or *daughter,* depending on the context in which it is used. In this case, I use the phrase "young women" because in my experience the ages of members of such ensembles can range from ten to thirty, and members of the ensemble associated with the state radio station usually occupy the latter half of that age range (see figure 2.1, which shows Ro'za opa rehearsing with the state radio station's young women's dutar ensemble). This radio ensemble is usually thought to exist under the rubric of traditional music, despite its Soviet roots and the large size of the ensemble. It represents a gray area between the two styles, especially now that it is directed by Ro'za opa, an arranged folk musician who often seeks to express the commonalities between the two styles. Furthermore, the ensemble's association with youth is indeed important in this instance, and women are encouraged by the administration to shift to other ensembles once they reach thirty or so (Hodjayeva 2009b).

Figure 2.1. Ro'zibi Hodjayeva (left, with frame drum [doyra]) rehearsing the Uzbek state radio station's young women's dutar ensemble. Photo by author, 2009.

This gendered marking of dutar ensembles also translates into Russian language discourse, where they are called *ansembl dutaristok* (ensemble of female dutarists). The Russian descriptors lack the specific reference to age in the title, but nonetheless, most performers in such ensembles are referred to in both languages with the term indicating young, unmarried women.

Interestingly, these ensembles blur the strong institutional lines between traditional music and arranged folk music. As mentioned in chapter 1, all-dutar ensembles are common in traditional music departments, as they are in arranged folk departments. I have seen more mixed-gender all-dutar ensembles in traditional music departments, although people often still refer to them as girls' dutar ensembles as a general category. Clearly this ensemble and its associations with femininity have a symbolic hold on both musicians and nonmusicians with whom I spoke: it is a category that is understood as gendered, even if the instrument itself is associated with both men and women. The collective unison performance of the dutar (or a harmonized arrangement, if using a consort of reconstructed dutars) is most associated with young women, and it bridges the divisions between arranged folk music and traditional music because this ensemble is identified with both styles. The ubiquity of the notion that dutar ensembles are a women's ensemble may be what led some people (especially nonspecialists) to describe the mixed-gender dutar ensemble that I lead at the University of California, Santa Cruz, as exotic for its inclusion of men, and also why my performance of the dutar is often remarked upon as something quintessentially feminine and Uzbek.

This elision of age, gender, and national identity is not necessarily unique to the Uzbek context, although certainly this particular manifestation is. Anthropologist and cultural theorist Anne McClintock discusses the "intense emotive politics of dress" regarding women's larger role in performing national identities through the public display of national dress (McClintock 1997, 97). This is certainly present in Uzbek contexts across musical genres. Indeed, there are additional aspects of cultural expression beyond costuming that also seem to have intense emotive qualities, including the strong feminine and national associations with the dutar, especially as played by youths in groups.

In the same chapter, McClintock goes on to note that national discourses, as they grapple with notions of traditionality and modernity, often present the "contradiction in the representation of *time* as a natural division of *gender*" (1997, 92). Although McClintock is clearly referring to a traditional past redolent of hearth and home that is associated with women and a public modernity associated with men, this issue of time is worth considering for the extreme value placed on youth by these dutar ensembles. Uzbekistan is hardly the only nation in which youth is praised and valued; the focus on youth and femininity is something that film scholar Zhang Zhen notes as symbolically important in late twentieth-century China, with a phenomenon called the "rice bowl of youth," where young women are specifically sought for high-paying jobs in urban centers where youth and beauty are highly valued (Zhang 2000, 94). She notes that within this phenomenon, "[F]eminine youth [is] fashioned as the timeless object of male desire [and] is simultaneously the trope and implementation of modernization and globalization with Chinese characteristics" (2000, 95).

It seems no coincidence that young women are chosen to represent a specifically non-Western modernity that engages with symbols of tradition and nation in both the Chinese context (with the "rice bowl of youth") and the Uzbek setting (with the dutar). However, in modern Uzbekistan, the combination of gender traditions, nation, modernity, and youth is unique in terms of post-Soviet manifestations of a modern femininity that embraces a sense of renewed and remade tradition. It is also worth noting that in music's role in the Uzbek national project, there is a strong assumption of a male gaze in terms of the marketing of national identity, one that appreciates youth, beauty, and pleasant, uplifting, yet traditional sounds.

This representation of young women performing arranged folk music on a single instrument thus contrasts significantly with ensembles that perform traditional music, which often feature older solo vocalists, and in which most of the performers are still men. Young women's dutar ensembles represent a different relationship to notions of modernity and history than that implied by maqom ensembles. Indeed, reconstructed dutar ensembles' employment of written scores for the learning and dissemination of music allows the ensemble to sidestep what are acknowledged as traditional modes of transmission, specifically the oral-imitative teaching methods used in the master-apprentice system (one in which, as mentioned in chapter 1, the vast majority of masters are male).

The Creation of Arranged Folk Music in Uzbekistan

Arranged folk music performed on reconstructed instruments—whether involving groups of young women playing different sizes of dutars or large folk orchestras that include a variety of reconstructed instruments—has a distinct history that emerged in Central Asia during the 1930s, when similar developments were underway throughout the Soviet Union. The phenomenon itself, however, has its roots in the late nineteenth century, with the founding in Russia of *balalaika* (plucked metal-strung lute) orchestras and the resulting reconstruction project that created symphonic-style folk orchestras.

Pre-Soviet History

Aspects of arranged folk music, including instrument reconstruction, temperament, and employment of Western harmony, may be traced to the pan-Soviet reconstruction projects in the 1930s, but the practice of altering instruments in order to allow ensembles to perform harmony (or at least double at the octave) is one that has roots before the Soviet era in both Uzbekistan and Russia. During the first two decades of the twentieth century, while Central Asia was still under Russian colonial rule, Yunus Rajabi experimented with larger versions of plucked lutes that could double the melodies performed by maqom ensembles at the octave. It was not a widespread practice at the time, but sources on Uzbek folk orchestras cite this as an origin point for the reconstructed folk instruments later used in the Soviet and post-Soviet periods.[1]

The other important origin point often cited for folk orchestras and reconstructed instruments is the reconstruction project begun in the nineteenth century by nobleman and Russian balalaika player Vasiliy Andreev (1851–1918). Andreev was the innovator of the Russian folk orchestra, masterminding the reconstruction of the balalaika into consorts that correspond with vocal ranges, feature equal-tempered tuning, and are made of materials meant to project within concert halls.[2] He began this project in 1887 with a group of seven to eight balalaika players, and gradually expanded from there. Andreev worked hard to popularize this approach, which mimicked the Western symphony orchestra, seeing it as a way to "resurrect" folk instruments. His work in the late nineteenth and early twentieth centuries did not catch on immediately, but once the Russian army embraced it, the ensembles quickly grew in popularity (Olson 2004, 16–17). There was also a rise of folk choruses in the late nineteenth century, the most famous of which were led by Dmitri Agrenev-Slavianskiy and later by Mitrofan Piatnitskiy, whose repertoire included many songs, such as "Kalinka," that have since become classics in the Russian folk song canon (Olson 2004, 28–29).

Soviet-Era Innovators: Andreev and Petrosiants

Andreev's work continued after the Bolshevik Revolution, but his balalaika ensembles, along with the folk choruses mentioned previously, needed to align themselves with the ideology of the Communist Party and the newly founded Russian Association of Proletarian Musicians (RAPM), which in the late 1920s sought to stifle the performance of Russian folklore because of its perceived cultural "backwardness" (Russian: kul'turnaya otstalnost') (Olson 2004, 37). By the 1930s in the Soviet Union, the stage was set for the flourishing of folk orchestras, projects that supported Soviet ideology by taking instruments common to peasants and nonbourgeois peoples and "elevating" them to a standard associated with high quality and international renown. This elevation process inevitably brought the instruments, composers, and musicians into conversation with Western art music.

Many people in a variety of Soviet republics began arranging folk music and dance for concert performance. Slavic studies scholar Laura Olson comments on this process of marrying musical production with government ideology. "According to official rhetoric [in the 1930s], socialism had been achieved and class no longer existed as a legitimate category. However, one remnant of the pre-socialism days was allowed to remain—nationality. Socialism now included the 'brotherhood of the peoples,' the idea that all (except the Russians) were equal. The Soviets invested enormous time and energy into the production of national consciousness among the citizenry" (Olson 2004, 37). This process happened in the other republics, such as Kazakhstan (Rancier 2009a, 115–24), although the most remarked of the folk orchestra models came from Russia, where the phenomenon originated, and where many major figures hail from. Igor Moiseyev is perhaps the most famous folk dance revivalist of the era, as Dmitri Agrenev-Slavianskiy and Mitrofan Piatnitskiy were for their folk choruses (of which Piatnitskiy's was given the moniker "ethnographic" [Russian: etnograficheskiy]).

The 1930s was a very important time for bringing the arts in line with Soviet values. Soviet-trained ethnomusicologists Izaly Zemtsovsky and Alma Kunanbaeva describe the atmosphere of this era: "Folklore in the USSR was called upon to help in the building of a new culture, 'national in form and socialist in content.'... Whatever and whoever did not suit this model was to be reoriented or eliminated" (Zemtsovsky and Kunanbaeva 1997, 6). The reconstruction of instruments and the arrangement of folk songs into polyphonic symphonic works were important ways to mold folk culture into a Soviet image. Indeed, this process of harmonizing folk music was framed in terms of the creation of important culture for the Uzbek people (and on their behalf). As local Soviet-era musicologist S. Zakrzhevskaya notes, "The problem of harmonization in Uzbekistan is extraordinarily important, for harmony is tied to the formation of a modern Uzbek national musical style" (Zakrzhevskaya 1968, 212). This rhetoric pervaded the Soviet era, and folk orchestras and their polyphonic music were emblematic of the ideological project of using culture to emancipate the workers.

In Uzbekistan, the primary figure associated with the Soviet-era innovation of reconstructed folk instruments and their new capabilities is Armenian acoustician Ashot Petrosiants (1910–78). He founded a musical instrument laboratory and museum in the Tashkent Conservatory that continues operation in the current independence era. His philosophy expresses the educational value of the creation of such instruments because they would help educate the folk in harmony and polyphony: "Folk instruments, being at the same time popular and associated with the masses, had to play an important role in the wide propaganda of musical literacy, in the development of multivoiced performance, and in the development of the talent of the folk" (Petrosiants [1951] 1990, 5). It was this synergy between peasant/folk instruments and polyphony that clearly fit into the government's ideological project of uplifting the folk and educating the masses. This approach, marketing such instruments and ensembles as educational tools, was the primary strategy promoted in the promulgation of reconstructed folk instruments and arranged folk music. Later in Petrosiants's volume on the reconstructions of folk instruments, he makes this explicit, saying: "The reconstruction of Uzbek folk instruments gave us the possibility not only to develop Uzbek culture, to involve wide masses of the folk in active musical activities, but also to contribute to the spiritual life of the peoples of the Soviet Union" (Petrosiants [1951] 1990, 6).

This heady mix of mass musical activities tied to the soul of the people made folk orchestras a powerful metaphor for the progress that the Soviet system brought to "backward" peoples, as it implied more than mere technological or intellectual development.

In 1938, Petrosiants founded his first official Uzbek folk orchestra that performed polyphony at the Uzbek State Philharmonic (Russian: Uzbekskoy Gosudarstvennoy Filarmonii).[3] At the time he was serving as an instructor at the Tashkent Musical Technicum (Russian: Tashmuztekhnikum), an institution of higher education sometimes considered a precursor to the conservatory, which also had more focus on pedagogy than concert performance (Sobirova and Abdurahimova 1994, 12). He later became an instructor at the Tashkent Conservatory, where he was already working on reconstructed instruments. The conservatory was founded in 1937, but provided education at that time only in Western art music. In 1949, the Department of Arranged Folk Music opened, ushering in an era when folk orchestras flourished in the Uzbek SSR (Sobirova and Abdurahimova 1994, 36).

Faizulla Karomatov, a musicologist and founder of the traditional music department in the conservatory, remembers this period of development, with traditional music ascendant until the 1920s. After that, the focus shifted toward arranged folk music and Western art music, eventually resulting in an educational system devoid of traditional music from World War II until the 1970s. This shift was conscious and ideological, and in a 2005 conversation, Karomatov described the progression clearly. Until the purges of 1937, traditional music was quite prominent and in 1926 a system of schools of music opened. The first school focused on traditional music, and Karomatov was part of that system of education. According to him, the shift toward reconstructed instruments took hold only after World War II. At that point in his account, Karomatov stated, "Slowly [only] the arranged folk instruments that had been reconstructed [were left]. At that point they called [traditional music] 'backward,' and asked whether or not it was still needed" (Karomatov 2005). The use of the term *backward* (*qoloq*) to describe traditional music was fairly common at the time, and it provides insight into the utility that the government saw in the reconstruction projects. This act of uplifting "backward" music to an international standard became part of the project of uplifting peoples who were seen as backward and uneducated.[4] In 1971, in one of the earliest English-language articles on Central Asian music, ethnomusicologist Mark Slobin noted the same rhetoric in scholarly musical discourse, explaining, "It seemed to the Soviet writers I read that Uzbek music was a largely unacceptable remnant of a 'feudal' past, which must change with the times" (Slobin 1971, 7). This connection with ideology is important to consider, but just as Karomatov emphasizes the ebb and flow of traditional musical practices during the Soviet era, even Slobin noted that the task of reconstruction and modernization was largely run by Uzbeks themselves and thus hard to dismiss as solely a forced project from Moscow. Therefore, even during the Soviet period, the specific proportions involved when blending nationalism with notions of international prestige (via ties to Western art music or, as Slobin puts it, the desire to "sound as much like Tchaikovsky as possible" [Slobin 1971, 7]) were in constant negotiation.

Arranged Folk Music and Soviet Inclusion of Women in the Workplace

A key aspect of this nationwide government project to bring culture to a higher level corresponded with a move toward what was seen as equal participation for women, at least in the workplace. Beginning with the hujum unveiling campaigns of the 1920s, the inclusion of women in Soviet-era ensembles was very important to the government's strategies of women's liberation. Women engaged in all kinds of musical performance spoke proudly of the opportunities that the Soviet Union had afforded them, but the folk orchestra, as a Soviet ensemble, required a public performance of this policy of gender equality. As such, after World War II, conservatory director Muxtor Ashrafiy took a delegation out to cities and towns throughout the Uzbek SSR searching for talented youth, especially girls. Conductor and chang (hammer dulcimer) player Faizila Shukurova remembered proudly when Ashrafiy came to her home city of Samarqand in 1960 and chose her for the conservatory's preparatory program when she was only fourteen years old (Shukurova 2008). Many women like her have been proud to be on the vanguard of women in the musical profession. According to Faizila opa and others, music was one of the more difficult professions to attract girls into because of the requirements of public performance on stage and of the associations with "easy women" (Shukurova 2008). At the same time that women are now accepted in all types of professions in Uzbekistan, this association with loose morals, and the concern that public performance ruins girls, still persists. It means that highly successful public performers have had to make a deft negotiation between traditional morality and modern institutions that value women's equal participation in the workplace.

In her travels throughout Central Asia in the 1920s, US journalist Anna Louise Strong noted and praised the Soviet educational system and reported on a music high school in Samarqand in particular, noting that the students "[go] forth to sing and dance propaganda into the villages" (Strong 1929, 80). She later writes of a spectacle put on by students of the same school at a train station, and notes the specifically coed nature of their performance. She characterizes the melodies performed as "the monotonous music of Central Asia, often tiresome to a European," but comments that the texts sung to the "monotonous" traditional melodies reflect the new values of the Soviet state (Strong 1929, 117). She describes the spectacle as a whole as "modern," and goes on to translate one such song, which she describes as having strong rhythm and being sung by a man and woman facing each other.

> Where, O where is the maiden?
> Where, O where is the maiden? . . .
>
> Here, O here is the maiden.
> Here, O here is the maiden. . . .
>
> You are given as a bride to an old man,
> Who offers a fine rich kalym (bride money). . . .
>
> I won't marry an old man,
> And kalym is now forbidden. . . .
>
> Who then will marry the maiden?
> Who then will marry the maiden? . . .
>
> I will marry a Comsomoletz
> I will marry a Comsomoletz (young Communist and very modern). . . .
> (Strong 1929, 118–19)

Strong's observations about musical productions that included traditional melodies fits within Karomatov's description of the 1920s as it allowed space for traditional music even in the ideological project of representing Soviet Turkistan musically. In this case, the rhetorical shift toward modern values does not require a complete rift from the previous musical forms, but simply a commitment to forsake other traditions (like the bride price or "bride money," as Strong translates the Uzbek term *kalym*). This transition had a serious impact on women, who became an important symbol for progress toward modernity. Such "emancipatory" movements did not come without a price, creating for many women a double burden of home and career life. Musician and conductor Faizila Shukurova remembers her musical education and experience with pride, while also noting the challenges of maintaining a career, a family, and keeping a home.

Now, in our lives, there are a lot of advantages. We can, without a problem, leave the house, work, wear whatever we want, play music. However, there are difficulties too, since there are troubles with the family, since all the family work remains. In the past men would do everything needed in the public sphere, even go to the bazaar and buy everything we needed for the house, groceries and everything. Now there's quite a burden on us women! (Shukurova 2008)

Soviet Histories Remembered by Women Performers

As Strong notes, the inclusion of women in public musical performance was an important step in publicizing a notion of Uzbek Soviet modernity. It was one of the more challenging aspects of the larger emancipatory cultural project associated with the hujum. Although the consultants who contributed to my research were not yet born during the 1920s, many do credit that generation of women with helping to create a foundation for the career opportunities that they enjoyed in the later Soviet period in the 1960s, 1970s, and 1980s. Much like the reminiscences of Malika opa in chapter 1, the musical histories of chang (dulcimer) player and conductor Faizila Shukurova, folk orchestra conductor Firuza Abdurahimova, and dutarist Ro'zibi Hodjayeva provide a view of the Soviet musical education system as one that focused on bringing more women into public performance, even pushing them to play instruments not often associated with femininity (as opposed to the dutar, which was). However, it is notable that the instruments these women began studying (the Kashgar rubob [a shorter-necked plucked lute] and the chang) have now become a sort of new norm for women's performance in the twenty-first century. During my research, I met schoolgirls and female conservatory students who studied dutar, rubob, and chang, but none who studied the gijak (bowed fiddle) or the doyra (frame drum). It is possible that such performers exist, and certainly many students of both genders play the doyra casually, without formal lessons. However, in the conservatory and in various kollejs and music schools, the doyra studios are populated solely by men. As a result, these reminiscences from women who studied arranged folk music during the Soviet period can be seen as reflecting an important time when a new norm for women's performance was solidifying.

Faizila Opa's History

Faizila Shukurova remembers her progress through the Soviet educational system in the 1950s and 1960s fondly, noting that it was a distinct privilege that her parents lacked. She specifically mentioned that her parents did not go to university because they came of age during the war. This motivated her parents to push their children to take advantage of Soviet programs that brought bright students from the provinces to central cities for further education in kollejs and universities (Shukurova 2008). Part of her childhood memories include dancing to her father's dutar playing and being encouraged to pursue music, even though she did not come from a family of professional musicians.

Faizila opa emphasized that music was an especially challenging profession for women to break into because of the social stigma associated with women who perform music or dance in public, come in contact with "strange men," and thus gain a reputation for a lack of morality. According to her, the first women musicians were actresses who would sing—that was the breakthrough moment. When the conservatory opened, it attracted women, usually Russians and Tartars, but few Uzbeks. It was not until her childhood in the post–World War II era that there was a large orchestrated push to bring young Uzbek women into musical higher education, around forty years after the hujum focused on unveiling and on encouraging women's participation in the workforce.

While Faizila opa was a student in school in Samarqand, composer Muxtor Ashrafiy was the director of the conservatory, and he sent a delegation to invite young Uzbek students to the conservatory, especially women because there were so few of them. As a result, Faizila opa only studied for one year in Samarqand and then was taken to Tashkent for further study. She remembers playing the tune "Yoshlik" (Youth) for the commission, after which she was accepted to the conservatory at age fourteen for a two-year preparatory course. While in Tashkent, she lived with her three sisters, all of whom were eventually sent from Samarqand to study in Tashkent. She remembered difficult good-byes at the train station, when her mother would send them off with huge bags of flour and jars of homemade jam (Russian: *vareniye*).

It was rare at the time for women to choose a musical profession, and unheard of for a girl to play the chang. Faizila opa's family was supportive of her innovative choice and even sold their cow to buy her instrument, which was much more expensive than plucked string instruments like the dutar or Kashgar rubob. Faizila opa still has that first chang, and remarks that it was made by a "very good Russian instrument master who was living in Tashkent" (Shukurova 2008). Many of the instrument makers and early pedagogues of arranged folk music in the Uzbek SSR came from Russia and Armenia, and later taught Uzbek instrument makers.

When she arrived at the conservatory, Faizila opa became the first girl to study chang in the halq cholg'u (folk performance/arranged folk music) department, and she was one of only ten girls in her class across all instruments. Remembering her early days in the halq cholg'u department (founded in 1949), which she joined in 1960, she said that many of her teachers were the first graduates of the department and were hired to teach immediately after graduation. She also mentioned playing a wide range of music, the only requirement being that it was written in Western notation: "In the halq cholg'u department, very few of our Uzbek national melodies had been notated at that time. As a result, we played more European works and folk compositions from other republics, such as say, Azerbaijan, and the Georgian republic had its own works, and more Kazakh and Kyrgyz ones. For us, if it was notated, that's it, we could play it!" (Shukurova 2008). This emphasis on European art music and on arranged folk tunes from other cultures has certainly continued, despite the wealth of Uzbek folk music now arranged for all manner of ensembles. As discussed later in this chapter, the multicultural repertoire focus has remained, while the discourse surrounding it necessarily evolved from pan-Soviet pride to international relevance that supports national projects.

After graduating from the conservatory in 1967 with degrees in both chang performance and conducting, Faizila opa joined the folk orchestra associated with the state Filarmonia (philharmonic association). She tells a triumphant story of her participation in pan-Soviet and international tours and competitions known in Russian as *dekadas* (festivals/competitions held every ten years). When describing the exhilaration of these tours and competitions, she gave her version of the comment made by cartoonist Robert Thaves in his comic strip *Frank and Ernest*—that Ginger Rogers did everything Fred Astaire did "backwards . . . and in high heels." Although I do not think that Faizila opa was aware of this iconic saying in English, she described her great pride in being one of the few women instrumentalists participating in these tours and competitions, and the only one performing on a heavy and demanding instrument like the chang. Faizila opa would leave for tour "with my suitcase in one hand, my chang in the other hand, my purse over my shoulder, and high heels on my feet! I was young, and I could handle such burdens" (Shukurova 2008). She also remembers running with all her gear out of the bus after the nightly concert to try to get to the best hotel room. She would inevitably end up on the third floor of the hotel, jostling for position with all the men, dragging her heavy instrument all the way.

Firuza Opa's History

Firuza Abdurahimova is a powerful force in the Uzbek music scene. One of Ashot Petrosiants's best-known students, she bravely founded a privately funded chamber-sized folk orchestra in 1994, during the aftermath of the dissolution of the Soviet Union. She named it the Sogdiana Uzbek Chamber Folk Orchestra (Sug'diyona O'zbek Xalq Cholg'ulari Kamer Orkestr [Sogdiana Folk Orchestra, for short]) after the Sug'dian civilization, considered a powerful ancient Iranian people who were subjugated by Alexander the Great, and who established their capital in Samarqand (in present-day Uzbekistan). By naming her folk orchestra after such lofty historical forebears, it is clear that Abdurahimova locates her ensemble within the national narrative that invokes Uzbekistan's rich and ancient history at the same time that she posits a strong modern ambassadorial purpose for the group. The Sogdiana Orchestra has obtained recognition and won competition prizes at a variety of international venues, and has now received state sponsorship as a result of all its success. The ensemble currently rehearses at the conservatory, where Abdurahimova teaches conducting as well.

Abdurahimova's path to renown as an orchestral conductor began with her early recollections of her mother, who was a teacher at the local house of culture (Russian: *dom kultury*) in Navoiy, where she was born. Her mother would give talks at local collective farms about women's rights and was, as Firuza opa puts it, "a bit masculine," since she was driven and career-oriented. In addition to her modern orientation and her stance on women's rights, Firuza opa's mother played the dutar by ear, and encouraged her musical ambitions. In fact, her mother was the first person who told Firuza opa that she should become a conductor (Abdurahimova 2008).

Another inspiration for Firuza opa's career path (and someone she mentions as the possible source for her mother's comments) was Dilbara Abdurahmanova, conductor of the Alisher Navoiy State Opera Company since the late 1950s, who is discussed further in chapter 3. In a 2008 interview, Firuza opa paints quite a trajectory for the women of her family, noting her grandmother's walking around veiled in the paranja even while working at a factory, then her mother agitating for women's rights in collective farms, and finally her full participation in modern intellectual and musical life as a well-known conductor (Abdurahimova 2008).

Firuza opa's musical studies began at fifteen in Samarqand, where she entered the music high school (kollej/Russian: uchilish). She has been associated with the conservatory in Tashkent since entering as an undergraduate in 1969 and studying for a double major in conducting and rubob prima (the smallest and highest-pitched of the reconstructed rubobs). After finishing her graduate work there, she began teaching at the conservatory, and has been the director of the orchestral conducting department since 1994, the same year that she founded the Sogdiana Folk Orchestra. In the early years after graduation, she also worked with the Tuxtasin Jalilov State Folk Orchestra, which is directed by Faruq Sodiqov, another of Petrosiants's well-known students.

Firuza opa remembers the Soviet education system fondly and saw the creation of European-style education in Uzbekistan as an important step in the creation of a musically literate society.

> In the 1920s, when the Russians came, the first opportunity to create [music] schools occurred. In 1936 the conservatory opened, which was a very big plus for the development of our culture—a very big plus. The first of our literate musicians studied in Moscow, who then glorified not just Uzbek culture, but general Soviet culture, and they represented our culture abroad. Understand that was the first of our Uzbek literate musicians. (Abdurahimova 2005b)

The issue of musical literacy (discussed later in this chapter) is foremost in her discussion of the value of arranged folk music and of European-style education systems. The combination of rhetoric about musical literacy and about spreading knowledge of Uzbek culture abroad is also notable, especially when taken in conjunction with the focus on such early musicians working not just for Uzbek culture, but also for the larger Soviet cultural project.

Throughout our discussions and interviews, Firuza opa was always clear that she reveres her country's ancient traditions, but that it is important to innovate and to embrace the modern world. She mentioned the importance of maqom and traditional music, but also framed them as a jumping-off point for modern musical developments, calling maqom an important foundation that can be the basis for modern innovative compositions (Abdurahimova 2005b).

This focus on modernity is a common theme uniting the rhetoric surrounding folk orchestras and arranged folk music during both the Soviet and independence eras. Indeed, this approach to music that combines Uzbek and Western elements exemplifies the complexity that non-Western women engage with when trying to embody a non-European modern identity. Anthropologist Lila Abu-Lughod discusses Middle Eastern women's complex relationship with modernity, describing them as "suspicious about the way modernity is so easily equated with progress, emancipation, and empowerment of women" (1998, vii). But Abdurahimova and musicians like her see the incorporation of other musical elements as a vital way to allow a tradition to continue its development. As such, they embrace the modernity that Western harmony and temperament represent, not seeing it as threatening toward the essential Uzbekness of the music that they play.

The Soviets' didactic approach to publicizing arranged folk music as uplifting the masses is not prevalent in independent Uzbekistan. Symphonic-style music still has great appeal to those who continue to perform it, as well as to their audiences. However, the discourse surrounding the style and its value to Uzbekistan's national project changed as the rhetoric of Soviet ideology shifted to accommodate the new national project. The new priorities still emphasize the value of the blending of Uzbek folk elements with polyphony and equal temperament, but they do so in a way that emphasizes a new audience. Rather than this musical style being advertised as a way to educate the masses, it becomes a means to familiarize international audiences with Uzbek culture using a musical language that they can more easily comprehend than that of the nontempered heterophonic chamber styles associated with maqom and traditional music. This rhetorical turn is often emphasized by Firuza Abdurahimova, who writes in 2005 that the priorities of her ensemble (founded in 1994) are as follows:

- the revival and preservation of ancient performing traditions, along with their adaptation to modern performing contexts;
- the creation of rapprochement between Eastern and Western cultures;
- musical dialogue between the various peoples of the earth;
- the ability to familiarize non-Uzbek musicians with various Uzbek folk instruments;
- further development of orchestral performance technique on Uzbek instruments;
- encouraging the revival of traditions on manufactured folk instruments. (Abdurahimova 2005a, 7)

The stark change in language from emphasizing the education of the masses at the time of Petrosiants's work to the independence-era rhetoric involving valuing tradition and advertising Uzbek music to non-Uzbeks shows the overt shift in priorities after 1991.

Ro'za Opa's History

Ro'zibi Hodjayeva (Ro'za opa) claims a familial history of women's dutar playing, mentioning in interviews that her grandmother (who passed away before she was born) played the instrument. Ro'za opa credits her passion for music as a legacy of her father, who loved music even though he (and other family members of his generation) did not play musical instruments (Hodjayeva 2009b). She remembers that her father especially loved musicians from the northwestern region of Xorazm, in particular Komiljon Otaniyazov. "[Otaniyazov] had a really loud voice, and my father would play his recordings at home and the whole village could hear it!" (Hodjayeva 2008).

Unlike many women musicians from both the traditional music department and the arranged folk music department who began their studies on the Kashgar rubob (like Malika opa and Firuza opa), Ro'za opa entered music school in 1969 in her village of Krasnogorsk (a village within the Tashkent region), in the dutar studio. Her dedication to the instrument has not waivered, and she moved to Tashkent in 1974 at the age of fifteen to study dutar at the Hamza uchilish, continuing on in her studies at the conservatory in 1978.

Ro'za opa describes her family as simple people. Her father was a fireman and her mother stayed home with her and her five brothers. As a result, she worked as a dishwasher when she first went to Tashkent in order to pay for her room and board there, eventually joining the Dutorchi Qizlar Ansembli (Young Women's Dutar Ensemble) at the state radio station. After graduating from the conservatory, she began playing with the Tuxtasin Jalilov State Folk Orchestra (founded by Petrosiants), as well as the folk orchestra at the state radio station named for Doni Zakirov. In 1983 she was called to teach dutar in the halq cholg'u department of the conservatory. That was an exciting and busy time for her, and she mentioned in an interview in 2008 that one of the major influences on her pedagogical style was a leader in her department, Professor Vasilyev, who was of Russian ethnicity and a balalaika performer. She describes him as having impeccable technique and remembers that he taught pedagogy for both the Kashgar rubob and the dutar (Hodjayeva 2008). This clearly presents the range of reconstructed instruments across former Soviet republics as closely related, and indeed as descended from the original project of creating a balalaika-based folk orchestra. Ro'za opa is very proud of her pedagogical lineage and of the rigor with which she approaches performance and musical literacy. As with my other consultants in arranged folk music, she considers strong sight-reading skills and knowledge of (Western) harmony vital for professional musicians. Indeed, this widespread conviction is reflected in the curriculum of the conservatory, which requires courses in harmony and ear training for all students, not just those who focus on Western art music.

Another aspect of Ro'za opa's musical memories from the Soviet period involves performing at weddings, which she began doing in 1987 at the behest of the women in her neighborhood (Hodjayeva 2008). Interestingly, the account of her trajectory as a wedding performer began not with arranged folk music, but with traditional tunes, including the *tanovar* (a type of folk dance from the Ferghana Valley). Ro'za remembers this time fondly, stating that she did not think that she had a sufficiently good voice for wedding performance, but that the ladies in her neighborhood begged her to do it until she relented. Her first songs included "folk melodies" (*halq kuylar*), such as a variety of tanovars like "Ey Vo Sanam" (What a beauty) and the well-known "Ferghana Tanovar," as well as popular tunes within the framework of traditional music such as "Qora Qosh, Qora Ko'z" (Black eyebrows, black eyes) (Hodjayeva 2008). Hearing her account of all these traditional tunes, I asked what had changed because, as discussed in chapter 5, weddings that I observed in the early twenty-first century mostly featured pop tunes (estrada). Ro'za opa replied that "nothing changed, I still sing folk songs" (Hodjayeva 2008).

Despite this protest, she went on to admit that weddings had in fact changed in the postindependence era as synthesizers and minidiscs became popular and available in the 1990s. She presented the transition resulting in the inclusion of a great deal of pop tunes as an economic necessity because it was so much cheaper for one performer to bring a minidisc player and speakers with her, rather than paying a group of musicians to back her up. Popular music and "light music" has long been a part of the wedding scene in Tashkent, and maqomist Munojat Yulchieva described that as her inspiration to avoid performing at weddings as a developing vocalist (Levin 1996, 80). This tension between the prestige of maqom and traditional music and the entertainment value of estrada and light music is an important one. Achieving the correct balance within a given wedding performance is vital to keep all participants happy and thus guarantee the best compensation and an invitation to perform at future events. Ro'za's memories of weddings and the negotiation of light music versus folk tunes provide important insight into Soviet-era wedding celebrations, which existed largely outside government institutions that invested a great deal in the promotion of arranged folk music, and at which musicians performed a more diverse repertoire that included both traditional music and pop songs.

This is similar to the situation in Bulgaria near the end of the communist period there. Ethnomusicologist Timothy Rice describes the importance of weddings for musicians, in terms of both the musical innovation they encouraged and the profit provided to musicians. He mentions weddings specifically as events that were not absorbed into the state labor system and thus became important opportunities for individuals to earn increasingly large sums of extra money (1994, 241–43). Playing weddings as part of the "second economy," unofficial labor that is often more profitable than musicians' official occupations, continues in Uzbekistan in the independence era, alongside privatization of many sectors of the labor force. While Ro'za opa gains a great deal of prestige as the director of her various ensembles and as a virtuoso performer in orchestras and as a solo musician, performances at weddings help her support her family.

Locating Halq Cholg'u Ensembles within Larger Institutions

Performing European Masters on Reconstructed Instruments: The Appeal of the "Akademik"

In conjunction with Uzbekistan's larger national project, the conservatory system in Uzbekistan is markedly Uzbek in terms of disciplinary focus, language use, and demographics of students and teachers. However, it is clearly modeled on the European system. Knowledge of and ability to perform Western art music is highly prioritized across all the pedagogical tracks, which include traditional music, arranged folk music, Western art music, popular music (estrada), music criticism and journalism, and musicology. As noted previously, students in all departments are required to demonstrate fluency in harmony, sight reading, and solfège. These abilities, often referred to as "musical literacy" (Russian: *muzykal'naya gramotnost'*), are prized by members of all departments, but seem to be most focused on by students within the arranged folk music department.

This focus on musical literacy as defined by Western notation was also observed by Theodore Levin during his work in the region in the 1970s; he notes: "On the more professional level of conservatories and musical high schools, Western-style musical literacy is obligatory, and the use of Western notation is a *sine qua non* of the pedagogic system" (Levin 1984, 33). The priority on learning from Western notation was further reinforced by musicologist Rustam S. Abdullayev during a conversation about Uzbek music history. Abdullayev explained that the European educational system came to Uzbekistan in the 1920s, bringing ideas of musical literacy focused on notes and music theory to prominence. He went on to comment that "people began transcribing traditional melodies into Western notation. Until that time there was only rote learning, and the masters had to have a big memory" (2002). This use of Western musical compositions, notation, and language, especially by arranged folk musicians, causes them to label their practice "academic," seeming to contrast it with traditional music that does not depend as heavily on those systems.

This pride in an "academic" orientation that maps to fluency in the Western canon was emphasized to me in 2003, when I attended a concert in the conservatory's main concert hall. I took my seat in the audience, and a student whom I did not recognize sat down beside me. "I know you! You play the dutar," she said to me, "you're a student of Malika Ziyaeva's." I replied that yes, I was a dutar student of Malika opa's and that I had traveled from the United States to study Uzbek music. This student patted my arm and mentioned excitedly that she also played the dutar. When I asked if she studied with Malika opa and wondered why I had not met her before, she replied that she studied in a different department, in the "akademik fakulteti" (academic department). The was the first instance when I noticed that arranged folk music was being referred to as "academic" and was nonplussed by the term because I assumed that all the departments in institutions of higher education were "academic" as I understood the term translated in English. To clarify, I asked if she was a musicologist. No, she was not a musicologist, she said, she was a "dutaristka" (Russian for female dutar player), but she studied in the department that was academic and learned harmony and studied notation. I found this quite curious because she was clearly invoking what she perceived as a meaningful contrast with the traditional department, even though I knew that all my friends, teachers, and acquaintances in the traditional department knew how to read musical notation and took courses in harmony. The contrast that she was trying to draw seemed to focus on praxis rather than ability.

Clearly, "academic" is a moniker of pride for such musicians and connects to interaction with European composers and Western notation. Whereas those in the traditional department use a combination of written and oral traditions, arranged folk musicians use notation as a primary way of accessing and performing music. Written notation and one's ability to perform the music of European masters continued to underscore many of my conversations with those in the arranged folk music department. This phenomenon was also noted by Levin in his interactions with conservatory students and faculty in the 1970s, when he observed "the idolization of European masterpieces as a kind of musical rite of passage in the training of young ethnic music performers" (Levin 1980, 154). Indeed, as mentioned earlier, all students learn the music of European composers, and arranged folk musicians perform much European and American repertoire on their reconstructed Uzbek instruments.

Musicians who perform arranged folk music are involved in a very specific negotiation that allows them to posit strong ties with a rather convoluted web of sources for authenticity; these include both traditional music and Western art music, which underscores the universal value associated with this privileged tradition. By accessing both repertoires and performing traditions, halq cholg'u performers claim a place for a uniquely national symphonic musical style, even though it bears some similarities to other arranged folk traditions throughout Eastern Europe and Soviet Asia. This unique style also allows them to posit a modern Uzbek identity that is rooted in both traditional music (at least in terms of instruments) and the Western canon, with its emphasis on the written score. Firuza opa presented this argument, clearly stating her stance on traditional music as an important jumping-off point (rather than an end in itself), as well as arranged folk music's roots in European written tradition.

> Maqom is our ancient tradition, and if we deny this, we lose everything. We must preserve our traditions. However, if we stay only at the level of tradition, we stay away from the whole world.... The government now creates opportunities so that anyone who has the desire can engage with deep traditional culture, and anyone who wants to is allowed to engage with what we have now, which is already tied with a written tradition. Written tradition that indeed is based in European traditions. (Abdurahimova 2005b)

The high value placed on European masterworks is an almost constant thread running through discussions and performances of arranged folk music. My first introduction to the reconstructed dutar was seeing a young student of Ro'za opa's performing an arrangement of a Liszt piece on the prima dutar at lightning speed. Indeed, when arranged folk musicians chose pieces to perform for me, many chose from the repertoire of Western art music. This often confused me, as I was generally introduced as a researcher interested in traditional Uzbek music and maqom. Rather than playing Uzbek compositions or arrangements of Uzbek traditional melodies, it seems that students either chose Western art music as something that I would understand, or as something that would best show off their abilities.

Elementary Education's Focus on Arranged Folk Music

An experience of early education on arranged folk instruments is a factor that unites current performers of arranged folk music with many musicians who currently perform traditional music and maqom. The Soviet era offered only arranged folk music or Western art music in its educational institutions for a great deal of its history (until the opening of the Eastern Music Department in the state conservatory in the 1970s). Many of my teachers and consultants who currently teach and perform traditional music, such as Malika Ziyaeva, began their musical education on reconstructed folk instruments such as the Kashgar rubob; they read Western musical notation and learned composed pieces such as the "Andijon Polka," as well as pieces by Mozart, Bach, and Liszt. This focus on arranged folk music for students interested in Uzbek musical performance continues in post-Soviet elementary education.

In the independence era, general education textbooks for early grades focus mostly on music fundamentals, teaching students to read Western notation and using songs to help children acquire musical competence. The national music curriculum for the sixth grade includes a unit focused specifically on traditional music and the maqom repertoires; a unit on "contemporary music and its bases," which includes chapters on folk music and dance, as well as popular music (estrada); a unit on art musics of "Eastern peoples," including chapters on music from Turkic cultures (Turkey, Azerbaijan, and Turkmenistan), Iran, Arab countries, China, India, Kazakhstan, and Kyrgyzstan; and a final unit on European classical music that includes chapters on Mozart, the symphony, Beethoven, Chopin, and Glinka (Begmatov et al. 2001). The range of that year's curriculum is extremely broad, especially considering the other Uzbek musics that the curriculum covers, as well as Western art music. With its descriptions of folk music and popular music (which include pieces with symphonic orchestra), as well as its chapter on the maqom repertoires, the only institutionally standardized musical practice not mentioned in the text is arranged folk music. Although arranged folk music and reconstructed instruments are featured in textbooks for other years, it is notable that they are included neither in the section developed specifically about Western art music nor in that dedicated to Asian music. It seems that by combining aesthetic and structural elements of both musical practices, arranged folk music separates itself from either category.

This exclusion is an interesting aspect of the general education curriculum because to this day, so many students in music schools perform arranged folk music on reconstructed instruments as a result of the legacy of the arranged folk music focus of music education after World War II. Whereas the conservatory was the first to add traditional music in the 1970s, elementary and secondary education have adjusted more slowly. Now, even with traditional music encouraged in the national media and courses in it being offered in many music schools, arranged folk music still has a significant place in K-12 education. The smaller size of the soprano and alto versions of instruments is thought to fit smaller bodies better, and arranged folk music is still taught as a valuable part of many curricula.

Post-Soviet Strategies for Relevance

If national identity is articulated, as historian Ronald Grigor Suny says, "through the stories people tell about themselves" (2001, 866), then the alteration of the story of arranged folk music is indicative of a shift in how nationalism is experienced by the women who are actively performing it. Arranged folk music ensembles could be seen as losing relevance and popularity in the post-Soviet era, as government and media focus shifts from Soviet panethnic spectacles to musical productions that are generally viewed as rooted in national traditions. Arranged folk musicians, however, are savvy and engaged in promoting their ensembles within existing narratives of the Uzbek nation and its role in the world. Ensembles that continue to enjoy large audiences, institutional support, and good publicity describe their music as rooted first and foremost in Uzbek traditions, while playing an important role in educating international audiences about Uzbek music in ways that are approachable and modern. Women are quite active in promoting arranged folk music as a locus of modern Uzbek identity. In this, they are complicating representations of tradition that are so often associated with women; indeed, they are embodying the complicated and multilayered nature of women's participation in the post-Soviet national project.

If Suny's notion of nationalism extends to the music that people play for themselves and the songs that they sing about themselves, then the post-Soviet transformation of arranged folk music and its surrounding discourse is powerful and deep. Altering the Soviet era's concepts of uplifting "backward" music to the current goal of educating international audiences about the rich musical practices of the Uzbek nation indicates a profound shift in focus for the national project. The previous system sought to transform practices that were seen as insufficiently sophisticated for international audiences; thus it focused on members of the nation as the audience and those aspiring to international standards. The new audience for national performance is the global community. The world is being asked to understand Uzbek music, rather than asking Uzbeks to understand international musical aesthetics. Musical practices remain unchanged, but the surrounding discourse implies a very different listener to both story and song.

Folk orchestras are certainly part of the story that people tell about Uzbekistan's existence as a modern nation. They are often highlighted in concerts that mark national holidays, especially those memorializing World War II, such as Victory Day (Russian: *Den' Pobedy*) on May 9. These concerts tend to employ more Soviet-era imagery and repertoire than other holiday concerts, and represent a highly stylized embrace of Soviet Uzbek culture's Russian influences. Such concerts often feature operatic singers and patriotic songs in the Russian language as well as Uzbek. Uzbeks participated in World War II and in the process of honoring that legacy, a nationalism that integrates Soviet culture with the current manifestation of Uzbek culture is displayed. The Sogdiana Folk Orchestra as well as the state folk orchestra named for Tuxtasin Jalilov both have an important role in the musical recounting of that legacy and patriotic story. The national and historical foci of such concerts contrast significantly with the more international focus that these orchestras have developed in recent years.

Sogdiana Folk Orchestra's International Appeal

The Sogdiana Folk Orchestra truly acts on its assertions that the role of folk orchestras and of halq cholg'u music is to act as a bridge between international audiences and Uzbek music that may seem too foreign in its more classical or traditional forms. Director Firuza Abdurahimova is an adept promoter of her ensemble, and engages them with the international community in Tashkent, as well as taking them to international festivals and competitions.

One of the main ways that the ensemble interacts with the international community in Tashkent is via concerts given yearly in conjunction with one of the many embassies in the city. During the course of my fieldwork, I saw concert programs presented in the main concert hall of the conservatory in honor of the French, Italian, and Korean embassies, all of which were well attended and included remarks by foreign dignitaries, Firuza opa, and other conservatory administrators. These concerts were unique in that they did not include the typical combination of new folk orchestra pieces composed by Uzbek composers, arranged folk or classical tunes, or usually a couple of pieces by European composers. Instead, the embassy concert programs featured works by composers from the country of the embassy being honored; for instance, the French embassy concert in 2003 featured a suite from *Carmen* by Bizet and "Danse Macabre" by Saint-Saens. The Italian embassy concert in 2004 focused on arrangements of operatic classics by Verdi, Rossini, and others.

The concert in honor of visiting Korean dignitaries in 2005 was somewhat atypical because it presented Korean compositions as well as arrangements of well-known folk tunes from Uzbekistan and Korea, including the iconic Korean song "Arirang." Firuza opa's remarks at this concert showed her deft negotiation of the priorities of the current national project in Uzbekistan along with the important assertion of the international relevance of folk orchestras. In her speech, she mentioned how wonderful it is that Uzbek instruments can do such a respectable job playing Korean folk tunes, and asserted that it underscores music's universal value. She went on to enumerate the charge of collectives like the Sogdiana Folk Orchestra, saying, "The first order of the orchestra is to play Uzbek folk music, then music by Uzbek composers, and finally music of other peoples" (Abdurahimova 2005b). This clearly presents folk orchestras as they currently locate themselves both internationally and within the vital national project that so many musicians seek to ally themselves with. It also somewhat sidesteps the authenticity issue surrounding folk orchestras as they are marketed and received by foreign promoters. Regardless, there does seem to be a specific international audience that is interested in arranged folk music, perhaps the same audience that attends performances of Russian-based balalaika orchestras or tamburitzans (Balkan-rooted multicultural song and dance groups).

Beyond the simultaneity of national and international identity, it is also notable that the folk orchestra is often posited as a modern representation of traditional heritage. As a result, conductors, musicians, and students often present arranged folk music as a compromise between traditional and modern, as well as a middle ground that takes the best of both Uzbek musical aspects and European ones. Firuza opa did exactly this in a 2005 interview, when she discussed her orchestra as the continuation of a living tradition. She said, "I think that it is the most contemporary collective of the present day, even in the twenty-first century, in which one can create humanity. Do you understand? It is the most universal collective, and it can dialogue with every country of the world, and no one would consider that collective foreign-sounding" (Abdurahimova 2005b). In the same interview she discussed the issue of authenticity within traditional performance and the pressure that she feels from traditional musicians who criticize folk orchestral music for not being sufficiently true to traditional styles and values. She presents her argument, as mentioned earlier, in terms of the modern and in terms of the necessity for traditions to live, breathe, and change: "Of course ancient traditions are our foundation. But meanwhile, we have such riches of musical instruments. To keep them under locks by ancient traditions means that we refuse to develop" (Abdurahimova 2005b).

This is a contentious debate that often underscores the worry that one style will usurp prestige or resources from the other, as much as it is a debate about which style deserves to be labeled traditional or modern. Indeed, traditional musicians such as Malika opa and her students often express the idea that music performed heterophonically on nonreconstructed instruments also engages with modernity and continues to be a viable, lively musical practice. In light of such tensions and challenges, Firuza opa makes convincing arguments as to why her collective maintains its relevance in the post-Soviet era, with its connections to international communities. She is also one of the most important public faces involved in presenting the story of Uzbek music to international audiences.

Firuza opa, Faizila opa, and the other women in this book have become symbols of nationality and upstanding morality in their daily home lives at the same time that they actively perform national identity via the musical stage. While performing with her ensemble and gaining international renown, Firuza opa simultaneously maintains a home and a family and projects an appropriately modest and professional feminine persona. As a result, she and others like her embody third-wave feminist Chandra Mohanty's assertion that "[w]omen are not only mobilized in the 'service' of the Nation, but they also become the ground on which discourses of morality and nationalism are written" (Mohanty 1998, 495). This grounding of moral and national discourse becomes especially evident in the training of young female musicians with an emphasis on modesty, such as wearing appropriate concert dress that often employs national fabric whereas men perform in Western-style shirts and ties. Furthermore, musicians such as Firuza opa and Faizila opa were clearly mobilized in the service of first the Soviet nation, when they were selected for groundbreaking places in music education that would bring women publicly into professional musical circles. This mobilization has continued in the independence era as they are continually spotlighted in the media and in musical discourse as evidence of the continued project of uplifting professional women.

The Dutar Ensemble at the Japanese Business Center

With the renewed focus on international audiences and on the ability for reconstructed instruments to appeal to members of other cultures, it might seem surprising that the ethnic makeup of folk orchestras and dutar ensembles remain overwhelmingly Uzbek and Tajik. There is, however, one ensemble that bucks this trend and truly embodies the current value placed on arranged folk music's ability to introduce Uzbek culture to foreigners—Ro'za opa's dutar ensemble at the Japanese Business Center, which is housed in a large complex that includes Tashkent's Intercontinental Hotel. Ro'za opa founded the ensemble (which she calls a young women's dutar ensemble) in 2005 as a dutar "course" at the business center (Hodjayeva 2008). While I was in Tashkent in 2008, Ro'za opa excitedly described her new project, teaching the dutar and Uzbek music to a group composed mainly of the wives of the Japanese businessmen who work at the center for two-year shifts. This temporary nature of her students' stay in Tashkent was the one negative aspect of the ensemble that Ro'za opa mentioned during an interview in 2009 because it means that she misses her dedicated students who have moved back to Japan (Hodjayeva 2009a).

After learning of the ensemble in 2008, I began to attend their weekly rehearsals on Wednesday nights, where I met a group of about half a dozen women and one man whom Ro'za opa described as enthusiastic enough to take up the dutar after working hours are over. The creation of the ensemble at the Japanese Business Center was quite a coup for Ro'za opa, and she is very proud of her students' accomplishments, as well as the salary that she is paid, which exceeds her pay rate at either the conservatory or the state radio's folk orchestra. Indeed, Ro'za was so proud of her new ensemble that she put a photo of the group on the cover of her new book *Dutor Taronalari* (Dutar melodies) (Hodjayeva 2007). In the introduction to her book, which presents a collection of arrangements of traditional tunes and precomposed works, she combines the rhetorical strategy of international appeal with descriptions of the dutar's unique qualities and implies the universal value of Western art musical composition. She says, "The sound of a professionally performed dutar is incomparable. It has characteristics at the level of other world musical performing styles. This is especially true of Eastern and European composed works that use dutar melodies to achieve emotion and meaning. This type of understanding [of the dutar's unique qualities] is becoming more and more evident" (Hodjayeva 2007, 3).

Although many of Ro'za opa's other dutar ensembles switch between pieces using "traditional" dutars and those using reconstructed dutars, often of different ranges that involve Western harmony, the ensemble at the Japanese Business Center featured only the reconstructed dutars. Also, in terms of repertoire, while the other ensembles performed newly composed pieces by Uzbek composers, arranged folk tunes, and arrangements of material from Western art music, the rehearsals that I observed in 2008 and 2009 did not include any Western art music. Rather, they focused on composed and arranged Uzbek pieces, as well as an arrangement of a Japanese song "Shima Uta" (Island song) that the students were especially proud of. (See figure 2.2, Ro'za opa leading a rehearsal at the Japanese Business Center.)

Figure 2.2. Ro'zibi Hodjayeva (far right) leading a rehearsal of her ensemble at the Japanese Business Center in Tashkent. Photo by author, 2008.

"Shima Uta" already had an international history before its performance in Tashkent, which I heard in 2008. In 1993, Kazufumi Miyazawa, the lead singer of J-pop band the Boom, wrote the song in memory of the Okinawans who experienced the US invasion during World War II. The folk pop song gained popularity in many countries, even serving as the theme song for the Argentinian soccer team during the World Cup in South Korea in 2002 (Fisher 2003, 43–47). As a result, it was a natural choice for Ro'za opa's Japanese dutar students, who are enamored by the cross-cultural possibilities of the reconstructed dutar ensemble, and possibly also because the reconstructed dutar has a timbre reminiscent of the Okinawan *sanshin* (three-stringed plucked lute) that is often heard accompanying the song in recordings. Performing arrangements of other cultures' songs is a popular strategy for engaging with international audiences, and it allows the innovations of the Soviet era to take on a global sensibility that fits with the cosmopolitan modern identity of many Tashkenters.

Such a process of shifting priorities in the independence era is not unique to Uzbekistan. Ethnomusicologist Peter Marsh discusses similar phenomena in regard to the Mongolian horse-head fiddle and its trajectory in musical narratives of cosmopolitanism. He notes especially the shift in the 1990s from the "epochalist promises of the Soviet Union" to the "moral authority" of the "deep past" (2009, 122). He goes on to describe a sort of folk revival that includes the creation of a new version of the instrument by presidential decree, a post-Soviet process that sounds much like the reconstruction or modernization projects that Petrosiants began in Uzbekistan in the 1930s, with its own twist that emphasizes a unique Mongolian national historical imaginary (Marsh 2009, 137–42). Marsh emphasizes that both the era of Soviet influence in Mongolia and the post-Soviet period have been immersed in a cosmopolitan project that features an "imagined connection that people sense they have with a broader translocal or international community, but which is manifest in distinctly local ways" (Marsh 2009, 7). Marsh is astute in his analysis of the Soviet experience as one that is inherently cosmopolitan, and also in his observation that the post-Soviet period manifests this cosmopolitanism in a different way. Such an observation could be made about Uzbekistan as well, and perhaps even about urban culture in Central Asia long before the ascendance of Russian and Soviet power. Uzbek national identity is always in the process of reacting to (and performing for) international standards and global norms, and has been since the formation of a coherent national identity during the Soviet era. However, the new cosmopolitanism in Uzbekistan, Mongolia, and elsewhere seeks a place in the world for savvy global citizens that privileges different rhetoric and different types of performance than were rewarded in the Soviet era. As a result, Firuza opa and Ro'za opa's projects engaging European and Japanese audience members and performers embody this new cosmopolitan perspective, which privileges the historical rootedness of the dutar and other traditional instruments while also embracing modern song forms and symphonic sensibilities.

This cosmopolitan identity that involves perceived contact and dialogue with a host of other peoples and nations allows female musicians to both perform their own national identity and engage with ideas and identities that may not be encapsulated within the expectations resulting from the norms of tradition and appropriateness associated with Uzbek music. If arranged folk music represents an interaction or dialogue between Western art music and Uzbek folk music that began during the Soviet era, then the dispersal of this musical practice via embassy-sponsored concerts and classes at the Japanese Business Center allow for the continued growth and relevance of the genre, while also permitting the women who perform it access to international (or at least other nations') ideas about prestige, musical performance, and gender.

Conclusions

The differences between traditional and arranged folk music are deeply defended and emphasized in institutional settings like the conservatory and state performing ensembles. However, there are strong elements of overlap, especially regarding gendered performance. The role of the dutar as a feminine instrument is a key aspect of women's musical legacies that is capitalized on by performers in both traditions.

Although the ustoz-shog'ird master-apprentice system is not seen as relevant to the transmission of women's traditions in terms of canon formation and processes of legitimation, the legacy of the hujum manifests itself again in the fact that arranged folk musicians, most especially Firuza Abdurahimova, are able to carry on their teachers' legacies. The notion that women are the natural carriers of their teachers' legacies is an important innovation in musical discourse, when one considers how many of the musical chronologies and histories catalogue men's activities. Furthermore, it is this generation of women who came of age well after World War II who are guiding the direction of arranged folk music in the thorny and uncertain ground of post-Soviet Uzbekistan. The shift toward an international focus seen in both Firuza opa's Sogdiana Orchestra and Ro'za opa's dutar ensemble at the Japanese Business Center is indicative not only of the importance of musical genres maintaining relevance in the midst of political change, but also of women's place at the forefront of projects that define musical genres and the kinds of meaning that those genres are able to evoke.

Arranged folk music, although not connected with various international organizations invested in preservation-based projects and their inherent obsession with authenticity (like UNESCO and the Aga Khan Foundation), which are generally drawn more to traditional music and village-based vernacular music, is still able to reach out to international organizations and audiences. Mostly this work is done through connections with foreign companies and embassies within Tashkent, but it also involves participation in festivals and competitions abroad. Although arranged folk music does not have a wide international audience, this is poised to change somewhat as a result of the efforts of Firuza opa and Ro'za opa.

Through passionate musicians and conductors, this genre continues to thrive in modern Tashkent. Arranged folk music could have been viewed as a relic from the Soviet era, a failed project from a failed state. Instead it is reborn, reimagined as a collaboration between peoples, a project seeking to connect folk music to larger discourses as it expands to fill symphonic ensembles. This cosmopolitan and modernized reworking of a project rooted in the Soviet ideological project to "uplift" the folk music of the Uzbek people is proof that musical change can be easily located in the realm of discourse and rhetoric as much as it involves alterations in repertoire and playing style.

This modern and innovative focus means that arranged folk music does not need to imagine a pre-Soviet history that includes women as equal public practitioners. With its genesis in the 1930s after various emancipatory projects were already in full swing, the histories that arranged folk musicians discuss are more personal (most musicians I spoke with, besides conservatory students, have living memory of Petrosiants) and also more focused on modernity. Arranged folk music exists in a framework in which women were always already expected to be visible practitioners, as they have been. Although not gaining international renown in the same fashion, with the same gendered, national, and musical metaphors as traditional music, women like Faizila opa, Ro'za opa, and Firuza opa still create a musical space for the performance of Uzbek femininity and work to support a national narrative that is modern and uniquely Uzbek. Although it may be influenced by and based on Western frameworks, the goal of such a project is the creation of musical performance that is modern, Uzbek, and global all at once.

3 Like Tereshkova in the Cosmos

Women at the Forefront of Western Art Music

On November 27, 2003, I went to the conservatory to observe a dutar ensemble class taught by Malika opa in the traditional music department. Arriving to find that class had been canceled, I saw that Firuza (one of Malika opa's dutar students) was sitting at the piano picking out the melody line of what looked like a light classical piece in 6/8 with a moving bass line that could have been composed by Muzio Clementi. I sat down at the piano with her and offered to play the left-hand part. She agreed, so we started to play the piece together. I quickly got very confused, as it became clear that we were not playing in the same meter. It was notated as 6/8 with a dactylic feel, using a series of paired eighth and quarter notes. However, the written rhythm did not line up with what Firuza was playing. Thinking the piece to be something similar to what I knew of Clementi or C. P. E. Bach, I reconfirmed the meter was 6/8, and we started again.

As we went on, I noticed Firuza continuing to play the dotted rhythms differently than they were written. She articulated the melody in a syncopated duple that sounded much like the Arab mode maqsum (a four-beat rhythm often expressed using the syllables "dum" and "tek" that has syncopated accents within the first two beats and the last two beats matching the pulse: DT-TD-T-). I struggled to match the bass line to her seemingly eccentric iteration of the melody. After we came crashing to another stop, I asked what the piece was and who wrote it. Firuza informed me that this was an arrangement of a folk song that she knew. She then sang a bit for me that was definitely in 4/4 and featured a great deal more ornamentation, flexibility, and sliding between the notes than what the cleanly notated score provided. After hearing her rendition of the tune, I sheepishly apologized for trying to question or correct her reading of the score, when the piece was clearly something known from the oral tradition and not dependent on the score or created for the keyboard.

This moment in 2003 emphasized the multilayered nature of Uzbek musical culture to me and made it clear that musical notation and instrumentation are not always what they seem to be. Certain assumptions that I gained from my conservatory education in the United States do not apply, even when examining a performance within the framework of Western art music. The piano is often experienced as an Uzbek instrument, despite its equal-tempered limitations. It is used to teach vocal lessons in the traditional music department, even though vocal lines often require significantly more flexibility than can be reproduced by the instrument. The piano is also used to accompany performance exams and solo recitals of students in the halq cholg'u department. All students of the conservatory are expected to develop rudimentary keyboard skills and to be able to read Western notation fluently. This has been true since the Soviet period, as Levin notes, calling Western notation "a *sine qua non* of the pedagogic system" (1984, 33). As a result, Western art music provides an often-unacknowledged foundation for the diverse styles and repertoires offered through educational institutions. Western notation represents a lingua franca that all are expected to gain fluency with, and the piano is experienced as a flexible enough instrument to be able to engage a wide range of musical styles, at least in terms of pedagogy.

As ethnomusicologist Ter Ellingson notes, "Cross-cultural transcription began as a tool of colonial acquisitiveness.... Transcription thus began as a medium for capturing and preserving exotic sensory experiences" (1992, 110, 112). This holds true in the Uzbek situation, with the earliest musical notation coming from Soviet-era male musicologists transcribing Uzbek male musicians' performances into Western notation (Uspensky 1924 is the prime example). This practice of transcription was important for the elevation of Uzbek music to official and scientific levels. This means that notation, even descriptive transcription, is venerated as Western art music places the score as the final location of a composer's musical intention, even though in the case of Firuza's folk tune, the transcription is clearly inadequately descriptive and less effective than the oral tradition in transmitting important musical detail. Nonetheless, musical literacy in the form of fluent reading of Western notation continues to be a mark of musical training and excellence for all professional musicians in Tashkent.

Western art music, with its emphasis on musical literacy and professional training, has maintained continued relevance throughout the twentieth century. There has been a clear project to produce Uzbek Western art music, one that retains prominence in independent Uzbekistan. This project has involved getting composers engaged not just in arranging folk tunes for Western instruments, as in the case of the piano piece that was so easily mistaken for Clementi, but also in the creation of a sense of Uzbek style in composition. Similar to many other cultures that also engage with Western art music, the majority of Uzbek composers, and indeed all of the early composers, were men. However, in Uzbekistan, from remarkably early in the Soviet period, women have been important figures in the performance and promulgation of Uzbek compositions.

The History of Western Art Music in Soviet Uzbekistan

The colonial era in Uzbekistan brought a great deal of Western art music to Central Asia, including military bands and other forms of entertainment. With the transition to the Soviet system in the early twentieth century, it became important for Western art music to be considered a project of national pride, rather than one brought in by a colonial force. As a result, local composers and musicians needed to be cultivated.

During the early Soviet period, in addition to the push for reconstruction projects and the arrangement of folk music previously discussed, there was also a strong push for the creation of art music by Uzbek (and other Soviet minority) composers. Just before World War II, the creation of the first operas was hailed as an important step in the creation of Uzbek art music. Local musicologist Tamara Vyzgo described this as helping address the challenge of "cultivating new expressive paths for Uzbek music" (Vyzgo 1972, 174). These works and their performance at the newly constructed Alisher Navoiy Theater in Tashkent were important developments for the Uzbek Soviet people.

Further, links between state-sponsored ensembles, such as the opera and ballet companies associated with the Navoiy Theater, and other institutions, such as the Composers' Union and the conservatory, were palpably strong. Indeed, the composer of the first Uzbek opera, *Buran* (The storm), was Muxtor Ashrafiy (in conjunction with his teacher and mentor, Russian composer Sergei Vasilenko, and with a libretto by Kamil Yashen). Ashrafiy later became the director of the conservatory. The creation of *Buran*, which premiered on June 11, 1939, and its successors was seen as a great success for collaboration within the musical community of Tashkent. Vyzgo commented on this, saying, "The first Uzbek operas, *Buran* and *Leili and Majnun*, were composed in a community of Uzbek and Russian musicians, laying down the basis for future developments in Uzbek musical theater. [These musicians are] helping [one another] through successfully mastering complicated genres of professional art" (Vyzgo 1972, 191). In this case, Vyzgo is framing professional art in terms of the creation of an Uzbek Western art music, clearly ignoring the centuries of professional musicians who performed maqom. The successful creation and performance of operas and symphonies implied the successful raising up of Uzbek music and musicians to an international standard, bringing their works into a more global arena.

Unlike many of the operas coming out of Central Asia and the Caucasus at the time, which based their libretti on fairy tales, *Buran* is a historical and patriotic tale about an uprising in the Jizzax region of Uzbekistan in 1916, but it also included an ill-fated love story between Buran's son Jura and his wife Nargul, who both die in the tragic final act (Pekker 1963, 79–82). True to the style of the time, it incorporated transcribed folk melodies, many coming from the Jizzax region in an attempt to capture a sense of the local culture (Iskandarova 2009).

Laila and Majnun (The madman and Laila, or Madness for Laila) is a fairy tale about a man who was overcome by fervent love for a girl named Laila, writing many poems in her honor. After her father refused to grant her hand in marriage, and upon hearing of her marriage to another man, Majnun began wandering the desert, eventually perishing in the wilderness. This story has been transmitted by a variety of poets, including the famous Uzbek Poet Alisher Navoiy throughout the region and the Ottoman poet Fizuli (1494–1556), and has been a very popular source of material for compositions. The most famous of these is the first Azerbaijani opera by Uzeyir Hajibeyov (1885–1948), which premiered in 1907 and incorporated elements of Azerbaijani mugham (Naroditskaya 2002, 93–94). This variant was extremely popular in the region and was performed in 1916 in Tashkent (Pekker 1963, 90). Hajibeyov went on to write a second "mugham opera" in 1938 (*Keroglu* [Son of a blind man]), which was also critically acclaimed. Hajibeyov has been much lauded for his reform and development of Azerbaijani culture, and his early opera is seen as an especially significant achievement (Naroditskaya 2002, 99). The story of Laila and Majnun was also reworked in the Uzbek republic in the 1930s. Sh. Khurshid penned the libretto, and Reinhold Glière was the official composer, working in consultation with Talibjon Sadikov, who transcribed and arranged folk tunes for the opera (Pekker 1963, 90–91).

Indeed, Laila and Majnun was a popular source for plot material in other Soviet musical productions. It was the inspiration for a symphonic poem by Azerbaijani composer Gara Garayev (1918–82), and for a ballet composed by Tajikistan's leading composer (of Armenian descent) Sergei Balasanyan (1902–82). Another fairy tale–based opera describing ill-fated love, *Farhad and Shirin,* was composed in Uzbekistan by guest composers/arrangers

Mushel and Tsveifel based on "three thousand bars of folk music" transcribed by Russian musicologist and composer Viktor Uspensky. This was presented along with nine other Uzbek operas at a 1937 festival in Moscow (Frolova-Walker 2007, 319). To get a sense of how select the circle of musicians engaged in these projects was at the time, Muxtor Ashrafiy directed the opera and Tamara Khanum was a featured dancer in the production (Pekker 1963, 64).

Just as local iterations of Western art music developed under Russian guidance in Uzbekistan and Azerbaijan, similar processes occurred in the other Soviet republics in the 1930s. A great deal of nationalist opera and ballet premiered then. In fact, most of the Central Asian republics produced their first "national" operas in that decade, as a result of government priorities and oversight of the process of creating works that would represent both nationalism and socialism well. Sociologist Rafis Abazov provides a helpful list of similar processes and operatic and symphonic work from the Uzbek and all other Central Asian Republics during this period (Abazov 2006, 144–45). In this, we can see that Uzbek composers and performers were participating in larger pan-Soviet processes of discursive and musical development.

These developments in the 1930s were furthered in the post–World War II era. Indeed, Soviet interest in the development of Uzbek compositions, composers, ensembles, and students continued full force, with a dekada (Russian: decade/celebration) of Uzbek arts and literature occurring in Moscow in November 1951 (Babaev 1952, 45). In describing the successes of composers in Uzbekistan (of both Russian and Uzbek heritage), composer S. Babaev notes that: "The Composers' Union is continuing its work plan to create operas, ballets, music dramas, and comedies. It is this level of creative activism that brings the union closer to its life purpose of contemporization [modernization of Uzbek music]" (Babaev 1952, 45). Indeed, in this article, the all-important rhetoric of modernity and high art is employed to praise the developments of the past three decades in the Uzbek SSR.

Opera and ballet continued to receive significant attention from scholars and reviewers, perhaps because of their ability to represent ideas visually as well as sonically. An article in the journal *Sovetskaya Muzyka* (Russian: *Soviet Music*) favorably reviews the premiere of G. Mushel's ballet *Ballerina*, describing the care that was taken to incorporate Uzbek folk themes and rhythms into many aspects of the work: "[T]he language and . . . the expressive legacy of [Mushel's] music are very close to Uzbek folk vocal works" (Karelova 1952, 60–61). In this case, it is clear that the incorporation, or the "hiding," of folk elements within Western art compositional forms was considered an important way to express the sophistication and uplifting of local forms. The article ends with the hopeful proclamation that as "[s]pectators received the spectacle well . . . one can hope that [the] new Soviet Ballet will take a lasting place in the contemporary repertoire" (Karelova 1952, 63).

Thus began the project of incorporating Uzbek composers into a Western art music canon, one that embraced the "great men" usually implicated in such constructions, such as Bach, Beethoven, and Mozart, but also including a number of Russian composers, such as Glinka and Borodin, who are often marginalized in Western European and American representations of the canon. Indeed, Russian composers and pedagogues were seen as important models in the crafting of Uzbek Western art music. Clearly, canon building was important in all the styles of music performed in the Soviet era, from classical maqom to European classical music. These canons were created and maintained primarily by men, standardizing repertoires composed by men and largely performed by men.

The creation of a canon that was inclusive of Uzbek and other Soviet composers was an important step in establishing the authority of Soviet cultural products. Ethnomusicologist Philip Bohlman discusses the importance of canon in a more general context, saying that "[c]anon, indeed, seems to possess a certain immanent power—an imperative and concomitant ability to ascribe law and order to music—that yields discipline or, better, the discipline. Canon establishes authority" (Bohlman 1992, 201). The construction of a Soviet Western art music canon helped reinforce cultural ties from the margins to Russia, using art music and its pedagogy as a way of linking cultures in a manner that established Russian leadership and hegemony without overtly colonial implications. This noncolonial framework was effective because Uzbek composers were writing their own music, highlighting their own heritage, often incorporating melodies and other musical elements that were seen to stem from the folk in Uzbekistan.[1] That they were writing in European styles with European instruction complicates the notion that this was a way to sidestep colonial structures. However, Uzbek performers of European classical music, like similar musicians worldwide, view Western art music as universally appreciable and thus belonging not simply to the West, but to all who practice it as well. It is this universal value and the opportunities for universal appreciation that represent the foundation of Western art music's continued prevalence and relevance in Uzbekistan.

This sense of a Western classical canon puts double pressure on non-Western women, who are not only other to the international standard established by Europeans, but also to the norm of male composer, conductor, and performer. Musicologist Marcia Citron addresses this issue of the power that canons have to enforce norms, noting that "canons are exemplary, act as models, instruct, represent high quality, endure, and embody at least some degree of moral and ethical force.... [C]anons exert tremendous power. By setting standards they represent what is considered worthy of inclusion" (Citron [1993] 2000, 15).

Western Art Music in Independent Uzbekistan

This European-focused approach to Western art music continues to a certain extent in the independence era, but it is tempered by the generations of Uzbek composers who have established themselves in the years following World War II. Indeed, the Composers' Union, headed by Uzbek composer Rustam Abdullayev, is very active in Tashkent, and helps to sponsor new music festivals and concerts at various venues throughout Uzbekistan. These tend to be well attended by composers throughout Uzbekistan and other former-Soviet states. However, as in the United States and parts of Europe, the discipline of composition continues to have a majority of male practitioners. Abdullayev invited me to accompany the delegation to a new music festival in Samarqand in 2003. Once again, most of the delegation was male, with one young female conservatory student in attendance, a vocalist who mentioned an interest in new music and composition.

The composers at events such as the festival in Samarqand present themselves as standing on the foundations of the Western canon. It is an interesting strategy for positing one's own international relevance by putting one's own work in a continuum with the great masters. Abdullayev, like many musicians who primarily play Western art music, emphasizes the universal value of high art and of the works from the Western canon. He rehearses that canon, declaring: "Rachmaninov is an absolute gem. You have to take care of masterpieces, no matter what nationality they come from.... We'd get nowhere without Bach, Haydn, Mozart, Chopin, Britten.... They're gems of universal value, for all mankind" (MacFadyen 2006, 56).

This dependence on the (albeit Russian-centered) Western canon also highlights the imbalance in reception between practitioners of Western art music and reception or adjudication via Europe. Uzbek composers are rather well known throughout the former Soviet states, but do not have as much opportunity to disseminate their work in Western Europe or the Americas. Perhaps this underscores a reason that Uzbek women have gained international renown as performers rather than composers—as performers and interpreters of the Western canon, they are lauded both nationally and internationally. Dilbara Abdurahmanova and Ofeliya Yusupova are able to achieve significant fame as interpreters of the canon and then are able to disseminate Uzbek works (such as Abdurahmanova's repeated performances of Muxtor

Ashrafiy's Uzbek opera, *Buran* [The storm], in Moscow and Germany). Thus they participate in shaping the national narratives that are emphasized to international audiences, even if they do not craft the music itself.

Despite an apparent dearth of women composers encountered in Uzbekistan, as mentioned previously, performance remains a decidedly prominent place for women in the realm of European art music in the post-Soviet era. Female students are well represented in the concerts and courses based on Western art music in the conservatory and other educational institutions. Furthermore, since the Soviet era, women have occupied important positions in the faculty and in state-run ensembles. These include conductor Dilbara Abdurahmanova and concert pianist Ofeliya Yusupova, who are discussed in the next sections. Their stories illustrate the complexity of discourse involved in women's performance of Uzbek European art music, which integrates notions of globalization, universality, modernity, and emancipation.

Dilbara Abdurahmanova

> When Tereshkova [(b. 1937)] became an astronaut, she sat just once in the spaceship. When she returned from space, she became the first woman in space for the rest of her life. And what more could she do? She remains the first female astronaut all the same. I was the first woman conductor to stand at the podium not just to conduct a symphony orchestra, but also [the first] at the podium for theater, opera, and ballet. Every day for forty-eight years I have stood at the podium and demonstrated this. Every day, with dignity, I stand in this place. This profession is such that if you stand up and make one significant mistake, then you lose everything that you have built up until then. Therefore I surmise that I have the most accountable/crucial profession in the musical world. Beyond that, I have to say that I was not only the first female conductor in the East, but also that I was the woman after whom more women in other countries came up in the ranks. There are now women conductors in Azerbaijan and in Kazakhstan. . . . I believe that I showed the East that women could also participate in this very difficult but rewarding profession. (Abdurahmanova 2008)

Dilbara Abdurahmanova's childhood provided an important foundation for her significant musical accomplishments, including her status as the first female opera conductor in Asia. Born to musician parents in 1936, the year that the Tashkent Conservatory opened, she grew up in the center of Tashkent's classical musical circle. Like Firuza Abdurahimova, her mother was unconventional and progressive, blazing a path for other women, including her daughter, to follow. In the 1920s, Abdurahmanova's mother was unhappy with the marriage that she was being pressured to enter, so she ran away to

Samarqand and joined the opera troupe there, where she met her husband. Abdurahmanova was born in Moscow in 1936, while her parents were in Moscow studying in order to create an operatic theater in Samarqand (they later relocated to Tashkent). She describes her mother's experience in the 1930s as burgeoning with potential and opportunity, explaining that the 1920s were a difficult time for women, but that by the 1930s and 1940s, women appeared on stage without problems (Abdurahmanova 2008).

Abdurahmanova began her musical schooling by attending the Glière State Music School (which is still open in Tashkent), studying violin and eventually becoming the concertmistress of the school orchestra. This meant that it was her job to lead the tuning and preparation of the orchestra before the conductor, Nina Tretyakova, arrived. As Abdurahmanova explains it, Tretyakova often ran late, so Abdurahmanova was told to rehearse the orchestra until she arrived. Eventually Abdurahmanova's talent became apparent, and Tretyakova allowed her to prepare a piece to conduct in the orchestra's concerts.

During this time, she was considering various directions for her potential career, and her opera-singing parents thought that perhaps she would be well suited to join the family profession. She describes her resistance not in terms of lacking talent or courage, but rather as lacking physical stature:

> It was important that I become an art worker, but what exactly I would do for a living wasn't important. By the time I'd turned seventeen or eighteen years old, my father [who was a tenor] wanted to prepare me to be a singer. I was categorically against it, however, because I didn't think that I was very attractive like a model, so I decided that I wasn't meant for the stage. I told my father that to be a singer I needed to be fifteen centimeters taller. (Abdurahmanova 2008)

Although Abdurahmanova is diminutive in height, her vibrant personality is unmistakable, and she clearly projects her place in the upper echelons of Tashkent's musical aristocracy.

Composer, conductor, and then director of the Tashkent Conservatory Muxtor Ashrafiy was a close friend of the Abdurahmanov family, and in 1955 he "invited" her to attend the conservatory after she finished at the Glière school. She began at the conservatory with three majors: violin, piano, and conducting, and after she finished, she began working as a violinist in a theater orchestra. She was a student of Ashrafiy's at the conservatory during the time that he became the principal conductor of the Alisher Navoiy's main stage in 1957 (Sharipova 2006, 33). As Ashrafiy further expanded his presence in Tashkent's arts circles, he ushered Abdurahmanova along with him. He was the one who encouraged her to take the position as head conductor at the Alisher Navoiy Opera and Ballet in 1976, a position she held until 1990 (Abdurahmanova 2008).

As she narrated her childhood, it became clear that her sense of presence and purpose is not a recent development. Abdurahmanova was a force of nature even throughout her schooling as she sought out mentorship and rose to prominence. In addition to Tretyakova (and later Muxtor Ashrafiy), Abdurahmanova's parents encouraged her to focus solely on her musical development rather than on the more pedestrian pastimes of young girls. "Women can't waste a second of their time," Abdurahmanova declared in our interview, elaborating on this assertion's relevance in her own life. "There are women who gossip—I don't have any girlfriends. All my friends are men. My mother said that 'tvoya podruga—partitura'" (a clever rhyme in Russian, meaning "your girlfriend is the musical score") (Abdurahmanova 2008). Clearly the score was and still is Abdurahmanova's close friend, launching her conducting career from a remarkably early age, the result of opportunities afforded to her from the nascent and swiftly expanding quality of the arts in post–World War II Tashkent. She narrates the priorities of the time in terms of needing to develop arts that will be appreciated across the globe, not just local folk music.

> Our leaders cared that our operas would develop like art . . . art of international weightiness. . . . Because if all we presented was our own culture's art, after seeing our show, they'd receive us like an ethnographic troupe. Because you know, the Italians also have their own national music, their own mandolin, and so on. . . . But Italy entered the world stage, not because of their mandolin, but because of their opera artistry and because of their famous composers. . . . We [Uzbek musicians] also understood that in order to enter the global arena, we needed to strengthen our classical repertoire. (Abdurahmanova 2008)

It was the necessity of international standing that motivated the focus for Uzbek practitioners of Western art music, and that focus made the post–World War II era a very exciting one, with impressive developments. It is that ethos that created the current realities of musical institutions and educational systems that lay the foundation of structures in support of Western art music. This foundation in Western art music allowed participation in the international musical arena.

Throughout our 2008 interview, Abdurahmanova mentioned other accomplishments, including performances of Prokofiev ballets and Verdi's *Aida*; however, it was clear that Abdurahmanova views her role in the global musical sphere primarily as a promoter and performer of both Uzbek music and women's ability to succeed at the highest level of the musical profession and to attain international standing. She continued in her position as the principal director at the Alisher Navoiy State Opera and Ballet until just before the fall of the Soviet Union in 1990, a fourteen-year tenure that was considered quite lengthy. Since Abdurahmanova stepped down as principal director, she has continued at the Navoiy Theater, and still conducts many of the ballets there. In our conversation, Abdurahmanova explained that most conductors held that demanding position for only a few years at a time. However, Abdurahmanova had something to prove, and she wanted to ensure that no one missed the point. She refused to be seen as stepping down because she could not handle the job. Indeed, she expressed great pride in her tireless efforts on behalf of Uzbek art music, which she mentioned repeatedly as a source of great satisfaction in her life.

> I am a person of very happy fate! I can say that because I have reached the age of seventy-two, right? I am a person of happy fate, because I have put on so many interesting shows: national shows, contemporary shows, like works by Mustafo Bafoev and poet Omar Khayyum, like *Buran*, Ikaram Akbarov's ballet *Leili and Majnun* . . . there are so many on contemporary Uzbek themes. (Abdurahmanova 2008)

Abdurahmanova's emphasis on the glory of her career centering on the performance of Uzbek works results in a framing of Western art music's clear universal value and Uzbek practitioners' natural place in that elite milieu.

Membership in the modern and performatively emancipatory Soviet Union allowed for the flourishing of Western art music, Uzbek musicians, and women musicians especially, and the international value of Western art music continues to have great importance in Uzbekistan's era of independence. Although maqom and Uzbek folk music have gained standing in the media and culture of post-Soviet Uzbekistan, the accomplishments of Uzbek composers and performers of Western art music have not lost their significance. Indeed, Western art music is still seen by many as the best way to engage in cross-cultural communication and understanding via the arts. As a result, Abdurahmanova made much of the international nature of her orchestra and the resulting necessity for Russian as a lingua franca. As discussed later, the orchestra for her productions includes people from almost all of the former Soviet republics, so Russian is still the clearest way to communicate professionally. Following the previous quote, Abdurahmanova went on to comment on the bilingual realities in two other postcolonial nations, India and Algeria, but specifically did not tie the issue of colonialism to her discussion of her orchestra, the language, or the repertoire that they play. Like many I spoke to in Uzbekistan, she seems to want to separate the Soviet experience from notions of colonialism.

Abdurahmanova clearly takes pride in Uzbekistan as an independent nation, but sees the Soviet period as a time when the arts, especially Western art music, flourished, thus making it an important period of cultural development. As a result, for Abdurahmanova and many musicians like her, ordinary critiques of colonialism fall flat. Indeed, it is important that participation in Western art music seems natural for these women, and could be seen as part of the project of "salvaging modernity by asserting its indigenous pedigree [that] takes multifarious forms" (Kandiyoti 1998, 271). As gender studies scholar Deniz Kandiyoti notes, women play an important role in naturalizing modernity, especially as modernity, gender, and nationalism intersect. Western art music, as practiced in Soviet Uzbekistan and independent Uzbekistan, can be seen as one of the central nodes of the nexus between the three concepts.

In order to continue this legacy of excellence, after stepping down as the principal director at the Alisher Navoiy Theater, Abdurahmanova took a teaching position for the first time. She is now able to model her passionate and rigorous approach to opera conducting for students at the Uzbek State Conservatory. Pianist Ofeliya Yusupova served as the director of the conservatory in the 1990s, and it was she who invited Abdurahmanova to start a preparatory opera program there. She is quoted in Abdurahmanova's biography as saying, "You've already done everything in the theater. Now it is time to work in the conservatory. . . . You need to pass on your experience and knowledge to young people" (Sharipova 2006, 138). As a result, in 1994, Abdurahmanova became the head of the opera program there, where she continues as a role model of women's musical successes.

Ofeliya Yusupova

Like Abdurahmanova and many others who grew up in the region after World War II, pianist Ofeliya Yusupova benefited from the trail blazed by Uzbek women in the 1920s. She has an early history similar to Abdurahmanova's, except that her family was not made up of opera singers from Samarqand. Rather, Ofeliya Yusupova's parents were teachers in the city of Tashkent. Her mother taught Uzbek literature and her father taught mathematics; both were members of the intelligentsia, as Yusupova describes it: "My mother was a member of the first generation of the intelligentsia. One of the first generation to receive an education and to throw off the paranja [veil]. Her mother, my grandmother, actually threw off the paranja and none of her children wore it. She studied here and then even went to Leningrad for graduate school" (Yusupova 2008). It is worth noting the importance of study in cosmopolitan cities for the parents of Yusupova's generation. Like Abdurahmanova's parents, who studied opera in Moscow to prepare for the establishment of an opera theater in Samarqand, Yusupova's family is markedly intellectual and cosmopolitan, with their ties to education from Russian institutions.

This was the result of a push in the 1920s and 1930s to educate the most accomplished students from the outlying republics in Moscow and Leningrad. It was an important policy that helped disseminate Soviet ideals and artistic standards. Although identification with the bourgeoisie was dangerous during the Soviet period, membership in the literati was less so, and continues to be a source of pride for those who, like Yusupova, feel that identifying as an intellectual is crucial to their identity.

Highlighting their ties to the European cultural elite, Yusupova's parents named their daughter Ofeliya after seeing a performance of Shakespeare's *Hamlet* near the time of her birth (Yusupova 2008). Yusupova remembers her childhood fondly and highlights the high-quality, tuition-free education that she received. Although her parents were not professional musicians, they encouraged her pursuits. She is quoted in her biography as saying, "[F]or me, there was never any kind of question about who I would be when I grew up. From childhood, I knew that I would be an artist, I just didn't exactly know what kind. I loved to sing, dance, and later, to play the piano. Therefore I mixed my education between music school and the choreographic music high school" (Yusupova, quoted in Kalmykova 2001, 12). Yusupova's aunt took her to the opera and ballet as a child so that she felt comfortable in musical surroundings. In 1956, she graduated from the Uspensky Music School in Tashkent and was accepted to the Moscow Conservatory (Kalmykova 2001, 13).

In 1960, she transferred to the Tashkent Conservatory and finished her bachelor's and graduate work there (Kalmykova 2001, 15). During our interview, Yusupova remembered her education in Tashkent and Moscow fondly, and highlighted the elite nature of her education: although higher education was tuition free, entrance was extremely selective, especially to institutions like the Moscow Conservatory (Yusupova 2008). She began working as a concertmistress (in this usage, one who rehearses the orchestra) with the conservatory orchestra when she transferred to the Tashkent Conservatory in the fifth year of her bachelor's program. Yusupova also married her husband at this time, at age twenty, which she described as typical of that era (Yusupova 2008). In addition to family life and work as a concertmistress, she began teaching at the conservatory and working as a pianist and soloist for the Uzbek State Philharmonic in 1962 (she worked at the philharmonic from 1962 to 1970) (Kalmykova 2001, 16).

Ofeliya Yusupova often championed the works of Uzbek composers, and has given performances in a variety of countries throughout Europe, Asia, and North America. Like many successful musicians, she had to balance a wide variety of professional duties (all while supporting a family and bearing two children). In 1993 she premiered Rustam Abdullayev's Third Piano Concerto in Bangkok, Thailand (Kalmykova 2001, 18). Yusupova's biography highlights the impressive range of concertos that she performed with symphony orchestras in Europe, Asia, and North America, including those by Bach, Beethoven, Grieg, Abdullayev, and other composers from the former Soviet Union (Kalmykova 2001, 19). As a result of her touring, Yusupova can be seen as an important representative for Uzbek art music, even though she was not composing it herself. Again, although it was mostly men who established themselves as composers in the Soviet Union, women played an important role as the face of the nation in their performances of their works. Certainly her biographer notes this, declaring that "the propagandizing of [Uzbek composers'] works appears as a dominant theme in [Yusupova's] performing career" (Kalmykova 2001, 19).

After a successful performing career, Yusupova began to focus on administration, and eventually became the director of the Uzbek State Conservatory during its important transition period from the Tashkent Conservatory (part of the USSR) to the state conservatory of the independent nation of Uzbekistan.[2] During her tenure as director, from 1987 to 1997, she oversaw the creation of new departments (such as music journalism and criticism), and the official national transition from Cyrillic to Latin script in 1995. Like Abdurahmanova, she also made space for women to follow her into the upper echelons of administration, with Dildora Muradova serving as the director of the conservatory while I was in residence there in 2004 and 2005.

Women like Yusupova and Abdurahmanova continue to play an important role in the representation of Uzbekistan as an important cultural center with artists who are capable of attaining the highest international standard. Indeed, the value afforded to their contribution is made evident by the fact that both women are the subjects of published biographies, an honor not bestowed on many of the other highly accomplished women in Tashkent's musical circles. Indeed, this gives testimony to the import that Western art music is afforded in Tashkent, as its prestige is seen as internationally accepted cultural capital. The ubiquity of Western art music throughout the world gives weight to performers' accomplishments as they are coopted to support Uzbekistan's national project.

Russian as the Language of Western Art Music's Discourse in Tashkent

As noted in the Introduction, language is a key area where one can display a nuanced cultural orientation. In discussions with traditional musicians and folk orchestra performers described in previous chapters, the musical discourse occurred primarily in the Uzbek language, often with smatterings of Russian used to reference Soviet ideas or history. Because most adults in Tashkent are polyglots, speaking Uzbek and Russian as primary languages, there are opportunities for nuance that only code-switching provides. Although it is expected that Uzbek-identified adults in urban centers speak both Uzbek and Russian, many also speak one or more languages such as Tajik, Arabic, Turkish, French, or German. The sheer number of languages that people have a conversational knowledge of is testament to the long cosmopolitan history of urban centers in Central Asia. The ordinary nature of multilingual fluency in Tashkent displays the population's proclivity for becoming conversant in other cultural idioms.

Also, it is worth noting that students in primary schools are currently taught with Uzbek as the primary language, usually adding Russian language classes later, and giving students the option of others (such as Japanese or English, two languages that children of my acquaintances studied) as optional after-school activities. Despite the continued emphasis on Russian fluency in schools, I did notice some students in kollejs and the conservatory struggling more with Russian than adults who were raised and educated in the Soviet period. This probably stems from the societal focus on the Uzbek language, such that it is very possible to grow up in Uzbekistan without a sense of immersion in the Russian language.

These multiple fluencies and instances of code-switching allow musicians to underscore aspects of their arguments or cultural orientation in implicit ways. Many of my consultants expressed a preference for either Uzbek or Russian, while others claimed that it was all the same to them, no matter which language we communicated in. Despite the diversity of linguistic preference, patterns and norms were clear (and often unspoken). All of the lessons and interviews conducted with members of maqom ensembles and traditional musicians were conducted in Uzbek (except in 2002 when my Uzbek language skills were not sufficient for those tasks). Interviews and lessons with members of folk orchestras and the halq cholg'u department occurred in either language, with younger musicians preferring Uzbek and senior musicians using either. Occasionally someone would express a preference for either Russian or Uzbek, but ambivalence was far more common. Most would switch between Uzbek and Russian, depending on the topic at hand because so many found the Russian language most conducive to discussions of the Soviet period.

Western art music was the exception to this trend of code-switching and ambivalence toward language use. When I began interviewing prominent women for this chapter, a strong preference was expressed for Russian, with conductor Dilbara Abdurahmanova noting that we would be discussing an international musical tradition and that Russian is an international language. Speaking in Uzbek, before switching to Russian for the duration of our interview, Abdurahmanova explained why she speaks Russian while working with her orchestra, declaring, "In our orchestra, there are people from many nations: Russian, Ukrainian, Korean, Uzbek, Karakalpak, Tajik, Turkmen, all kinds of people. Therefore, everyone speaks Russian. For example, in India, people speak two languages: Hindi and English, and in Algeria people speak [Arabic] and French. . . . [switching to the Russian language] So let's go ahead and speak Russian, since more people will understand it" (Abdurahmanova 2008). She did not explicitly discuss the issue of colonialism, but her defense of the Russian language involved the bilingual realities in two other postcolonial nations, India and Algeria. In her presentation, the lingua franca of Russian (or French or English) is necessary in order to participate in international endeavors.

She and pianist Ofeliya Yusupova are ethnically Uzbek and are most certainly fluent in both professional and conversational Uzbek, as current state policy dictates for most workplaces. In this case, Russian language can be seen as pointing toward a more European aesthetic that they value and associate with intelligent discourse. Russian is also often seen as an international language, which pairs nicely with the international qualities Uzbek practitioners ascribe to Western art music. Indeed, this reaching toward Europe, while questionable in national, postcolonial, and traditional musical frameworks, is completely natural for those engaged in professional performance of Western art music, a preference that already orients them toward Europe.

Russian Culture as a Link to Western Art Musical Lineage

Uzbek engagement with Western art music is at once transnational yet inherently local. There is distinct pride shown in ethnically Uzbek composers, such as the chair of the Uzbek Composers' Union, Rustam Abdullayev. Further, musicians and audience members invest much pride and meaning in the heritage that Uzbeks have as performers of Russian art music by canonic composers like Tchaikovsky, Shostakovich, Glinka, and Prokofiev. A glance at any season's program at the Alisher Navoiy State Opera and Ballet usually sees the company featuring works such as Tchaikovsky's *Evgeniy Onegin*, Prokofiev's *Romeo and Juliet*, or Glinka's *Ruslan and Lyudmila*, as well as canonic standards by Verdi, Bizet, and Donizetti and also works by Uzbek composers. Russian art music is performed with great pride and even a sense of heritage because many important Russian pedagogues from the Leningrad Conservatory took up residence at the conservatory in Tashkent when they were evacuated during World War II. However, the link between Uzbek practitioners of Western art music and their Russian counterparts predates World War II. The founding of the conservatory and the state philharmonic in 1936 and then the Composers' Union in 1939 meant that institutions were in place to support the influx of musical talent that arrived during the evacuations of World War II (MacFadyen 2006, 45). The legacy of the evacuation is strong and vibrant in institutions and communities around all areas of Western art music: symphony, ballet, and opera.

The process of making Western art music a local ethnonational project was deeply important and has taken root in significant ways. This aligns with many similar processes linked to globalization in the twentieth century and is especially noticeable throughout East Asia. Music theorist Yayoi Uno Everett notes that the incorporation of Western art music in the nations of China, Japan, and Korea existed within the larger context of modernization and westernization. Canonic concepts in Western art music, such as the individual genius of the composer and the importance of authorship and the written score, "radically redefined" the social function and context of music in those nations (2004, 7). She goes on to emphasize that the adoption of Western music and its accompanying value system ushered in a "new mode of elitism and sense of privilege for professional musicians . . . instituting a standard of excellence and technical proficiency in Western classical music, [and as a result] East Asians came to equate Western classical or popular music with 'music'" (Everett 2004, 8). This "domestication," as Everett describes it, is analogous to cultural processes that occurred in Uzbekistan beginning in the tsarist period with similar results (2004, 8). The Tashkenters I spoke with regard Western symphonies or piano sonatas as within the umbrella of the term *music* as much as they accept Hindi film music, Turkish pop, and their own venerated (and inherently bicultural) Shashmaqom as fitting within it. Indeed, with such a historically multicultural urban experience, it does not seem notable that Western art music should be accepted as music; it is more important that its value system has been so wholeheartedly embraced by the general public.

The prestige that Western art music enjoys globally allows affiliated musicians to describe their musical values as being part of a standard of universal beauty that all are supposed to be able to appreciate. In this manner, not only is Western art music domesticated, but it is also universalized; virtuosity, standardization, and individual genius are presented as unquestionable goals shared by humanity, rather than as goals that have a history, and have been disseminated through various pathways including colonization and modernization. The shift to a universalist view allows practitioners to sidestep complicated histories and engage with Western art music as musical tradition that non-Europeans can participate in and over which they can feel a sense of ownership.

This sense of ownership was intensified by studies with the Russian teachers and mentors, such as those mentioned earlier. Indeed, teacher-student links provide a sense of lineage, a sense of belonging within the Western canon. Rather than referencing recordings for credibility, it is the human connection between student and teacher (and students and a lineage of teachers) that provides some of the most meaningful ways that Uzbek musicians claim connection with and credibility for their performances of Western art music. The combination of the assumed universality of this music's value, along with a pedagogical link to European masters, provides a powerful sense of ownership.

The importance placed on Western art music in Asian cultures is not unique to Uzbekistan. As noted earlier, similar processes occurred in East Asia. Ethnomusicologist Jonathan Stock (1996), music theorist Yayoi Uno Everett (2004), and political scientist Richard Kraus (1989) trace the lineage of Western art music in China, specifically as located in conservatories. For various Soviet republics, Western art music was embraced as a way of engaging with the modern and uplifting populations that were seen as "backward" or uneducated. As discussed in chapter 2, this uplifting was accomplished in part via the creation of folk orchestras that were seen as bridges between the music of the folk and the universal value and rigor of European art musics. It was also accomplished by training indigenous populations directly in Western art music itself. This process had the possibility to be just as transformative as the one that brought Uzbek folk melodies into orchestral and harmonic/polyphonic settings. Chinese culture also saw Western art music as an opportunity for transformation, as Kraus notes: "[The] Chinese middle class... adopted aspects of European culture both as an emblem of its own modernity and as a key to transforming its weak and impoverished nation" (Kraus 1989, 3). Later in his work, he notes the status that Western instruments like the piano afford middle-class populations (Kraus 1989, 25). Despite the rhetoric of class equality that was pervasive during the Soviet period, there was still a strong affinity with Western music and musical instruments by people who viewed themselves as members of the intelligentsia.

In the Uzbek Soviet Republic, membership in the intellectual classes assumed fluency in and allegiance to European culture because the region was often described as lacking culture before the influx of European culture via Russian colonization and the rise of Soviet influence. Indeed, in 1974, Soviet musicologist Boris Jarustovsky stated this view clearly in his English-language article on the state of Soviet musicology. He places the Bolshevik Revolution as the tipping point when culture came rushing into the city of Tashkent: "Tashkent (the capital of the Uzbek Soviet Socialist Republic) had practically no professional culture of its own before the Great October Socialist Revolution, while now in the Institute the doctors of science F. Karomatov, T. Vizgo and some others are working, having published several important studies on the music of the Republic" (Jarustovsky 1974, 56). This Eurocentric view of culture and its values was a prominent story that has survived to a certain extent (and in certain circles) in the independence era. Clearly the notion that Soviet intellectuals brought about the first fruits of Uzbek culture is deeply problematic when one considers cultural accomplishments like maqom and Sufi poetry. However, when looking only within the narrow boundaries of European art music, it is clear that Russian and Soviet presence in Uzbekistan did indeed lead to significant musical achievements.

Historically, the Eurocentric narrative about culture was bolstered especially strongly in Tashkent by the influx of Russian and other European musicians and scholars during the evacuations of World War II. During the time when Leningrad and other besieged cities were evacuated to Tashkent, many local scholars and musicians were able to study under renowned musicologists and composers. Soviet musicologist Igor Boelza describes this process (and the narrative of cultural influx) in relation to composer-scholar Muxtor Ashrafiy:

> Uzbek culture derived much benefit from the sojourn of the Leningrad Conservatory at Tashkent [during World War II], and many of its professors were rewarded by the Uzbek government for their cultural activities. One of them who earned particular distinction there was Maximilian Steinberg, son-in-law and pupil of Rimsky-Korsakov.... Thus the Uzbek composer [Muxtor] Ashrafi, whose symphony earned him the Stalin Prize in 1943, studied theory and composition under Steinberg for a year and a half. (Boelza 1944, 357)

In this it is possible to see a Russian-centric version of the Western canon establishing and reinforcing new narratives of heritage and chronology in the artistic circles of Tashkent. It was extremely important to have teacher-student links to experts in the Leningrad and Moscow conservatories (much as traditional musicians mentioned in chapter 1 find it so important to establish teacher-student links with masters of the maqom repertoires).

Although the influx of Russian composers and musicians during World War II provided mentors during such an important time in the development of Uzbek opera, ballet, and symphonies, Russian culture did not provide a strong model for encouraging women to compose. Indeed, Soviet institutions that seemed so obsessed with the emancipation of women and bringing them into the public sphere spent very little time encouraging women into the field of composition. Of the many influential composers of the Soviet Union, Sofia Gubaidulina and Galina Ustvolskaya are the only prominent names, and both women were marginalized within the Soviet system. It should be no surprise, then, that Uzbek cultural organizations also did not emphasize the need for women composers. Instead, they focused on bringing women into various performance fields, allowing women to become prominent symbols of Soviet progress and national pride. The era after World War II was especially productive, and was the time when so many of the women discussed in this volume entered the conservatory and other musical institutions. Figures like Abdurahmanova and Yusupova take great pride in their contributions to projects of locating Uzbekistan as a culturally sophisticated nation engaged in the project of gender equality in public and professional life.

Jonathan Stock notes a similar process of building institutions for Western art music in communist China. He emphasizes that Western music's place in Chinese music making was later questioned because of its association with elitism, but that, even then, the conservatory maintained importance as an institution. He also highlights the central role of the conservatory as an inherently Western model in Chinese educational projects.

> In our understanding of the process of "conservatorization," it matters little whether specific Western musical techniques, instruments, or genres are adopted, or if indigenous repertoires are retained. What is significant is that the conservatory becomes a primary cultural institution at which musical change is effected and through which musical transmission takes place. The very notion of the music conservatory as a center for performance excellence carries with it the expectation that the music performed must itself be "excellent," able to stand, in the eyes of its practitioners and sponsors, beyond the purview of both the market place and the immediate context of its origin. (Stock 1996, 161)

The notion of excellence that transcends national origin is a common thread for musicians engaged in performing and/or creating Western art music. Musical value that does not depend on cultural or national group membership is greatly appealing to the Uzbek women I spoke with who perform Western art music and creates a sense of an intellectual linkage with Europe and beyond, even as it is employed in support of national projects.

One reason for the strong similarities in the processes of developing, standardizing, and canonizing musical practices in Central Asia and in China is the common ideological basis and also the Soviet Union's strong existing model at the time of the Communist Revolution in China. Chinese studies scholar Bonnie S. McDougall translated Chairman Mao's 1943 talks at a conference on art and literature. In them, Mao uses military metaphors to explain the importance of ideologically sound arts. "Our meeting today is to ensure that literature and art become a component part of the whole revolutionary machinery, so they can act as a powerful weapon in uniting and educating the people while attacking and annihilating the enemy" (McDougall 1980, 58). Both Stock (1996) and the essays in Everett and Lau (2004) discuss the rise of the conservatory in China and the importance of Western art music and European educational models in the institutionalization of music in China. In both communist frameworks, Marxist-Leninist ideology guided the development of new musical practices such that they would rise "up to level of world culture" (Slobin 1971, 7; quoting unnamed Soviet scholars). The level of world culture here is the norm of European symphonic music, and these ideological projects drove the creation of the modern Chinese orchestra and the folk orchestras associated with different Soviet republics, as well as their enshrinement in the European-style conservatory system.

Outside of the framework of communist ideology, complex relationships with Western art music within educational establishments exist in Europe as well. Ethnomusicologist Juniper Hill observed the challenges involved in creating folk music curricula within a conservatory system in Finland during her fieldwork there, noting, "Even as conservatory folk music programmes attempt to mitigate the influences of Western art music techniques and stylistic conventions, many Western art music standards and values still hold sway. These include ideals about transcendental artistry, individual innovation, technical virtuosity, and professionalism, as well as conservatory side effects such as competitiveness and elitism" (Hill 2009, 216). Although folk musicians from various places may balk at the notion of Western art music as an international standard, it certainly still functions in that manner in many places, including Uzbekistan. Furthermore, it has shaped the way that audiences understand proper concert behavior and how institutions frame their pedagogical goals. As mentioned in chapter 2, the whole notion of musical literacy in Uzbekistan revolves around fluency in reading Western staff notation and understanding solfège and harmony. In that sense, although Western classical music's role in Uzbekistan's musical landscape may have changed, it is still seen as an important touchstone for all musicians and an important genre for Uzbek musicians to specialize in in order to gain international renown.

Conclusions

Western art music pervades the Uzbek music educational system in specific ways. Despite a rise in disciplinary and generic diversity that occurred especially after independence, the language of music education and its pedagogical and aesthetic goals sit within the framework of the European system that the Uzbek institutions were based on. This European and specifically Russian heritage has specific resonances, even as the government and associated institutions seek distance from Russian-influenced Soviet models. Although Uzbek language now dominates conversations and official documents in the state conservatory, the deeper undergirding remains based on the European conservatory model.

This has specific stakes for women, and it is no surprise that female performers took up the challenge of gaining international renown in Western art music. As with the other professional musical styles discussed in this book, women began to achieve success during the Soviet era and have continued through the independence era. Figures such as Ofeliya Yusupova and Dilbara Abdurahmanova work tirelessly to maintain Uzbekistan's place on the global stage of Western art music. Although Uzbek composers may not be well known outside the former-Soviet states, performers continue to grapple for recognition in competitions and via tours.

Western art music allows women like Yusupova and Abdurahmanova access to the idea of a global aesthetic standard and a community around that standard, even when travel is difficult. It also provides a notion of high society and the intelligentsia that links well with both Soviet-era ideology and the rhetorical priorities of the regime in independent Uzbekistan. Specifically, the international standard and participation in a global community that may not necessarily focus on Russia is something that women like Abdurahmanova have been able to capitalize on in their projects. Indeed, Western art music is a flexible enough genre and repertoire that a shift in focus can embrace the ever-evolving rhetoric about how the arts best support national priorities.

4 "Greetings to the Uzbek People!"
Popular Music in Public and Private Settings

The lights in the Friendship of Nations Concert Hall in Tashkent focus on a stage with musicians on metal risers. On one side is a typical estrada combo, with musicians seated before their instruments: drum set, electric bass, and electric guitar. On the other side of the stage sits a keyboardist, a Turkish *saz* (plucked lute) player, and a *tablah* (hourglass drum) player, as well as two female backup singers in white catsuits (the male musicians wear trousers and button-down shirts).

The first song begins with an instrumental introduction featuring a steady, brisk, poppy beat as Rayhon, one of Uzbekistan's best-known young stars, descends to the stage as if from thin air above the hall on a red swing in the center of a giant heart. It is February 13, 2005, and the hall is filled with an audience eager to hear her perform hits from her nearly yearly album releases, as well as new songs from this year's album, *Faqat Muhabbat* (Only love). The audience cheers wildly as she descends to a stage bedecked with hearts and begins the title track of her new album, a catchy tune that overlaps nicely with the Valentine's Day theme. Although Valentine's Day is not an indigenous holiday, many are fascinated by the romantic connotations and enjoy the holiday nonetheless (perhaps more, because it does not carry with it the same cultural expectations that it does in the United States and elsewhere).

As Rayhon continues her song, the claps and cheers quiet down and the audience focuses its attention (and often its cameras and cell phones) on the action on stage. She dances and sings with a wireless microphone, strutting from one edge of the stage to the other. Her costume is flamboyant and red, and she dances a few lively steps as the vocals drop back for an instrumental interlude. Rayhon's concert was not advertised as a live performance (*jonli ijro*), so she lip-synchs to her own recordings and the musicians also seem dubbed (this phenomenon of depending on prerecorded tracks is called *fonogramma* in both the Uzbek and Russian languages). As a result, the intonation is recording-perfect and the instrumentation on the stage does not always mimic what the audience hears. However, this matters little to them; they respond enthusiastically to her emphatic facial expressions and enthusiastic dancing. It is clear that she is an accomplished performer and that the concert hall is full of enthusiastic and ardent fans.

One of those fans is a neighbor of mine, a seventeen-year-old who is overjoyed to be taken to this concert by a boy from her class. Rayhon is her favorite artist, and we have spent many afternoons in the kitchen with her mother and four sisters listening to the radio, singing along and chatting while preparing a meal or drinking tea. This concert is the highlight of her year, and I see her many rows in front of me, bobbing her head to the music and applauding enthusiastically at the end of each song. The concert continues with songs entirely in the Uzbek language, and Rayhon occasionally pauses and greets the audience, often to say, "I love you" and "Thank you!" in Uzbek, then filling in more complex discussion in the Russian language. Her repertoire is more mixed between Russian and Uzbek than tonight's all-Uzbek concert reveals.

Although her songs do not appear in world music textbooks or the scholarship on Central Asia, Rayhon G'anieva—known simply as Rayhon to the public—maintains an almost-constant presence in the Uzbek media and is hugely popular with young female audience members (among others). G'anieva performs addictively catchy estrada tunes with a strong dose of Turkish influence, hence the presence of saz in her concert and on many of her recordings. Rayhon's songs and those by similar artists represent the most common music in Tashkent's everyday soundscape. I have heard Rayhon in taxicabs, encountered her voice blasted from portable stereos in the bazaars, seen her *kliplar* (music videos) on television, and heard young people sing along to her tapes and her songs when they come on the radio.

During my time in Uzbekistan in autumn 2003, her single "Sevgilim" (My love), later to be released as the title track of her 2004 album, filled the airwaves. This song is an Uzbek version of the popular Azerbaijani song "Sen Gelmez Oldun" (You didn't come) composed by Alakbar Taghiev (1922–81). In 2003 and 2004, it was impossible not to hear the tune as one traversed Tashkent. Furthermore, the tune stood out as unique and memorable with its catchy, yet melancholy, Azerbaijani *balaban* track (the balaban is a double-reed instrument better known by its Armenian name, *duduk*). "Sevgilim" opens with Rayhon's plaintive a cappella voice, which quickly melds with the balaban in a slow, stepwise descending melody through the introduction. Then it transitions to a quicker tempo with the addition of synthesizers and drumbeats, but still retains the sorrowful and heartrending descending contour. The opening lyrics of the song declare:

> Sensiz yuragimda yuragimda armon qoldi sevgilim,
> Sensiz ko'zlarimga ko'zlarimga yoshlar to'ldi sevgilim,
> Sen kela olmasan sen kela olmasan
> Kunglarim aytmaydi sevgilim
> Sen kela olmasan sen kela olmasan
> Baxorim kaytmaydi sevigilim
>
> Without you, a hole remains in my heart, my love
> Without you, my eyes fill up with tears, my love
> You can't come to me, you can't come to me,
> My soul/heart doesn't say/sing my love
> You can't come to me, you can't come to me,
> Spring doesn't return, my love

Rayhon's hit songs were well known, widespread, and impossible to miss in daily life in Tashkent. As of 2014, she remains very popular, even after more than a decade on the scene. Although occasionally criticized for having an accent and making occasional mistakes when she speaks Uzbek—the result of her Russian-language education and upper-class economic status—she is considered by many to be uncommonly good-hearted and generous for a celebrity. This reputation bolsters her popularity, as she is seen as a helpful role model for youth and a "good girl." Despite her fame, she embodies many of the positive traits that Uzbekistan's national project seeks to emphasize when representing Uzbek womanhood: she is a powerful symbol of successful, wealthy, worldly, yet moral femininity. As a result, she is able to wield a great deal of attention and support from both audiences and institutions. G'anieva's official website displays photos of her visiting and performing at hospitals and orphanages, in addition to providing concert footage, publicity materials, and pictures of her recent wedding (http://www.rayhon.uz; G'anieva 2013). Rayhon started as an actress and later transitioned to a singing career, which may have influenced her extraordinary popularity because it provided an existing fan base and experience presenting oneself on stage.

Her history as an actress may be one of the reasons that Rayhon is among the many estrada vocalists thought to be dancers and pretty faces more than vocalists. Judgment in terms of appearance and image permeates women's experiences of performing estrada, from those who sing karaoke on the popular pedestrian boulevard "Brodvey" (Broadway) to wedding singers and pop sensations. This is nothing unique to Uzbekistan; image is an important part of the performance of popular music around the world, one that is deeply intertwined with the performance of gender identity (Whiteley 1997, xvii). However, the image required for female estrada singers in Uzbekistan is unique in that it demands both showy glamour and expressions of appropriately modest and patriotic behavior. Rayhon negotiates the performance of a tricky combination of traits: constantly smiling femininity, worldly modern sensibilities, traditional values, and patriotism.

Estrada's Development in Uzbekistan

To understand women's role in estrada, it is important to understand its roots as a genre in Uzbekistan. Estrada came to Uzbekistan via Russia during the Soviet period, although there is certainly evidence that colonial forces brought European music, popular song, and dancing with them to Uzbekistan (Burnaby [1874] 2001, 336–37; Graham 1916, 98). These Soviet-era roots include the creation of a state-run *Melodiya* record company headquarters in Tashkent, and Tashkent's reputation as the "disco capital" of the Soviet Union (Steinholt and Wickström 2009, 309).

The independence era has brought a shift toward private patronage, emphasis on Uzbek language, and Uzbek-specific nationalism, as well as the opening of a conservatory department in the discipline of estrada. Despite its new institutional standing and mobilization in support of the national project, many audience members and critics criticize estrada as borrowing too much from other cultures, specifically from Russia and Europe more generally. This is despite the presence of so many Turkish and Arab idioms in the musical sound, such as the rhythmic modes *saidi, baladi,* and *maqsum* in the drum machine and the presence of prominent saz and balaban/duduk tracks in many well-loved estrada tunes.

Furthering the transnational history of the genre, estrada in Russia got its name from the French term for *small stage*. As explained in detail in the introduction, estrada has become "a wide-ranging term that includes pop music but also applies to modern dance, comedy, circus arts, and any other performance not on the 'big,' classical stage" (MacFadyen 2002, 3). Even though its most common referent is still popular music, the word continues to function in the Russian language as a broad umbrella term for a variety of activities including popular song, vaudeville, juggling, comedy, and others because it is used in contrast to symphony, opera, and ballet, which use the "big" stage. However, in Uzbek usage, I've never heard it refer to any practice other than popular song performed for media of some sort. In Uzbekistan the term evokes large amplified concerts in venues like the Friendship of Nations Concert Hall, as well as more modest practices: singers honing their craft by performing at cafés to attract customers; wedding singers weaving traditional tunes for ritual seamlessly into performances of estrada so that young people can dance; and young girls gluing themselves to the radio, cheering and singing along when a new favorite is played.

Female vocalists performing estrada in urban Uzbekistan find themselves with a plethora of options for training (as do their male counterparts). The institutionalization of estrada in the conservatory and other educational institutions is an important project in the independence era. Debates over talent and skill arise in connection with estrada's place in music education along with other musical traditions that bear more prestige. Beyond these debates, estrada and its dissemination via both state-controlled and private radio stations is important for girls and young women as consumers and listeners. Their demographic importance brings the discussion from domestic media to the international world music scene, specifically to the careers of Uzbek pop icon Yulduz Usmanova and more recent world music phenomenon Sevara Nazarkhan. Both Usmanova's and Nazarkhan's training as traditional vocalists provides a great deal of their credibility internationally and within Uzbekistan. Another vocalist making a deft negotiation between the prestige of traditional music and the popularity of estrada is Gulzoda Hudoinazarova. As discussed later in this chapter, estrada's presence at the events that comprise an Uzbek wedding demonstrates the way that this genre, with transnational roots, is now an integral part of practices that are so often described as nationally and culturally significant.

Defining and Framing Popular Music in Central Asia

Popular music is often a difficult category to clarify, either in an academic framework or in the frameworks established by those who create and consume estrada in Uzbekistan. As mentioned, in Russian, the word *estrada* implies a range of activities that is more broad than the term *popular music* implies in English because it encompasses comedy, vaudeville acts, and other nonmusical pursuits appropriate for the small stage. However, in common usage in Tashkent, the terms map much more closely onto one another, especially when one defines popular music via its creation for media, as ethnomusicologist Peter Manuel does in his work on Indian popular music. "Since popular music ... is inherently and inextricably associated with the mass media, it can in many respects be more productively analyzed as a commodity, and as a form of media content, than solely, or even primarily, as an artwork to be judged by aesthetic criteria" (Manuel 1993, 7). In this commentary, Manuel presents popular music as important to a given locale because of its commodification and consumption via media, such that a merely aesthetic appraisal of its work in any given context fails to appreciate popular music's importance within a culture. He describes popular music as "inseparable from social identity," and notes that it garners its power from its ability to embody "encoded ideologies" (Manuel 1993, 6). Popular music scholar Simon Frith further emphasizes the commodified nature of popular music, saying that "popular music genres are constructed—and must be understood—within a commercial/cultural process" (Frith 1996, 88–89). This is important because the act of selling and consuming is not just part of the musical culture; in this case, it is the unifying element of popular music culture.

Turning from broader definitions to those specific to Central Asia, ethnomusicologist John Baily's definition of the term regarding the popular music of Afghanistan holds true to Manuel's framing with the media, implying though not underscoring the commoditization: "In one sense popular music *is* the music of the media, specifically, those kinds of music that have been created for the media, or in whose creation communication within a media network is important" (Baily 1981, 121). Working elsewhere in Central Asia, ethnomusicologist Rachel Harris describes Uyghur popular music in similar terms, defining *popular music* as music experienced primarily via technological media and intended for wide dissemination. She goes on to emphasize that this definition allows for more than the mere adoption of Western styles and forms, and focuses on "the diversity of local meanings and contexts of popular music, and the development and continuity of traditional musics made possible through the medium of technology" (Harris 2002, 266).

In contrast, ethnomusicologist Federico Spinetti unseats the notion of media's importance. Discussing Tajik popular music, he declares, "Technological mediation on a mass scale can hardly be taken as the distinguishing trait of the music in question." He further notes that a variety of genres enjoy mass mediation and thus could be described as popular if that is the primary defining characteristic (Spinetti 2005, 194). Indeed, mass mediation is something that all the genres in this book currently experience. However, estrada in Uzbekistan is notable in that it is created as a mediated commodity: live performance is not afforded pride of place in terms of the location of the music itself. With the proliferation of prerecorded backing tracks and lip-synching, the recordings are the primary consumable objects, whether purchased in cassette or compact disc form or received via radio or "live" concert. As a result, the function of mass media as the locus of the music itself is the vital differentiating characteristic of Uzbek estrada in comparison with other genres. That said, there are a variety of contexts where recordings designed for mass mediation are incorporated into live performances that have a distinctly local connotation.

The range of women's musical interaction with estrada spans from highly mediated celebrity-driven televised concerts to extremely local and nonprofessional street karaoke. A middle ground between the two extremes is also a rich area for inquiry about the ways women engage meaningfully with popular music: wedding music and café performances are both important inroads to the singing profession, though ones that carry complicated connotations in terms of morality and the policing of gendered norms. Furthermore, with its reputation for a focus more on entertainment value than talent or virtuosity, pop music represents an ideal venue on which to focus a discussion of Uzbek audiences and their consumption of media featuring female pop stars.

In addition, the institutionalization of estrada into music schools and the conservatory brings up the intersection of gender identity with ideas of credibility, prestige, hierarchy, and acceptability. Men also perform estrada and participate in its pedagogy at all levels, but it is women both as performers and consumers who represent its focus (this contrasts with the economic force behind Uzbek estrada, which is primarily made up of male sponsors). The result of women's star power and enthusiastic fandom is that this mass-mediated art form is used in varied and flexible ways, which often serve to underscore important ideas about femininity, especially those that apply across many contexts.

Institutionalizing Estrada: The Conservatory's Estrada Department

Estrada in independence-era Uzbekistan straddles state-run institutions and private industry. Uzbek artists perform estrada on privately owned record labels, on private and state-run television and radio stations, in state-owned concert halls, at state-sponsored competitions and holiday spectacles, at private wedding celebrations, and at privately owned cafés and nightclubs. But estrada is also part of the state conservatory of music, which plays such an important part in providing a central locus of professional credibility and hierarchy for musicians who perform all the musics discussed in the previous chapters. Perhaps it should be unsurprising that popular music would also be subject to official hierarchies and pedagogies, but it does seem an intriguing situation because popular music has not traditionally come within the purview of European-style conservatories, even those that have expanded their mission to include folk music, jazz, and improvisation, such as the Sibelius Academy in Finland. Indeed, estrada has not been part of the conservatory for long, with its department established only in 2002 when a new building opened to house the conservatory. The inclusion of a department of estrada in the new conservatory opened under the Karimov government was an important aspect of his larger project to develop "national estrada," something that was emblazoned on billboards and much discussed during my first few trips to the field. This project has continued resonance with the citizenry and is often referenced by non-estrada musicians as a reason the genre maintains pride of place in spectacles and the media. However, even before the opening of the new department in the new conservatory building, it was possible to study to be a pop star via the Kollej of Estrada and Circus Performers, an institution founded in the Soviet era that continues to embody the broader definition of estrada in the Russian language.

Some of the events held in the conservatory's estrada department illustrate important priorities of its arbiters in Uzbek institutions: those of transnational relevance and the performance of nation. These two priorities are programmed in much the same way, whether in a competition setting or during the juried examinations at the end of the school year. When I attended a number of competitions and exams in 2005, the range of sung languages was remarkable: English was very common, along with Russian, Turkish, French, and even Korean. In both contexts, however, each performer also sang at least one song in Uzbek, often one with patriotic overtones. Compared to the overwhelmingly Uzbek and Tajik demographics in the traditional and arranged folk music departments, the ethnic background of performers in the estrada department was much more diverse. It was also more clearly balanced in terms of gender representation in the department, with slightly more women performing than men. In the estrada department, as in those focused on Western art music, performers from Russian, Armenian, and Korean backgrounds joined those of ethnically Central Asian descent. Repertoire choices that I observed ranged from patriotic songs to jazz standards like "Mack the Knife" and a rendition of "Careless Whisper" made popular by George Michael.

Amid all this tension over credibility, talent, profit, and musical skill, in addition to all the changes in systems and institutions, the image of the smiling Uzbek woman proudly singing in her costume of national fabric is remarkably constant across disciplines and regimes. Notably, in estrada competitions and juries, the performance of femininity had a broader range than I saw in other juries, at least in terms of costuming and stage presence. Some female performers were reserved, while others made sweeping gestures and traversed the stage. None, however, challenged gender norms in observable ways. Costuming was more standardized in that it was always formal, but it involved either traditional forms of dress or modest modern attire. Women's dresses—and all did wear dresses—ranged from Western-style ball gowns and cocktail dresses to dresses in Uzbek national fabric in a variety of cuts. The diversity of attire underscored the hybrid and transnational nature of estrada performance in independence-era Uzbekistan.

Even with an established degree-granting program in estrada at the conservatory, a great many pop stars have other pedigrees. Women from various walks of life, including actresses, business owners, and traditional vocalists, want chances to perform estrada, and audiences seem willing to accept a wide range of backgrounds and levels of training. Following the lead of Yulduz Usmanova, who built a vastly successful estrada career in the 1990s after studying traditional music,[1] vocalists Sevara Nazarkhan and Gulzoda Hudoinazarova depend on their traditional music training for credibility even in those parts of their career that include estrada. There does seem to be a tendency for accomplished traditional vocalists to cross over into estrada—at least in practice if not in name—a phenomenon involving sponsorship, fame, and monetary compensation.

Beyond that, notions of tradition have a role to play in the presentation of women in estrada. Traditionally feminine images seem to meld easily with estrada as it is performed in Tashkent. The image of a female pop star in Uzbekistan draws a great deal from modern constructions of tradition that share common tropes of feminine identity with that of the female maqomist. Shared traits include the unfaltering smile, a focus on women as vocalists, and the employment of national fabric and national instruments in performances and publicity materials. In estrada, such national/traditional instruments are mixed with synthesizers and other instruments, amplified and mediated, whereas in traditional music performance gravitas is established with live, unaltered (though occasionally amplified) musical performance.

Tensions over Talent

This brings up the notion of talent and how it legitimizes one's art, an especially salient issue for women estrada singers. Although talent, technique, and expressiveness are required of all musicians, popular singers in Uzbekistan need to make explicit their credentials in order to be credible as more than just a pretty face. Of course, one could argue that musical talent has more weight within certain genres; certainly for the other musics discussed in this volume, talent, technical proficiency, and musical literacy (Russian:

grammotnost') are overlapping categories on which one's reputation as a performer is built.

It is worth noting that so many women in the upper echelon of estrada have musical backgrounds outside the estrada department or the estrada and circus kollej. Furthermore, its location in the conservatory has generated some debate. The recent inclusion of a department of estrada in the state conservatory of music brought the topic of popular music into numerous conversations among those affiliated with other departments. Although many reference Karimov's project to develop national estrada, others assert that the kinds of talent needed for estrada performance are not the same as those demanded by traditional music, arranged folk music, or Western art music.

These debates about disciplinary alignment and justification for placement in the conservatory are not always reserved for estrada. Indeed, similar barbed questions about musical literacy and technical virtuosity are often asked about traditional music's role in the conservatory because it is rooted in oral tradition. The answer to such issues is the same for estrada practitioners as it is for those of traditional music. Even if the genre has different aesthetic and technical requirements, all conservatory students are required to take courses in harmony and solfège, and are required to read music. Musical literacy, technical skill, and the development of talent are what the conservatory is designed to foster in its students, regardless of disciplinary alignment.

Ethnomusicologist Henry Kingsbury notes the fragility and supreme importance of the idea of talent in his study of the American conservatory system (Kingsbury 1988, 12–13). Estrada's lesser (or perhaps merely different) emphasis on talent seems to imply that genre is functioning differently and that people employ different metaphors when framing music (Rice 2003). Estrada first and foremost looks to music as mass-mediated entertainment. Emotional expression is highly valued, as is lyrical content and image. Talent and virtuosity are certainly lauded, but not a first-order necessity. This dissonance between each genre's ranking of the "music as art" and "music as entertainment" metaphors seems to create some of the tension and discomfort expressed when musicians engage a musical style outside their chosen specialty.

Indeed, the traditional musicians I spoke with were often suspicious of popular music, framing their discussions in polarities, with traditional music being healthy and moral versus estrada, which was framed as unhealthy and often leading to immoral behavior. Unlike many discussions of the risks of women performing in public, estrada's dangers threaten both sexes. A typical discussion that critiqued estrada went beyond the normal jockeying for acknowledgment of superiority that was common to dedicated practitioners of any of the genres. It is one thing to believe that one's chosen musical style is the most sophisticated and demanding; it is quite another to believe that practicing another style is damaging to one's health, good name, and spiritual development. This fear of negative effects is clearly intertwined with a range of issues, including the danger of assimilating colonial musical practices and losing one's own valuable culture, as well as the danger of pop music bringing young people together in immoral ways.

The perception of dangers lurking within popular music is a significant cross-cultural phenomenon that reaches back through history. Musicologist Susan McClary references Plato and Saint Augustine and their suspicions of all music when she notes that "[authorities'] reactions often verge on the hysterical when musicians depart from tradition to introduce novelties into the mix" (McClary 1994, 30). She goes on to call for popular music analysis that foregrounds the body as the locus when music does its work (and enacts its transgressions). She argues that pop music especially is linked with bodily practice (McClary 1994, 35–36). Certainly discussions of popular music in Uzbekistan focus more on bodies than any other genre, both in terms of judgment based on appearance and in terms of the perceived moral and physical dangers that become bodily risks.

Beyond the fear about poor health and immorality surrounding estrada, it does seem to be the most often criticized by both musicians and the general public with regard to talent. Most critiques heard from both professionals and audience members can be summarized as framing estrada as a genre that requires pretty faces, attractive dancing, and support from a rich sponsor; musical ability is not required. In this sense, for estrada a musical body is needed, but one that performs gender and nationalism appropriately; in many senses, musical sensibilities are more in the background of the discourse. Part of this may be linked with commodification: although supported by state media and the conservatory, popular music engages more with privatized industries—radio, nightclub appearances, wedding performance, media sales, and the sponsorship of artists are often outside the purview of state institutions.

Sponsorship is problematic in Tashkent. It has become another demonstration of patriarchal power because men represent the majority of the sponsors who shape the careers of women in estrada. Whereas once the Soviet state controlled the production and dissemination of estrada and other musics, now the patchwork of state and private endeavors mentioned earlier provide a more tortuous path to stardom. Finding a wealthy sponsor for one's work is often acknowledged as the only way to "make it" in estrada in the independence era. Indeed, individuals rather than corporations provide the bulk of sponsorship for albums, concerts, and other activities. Sponsors often provide musicians with apartments and stipends in addition to subsidizing their musical activities. In this case, the care and support of musicians has transitioned with the shift away from the Soviet system: it has moved from state support of musical endeavors to a largely faceless oligarchy controlling which pop musicians get the most publicity.

The Importance of Radio to Girls

Estrada performance is highly gendered and, in Uzbekistan, it does not provide a venue for artists to challenge gender norms. Estrada is an appropriate arena in which women perform acceptable, often nationalist, femininity. It is also an equally acceptable place for men to perform masculinity, as exemplified by Mo'min Oripov and Jahongir Foziljonov of the pop-hip-hop group Bojalar or Oybek Alimov of the mixed-gender pop duet Oybek va Nigora. The pop/rock dichotomy onto which a feminine/masculine dichotomy is often mapped in the United States and Britain, which has since been problematized by women's studies scholars (such as Coates 1997, 52–53), is not very relevant, as there is not currently a significant rock industry in Uzbekistan. Although some listeners do consume rock from other areas of the world, there is very little Uzbek rock available via media, especially when compared to estrada, which currently incorporates both pop and hip-hop elements into its style. Certainly popular music provides an important vehicle in which to display feminine values for the consumption and imitation of audiences.

In this case, an important audience for the music and the performance of feminine identity is young women. Analyzing popular music culture in the United States and Britain, sociologist and women's studies scholar Mavis Bayton noted, "Looking at popular music as a whole, women have been music consumers rather than music producers: the main role for women is that of fan" (Bayton 1997, 37). It would be remiss to exclude fandom and the act of listening from a discussion of women's roles in the popular music culture of Tashkent. Having attended quite a few pop concerts at the Friendship of Nations Concert Hall featuring female vocalists (Rayhon, Lola, Yulduz Usmanova, and so on), I can attest to the fact that young women comprise a large proportion of the audiences at these large concerts. In my personal interactions with Uzbek families, the daughters are also often the ones enthusiastically tuning in to the radio hoping to hear the latest single by their favorite artists. They often sit in the kitchen helping prepare a meal while singing along with their mother and any close female family friends who might also be there.

Even with the rise of mobile phones as a locus for one's music collection and the increase in home Internet use in recent years, radio still maintained an important presence in the Uzbek households that welcomed me.

Radio has been a constant companion in many homes (as is the television), and has often provided background music to help make household tasks lighter or provided entertainment when one is taking a break. Almost every kitchen I stepped into in Uzbekistan had a radio on, usually providing musical entertainment to a group of women and girls engaged in food preparation or other household tasks. It was an important site for listening, singing along, and discussing one's favorite songs and singers. Girls' enthusiastic responses to certain artists and songs on the kitchen radio provided me with an important study in early twenty-first-century pop culture.

In many households, the radio provides the main conduit for mediated Uzbek popular music, as the videos (kliplar) appear only intermittently on state-sponsored television, and purchasing cassettes (or now CDs) is a luxury that some forgo. Beyond that, there is a whole range of publicity materials marketed to school-aged girls that include school supplies like folders and notebooks with images of pop stars on them.[2] The result is that estrada stars become important companions and role models for young girls through their ubiquitous media and marketing presence.

Even though radio lacks visual representation, young women listening to the radio are very much aware of the images that each of their favorite artists is presenting. Further, it is the voice that carries a great deal of significance and emotional power for audience members. This is the same in traditional music, which frames all instrumental sound production in terms of vocal production and expression. Via the radio, vocal timbre and technique are two important ways that listeners differentiate the different artists. Frith discusses the centrality of the voice in the performance of femininity, for instance in the image of country singer Dolly Parton.

> But women performers in all musical genres have always been conscious of what it means to be spectacularly female. As a country singer, Dolly Parton, for example, doesn't only play on a male notion of femininity, but on *performing* the signs of vulnerability—the little-girl voice, the giggle, the nervous flounce—[which] makes their meaning problematic. . . . As is typical in country music, her voice (as opposed to her body), though a clearly physical sound, becomes the sign, the trademark even, of her stardom, the meaning around which all her other signs (the hair, the breasts, the gowns) are organized. (Frith 1996, 213)

Rayhon and others are clearly also aware of the need to be "spectacularly female" and the requirement to perform a type of femininity that involves a careful mix of strength, beauty, vulnerability, and smiling kindness. These attributes render female pop stars attractive role models for youth and appropriate representatives of a nation that values morality, beauty, and artistic talent (the lack of deviance or overt sex appeal is notable in Uzbek pop stars and has analogues in other countries, for example, Nancy Ajram in Lebanon). Such desirable feminine attributes apply not only to their physical image, but also to their vocal timbre, which has great immediacy for listeners. Indeed, Rayhon's rendition of "Sevgilim" (My love) performs this "spectacular" and vulnerable feat as much through the tremble in her voice and her urgent and sorrowful vocal timbre as it does in the lyrics that describe her waiting, unrequited, for her love.

At the same time that Rayhon's estrada is in many ways transnationally rooted in European and Turkic idioms, she is deeply engaged in the explicit performance of national femininity. She includes Uzbek instruments like the doyra (frame drum) in many of her songs as well as synthesized versions of other traditional instruments, like the surnay (shawm). The combination of glamorously modern and traditionally patriotic identity markers necessary for a successful Uzbek estrada diva is usually accomplished with costumes including dresses in national fabric with modern and less-modest cuts, as well as the de rigueur performance of patriotic songs in concerts and on albums (required for male artists as well). Many female artists go beyond the simple performance of nationalism via costuming, Uzbek lyrics, and patriotic themes in their songs. Rayhon, Sevara Nazarkhan, and Gulzoda Hudoinazarova all exceed the expected representations of national femininity and engage with Uzbek traditional material in ways that represent innovation both musically and in the portrayal of traditional aspects of the very modern practice of estrada performance.

The clearest example of this performance of national femininity in Rayhon's career comes from the track "Baka Bang," from the 2007 album *Sog'indim* (I missed you). This is a popular tune that was remixed for her 2009 album *Orzuinga Ishon* (Believe in your dreams). The title is onomatopoeic for the sound of the doyra. The lyrics blend both Uzbek and Russian text in a clever rhyming chorus: "Baka baka bang dor uynang, esli upadesh ne plach' vstan'" (Uzbek: Baka baka bang play the doyra; Russian: If you fall down don't cry, stand back up). The song features a duple rhythm (articulated on the doyra) that is commonly heard at weddings and other celebrations (tak taka dum dum taka taka dum dum). This is often referred to by musicians as simply the "folk rhythm," and would be recognizable not just to specialists, but to regular audience members as well; it strongly underscores not only nationalist platitudes, but also a larger sense of the sonic aspect of what it means to live in Uzbekistan.

The code-switching between Russian and Uzbek evokes the realities of Tashkent's bilingual populace, and the track also cuts in samples of a traditional music ensemble and a synthesized representation of the shawm (surnay) sound commonly heard at weddings. The result is a musical representation via estrada that evokes the desire for modern traditionality that is especially found in Tashkent's weddings. The video for this clip further plays with notions of tradition and modernity, showing a sad girl in traditional attire (not Rayhon), who is watching the object of her affections marry someone else. She then retreats to her room to watch some traditional music on a black-and-white television. Rayhon makes appearances throughout the video to encourage the girl not to cry and to stand back up. The video ends on a happy note with determined smiling faces on the protagonist and Rayhon. The feminine experience is clearly marked in both the song and the video, and the ostinato use of the folk doyra rhythm combines with Rayhon's poppy estrada vocal timbre to underscore the duality of the use of women as national icons who represent both the past and the present simultaneously.

This interaction between transnational and national/traditional identity is not unique to Rayhon. In fact, many female artists in Uzbekistan engage in similar negotiations. As is discussed later in this chapter, Yulduz Usmanova has been performing folk-influenced pop in Uzbekistan since the 1990s. Sevara Nazarkhan, in collaboration with the producers at Real World Records, also combines traditional musical repertoire with pop and electronica in a way that goes beyond other pop singers' engagement with the performance of Uzbek national identity. Gulzoda Hudoinazarova is a classical singer who has flirted with a career in estrada and is keen to write her own arrangements of traditional tunes in an effort to make them more relevant to the current generation. Aspects of folk and traditional music are used as powerful symbols in all four women's work not just to express nationalism, but also to emphasize their musical talent and their grounding in Uzbek history and tradition rather than European experience.

Complicated Nationalism and Mature Femininity: Yulduz Usmanova

Yulduz Usmanova (b. 1963) is arguably the most famous figure in Uzbek popular music at home and abroad. With the beginning of my research in 2002, I observed Usmanova after her career was well established (it began in the early 1990s). During my fieldwork, Usmanova performed a gala concert series every year in the Friendship of Nations Concert Hall in Tashkent (often lasting more than a week, as opposed to the two to three days of concerts offered by other comparable stars). These were well-publicized and celebrated events, and Usmanova was the subject of gossip and conversation by the women who identified as fans and followed her closely. As Levin notes, she is something of an "unlikely" pop star because she has roots singing folk songs in the Ferghana Valley, has a conservatory education from the Soviet-era Eastern music department, and has grandchildren (1996, 81). During my time in Uzbekistan, Usmanova's music was considered somewhat old-fashioned by youth, but many still admired her music and tuned in to hear her songs on the radio because she incorporated traditional instruments, rhythms, and melodies into her work, as well as writing songs that seemed concerned with everyday life (as she was doing when Levin interviewed her [1996, 81]).

My first experience with Usmanova came in 2002, when she was part of a large Independence Day concert that was televised during the celebrations on September 1. Usmanova was the headliner, featured last in the concert along with another well-established female vocalist, Nasiba Abdullayeva, and choruses of singers and dancers accompanying their songs. Before tuning in to this concert, I had had conversations with women lamenting Yulduz's loss of popularity because of rumors about her poor treatment of her husband. This combination of aesthetic appreciation and concern over a pop star's moral values and appropriate performance of national and gendered identity is a consistent theme in discourses surrounding female pop stars. It should be no surprise then that the acceptable version of pop stardom for women is attractive, friendly, and smiling, but not overtly sexy or overly rebellious (men are much more apt to present the image of a rebel in the context of Uzbek estrada, but still generally have more wholesome images than their male counterparts in the United States). This image of upstanding and optimistic morality did not change during my fieldwork. Usmanova was still engaging in that performance of acceptability and legibility and thus presented a great many concerts.

Such ideas about propriety do not seem to affect her popularity or her presence on state-run media; the next time I saw Usmanova perform was during a television broadcast of a Soldiers' Appreciation Day concert on January 14, 2004. It was another mass concert with a large variety of performers, including a traditional maqom ensemble and a military brass band. As a finale, the military band moved off to the sides and on came Usmanova with twelve dancers bedecked in shining colorful national fabric (*hon atlas*).

Usmanova was immediately swamped by people trying to give her flowers, but still managed to perform her song with enthusiasm.

In 2005, I attended one of the concerts held during Usmanova's spring gala at the Friendship of Nations Concert Hall, which lasted from April 23 to May 4. Her concerts were publicized as live and not lip-synched (*jonli ijro*). Her ensemble at this concert was huge, much larger than that of other pop singers I had seen at the same venue, and included a full symphonic string section, a pianist, and a typical five-piece band, as well as two frame drummers, a qanun (plucked zither) player, and performers who played Turkish saz and Kashgar rubob (both plucked lutes). Despite various rumors and detractors, Usmanova was given the most applause and attention of any performer I had seen at Tashkent's main concert stage, with throngs of people crowding the stage to give her flowers. Usmanova also addressed her audience completely in the Uzbek language, perhaps positioning herself consciously within a nationalist framework. She has enjoyed remarkable longevity as the queen of Uzbek pop, and provides a formidable foundation for other women to build on in Uzbek estrada.

Popularizing Traditional Music Internationally: Sevara Nazarkhan

Sevara Nazarkhan (b. 1978) is by far the best-known Uzbek pop artist to rise to international fame in the independence era. She has transcended the expected shiny smiling Uzbek feminine facade in order to present something more complex and true to life. Nazarkhan is known in Uzbekistan as a very competent estrada musician, one who is discussed with pride because of the vast skill that her training in maqom and traditional music brings to her performances. The large majority of her domestically released albums have been fairly straightforward estrada with poppy beats, thrumming synthesizers, and a smattering of patriotic messages. She is well regarded for releasing *Otmagay Tong* (Don't let the dawn come), an album of traditional music that includes performances of pieces from the Shashmaqom and related repertoires (2002). Audiences in Uzbekistan also have access to her international releases, which sound very different from her domestic ones.

Building on the fame and popularity of Yulduz Usmanova, who preceded her in the international arena and the world music category, Nazarkhan established her career in popular music with a sense of gravitas from her traditional roots and training. Like Usmanova, she studied in the vocal section of the traditional music department at the Uzbek State Conservatory.

Usmanova remains popular in Uzbekistan and gives well-attended concerts there; people still greatly respect her music and her business savvy.[3] Nazarkhan seems to share many of Usmanova's ambitious and savvy qualities in negotiating a career domestically in Uzbekistan as well as abroad via the platform of Peter Gabriel's Real World Records and WOMAD (World of Music, Arts, and Dance) festivals. On the international market, Nazarkhan has now released two albums on Real World Records, *Yol Bolsin* (Where are you going?) (2003) and *Sen* (You) (2007), and one self-published album, *Tortadur* (Stretching/pulling/melting) (2011).

All the albums feature Uzbek instrumentalists, generally playing traditional instruments, although *Sen* also includes the reconstructed bass *kobyz* (bowed lute) commonly heard in folk orchestras. The three albums represent a progression of sorts, with the first being shepherded along by well-known world music producer Hector Zazou (1948–2008). *Yol Bolsin* presents a set of standard traditional pieces with fairly straightforward traditional performance of their arching vocal lines, often accompanied by instruments such as the dutar, tanbur (plucked lute), and doyra, as well as by a variety of manipulated and synthesized sounds. In 2003, the album made something of an impact in world music circles, and Nazarkhan received some positive press in both the United States and the United Kingdom. In 2007 her second album was released, one that pulled away somewhat from the traditional repertoire. *Sen* features mostly creative remixes of the estrada tunes she is best known for domestically in Uzbekistan, such as "Korgim Kelar" (I want to see you) and "Kunlarim Sensiz" (My days without you), but also includes a version of Yunus Rajabi's famous song "Kuigai" (Ablaze). Nazarkhan wrote the majority of the material on this album, which was worked on by many of the same people who produced her debut world music album, *Yol Bolsin*. However, *Sen* did not receive as much attention from the press as her first international album.

In 2011, Nazarkhan engaged musicians from the Uzbek state radio and television maqom ensemble to self-publish *Tortadur*, which was released on the popular self-publishing website CDBaby.com. The material on *Tortadur* is similar to that of *Yol Bolsin* but without the added electronic and synthesized elements. The eleven tracks on the album include selections from the Shashmaqom and closely related traditional repertoire. In fact, this album is similar to *Otmagay Tong*, the 2002 Uzbek domestic album that preceded the international release of *Yol Bolsin* and included many of the same tracks without the added electronica. The tempi of the tracks on *Tortadur* are quite reserved, and it is mixed so that Nazarkhan's voice has a softer quality than on her more pop- and electronica-oriented releases.

The three international releases provide a variety of sonic representations of Nazarkhan, showing off the diversity of her output as well as the different approaches to marketing her to world music audiences. In a 2005 article, I note that in comparison to Nazarkhan's Uzbek release, which contains overlapping material with her first international release *Yol Bolsin*, her voice in these internationally oriented CDs is often subsumed by various electronic and synthesized sounds, which take the forefront at various points in the album, and serve to anonymize her unique vocal style and timbre (Merchant 2005). At the time of publication, there was a stark contrast between her domestic material, which included strict interpretations of traditional music or typical estrada with synthesized accompaniment, and her international releases, which layered the aesthetics of electronic and pop on top of renditions of traditional music. Before *Yol Bolsin*'s release, Nazarkhan's renditions of traditional music on her *Otmagay Tong* album—released only in Uzbekistan—conformed to the standard heterophonic and acoustic norms commonly heard in Uzbek media and institutions. The combination of these tunes with electronica in the world music treatment producer Hector Zazou created was something innovative and previously unheard of in the region.

Nazarkhan's more recent albums complicate this analysis, especially *Tortadur*, her self-published presentation of traditional tunes with none of the electronic processing. Dedicated to Hector Zazou after his death, this album's instrumental accompaniment is provided by members of the maqom ensemble of the Uzbek National Television and Radio Company in Tashkent, who perform the tunes in typical heterophonic style. They also interject virtuosic and filigreed interludes into Nazarkhan's mellow and down-tempo articulation of traditional melodies. In *Tortadur*, Nazarkhan provides a softer and in some ways more flexible interpretation of traditional repertoire that would be well known by any musician trained in the traditional music department of the conservatory (in fact, I heard many of the tunes from her album sung in the final exam juries I attended in that department). The mix of this album, in general, is soft and sparse, but Nazarkhan's voice is in the forefront whenever she sings.

Her second album, *Sen* (2007), also places her voice and her face much more in the forefront of her publicity materials and in the album's mix. Zazou did not participate in this album, and it lacks his hallmark electronica treatment (however, executive producer Bahrom Primkulov worked on both albums). This album presents an interesting bridge between Nazarkhan's Uzbek career, which trades on her credibility as a classically trained traditional vocalist but hinges largely on typical estrada, and her international persona, which often engages traditional musical material but presents it in a highly processed and less specific manner.

Nazarkhan has a diverse vocal repertoire, with experience in traditional music, jazz, pop/estrada, and the world music category that bridges most of those styles. Along with the range of styles, she has a range of images that support her roles in various performing contexts, which have evolved with her developing career. Although her early work with Real World Records was alarmingly anonymous in certain ways, she built a successful international career while splitting her time between Uzbekistan and the United Kingdom. She has needed a chameleonlike representation, at times linking her vocal timbre and feminine image to a large trope of global Asian womanhood (this often also involves romanticization about links to ancient traditions as in the liner notes to her 2003 album). However, as her career has developed, that generality has gained more individuality. It is possible to note in her latest self-released album a sense of other vocal styles influencing her very personal and tender renditions of classical Uzbek tunes. She manages to assert herself vocally as a transnational woman without leaving the confines of what is acceptable within the traditional performance milieu.

Nazarkhan has now been able to foreground internationally what she is often praised for in her domestic Uzbek career: her grounding in traditional musical technique, her unique voice, and her ability to sing in a variety of styles. She is a powerful national figure, but not bound by that nationalism when on the international stage, presenting herself musically as a woman with a multilayered identity that weaves nationalism with global imaginings of Asian femininity, as well as more individual aesthetics.

Negotiating a Career between Estrada and Traditional Music: Gulzoda Hudoinazarova

Gulzoda Hudoinazarova not only negotiates the demands of patriotism, sponsorship, and appropriate femininity required of female Uzbek estrada singers, but she also has a complicated relationship with the genre and a passion for maqom and art musics from across the world. She depends on her training and ability to sing traditional music in order to support her broader musical career and attract audiences who are more aligned with the musical values of traditional and folk music.

I first met her in 2003 when—as with Usmanova and Nazarkhan before her—she was a voice student in the conservatory's traditional music department. Hudoinazarova was one of the best of her cohort, gaining recognition for her interpretations of traditional songs and winning national prizes: a

Nihol (sprout—a national young person's music award) in 2003, second place in the Yunus Rajabi National Maqom Competition in 2005, and being named an honoree at UNESCO's Sharq Taronalari (Eastern Melodies) festival in 2007. By 2005, when she finished her bachelor's degree, her popularity in her home city of Bukhara gave her the opportunity to present a concert at the Friendship of Nations Concert Hall because she had found a sponsor, something that many vocalists have difficulty securing.

This concert was to launch her career because it came as she was completing her degree at the conservatory.[4] The program included traditional songs, such as "Chaman Ichra" (The flowering meadow), interspersed with estrada. This mix of traditional music and pop styling was reflected in the instrumentalists backing her for the concert: there was a coterie of traditional musicians on one side of the stage, including players of the *nay* (transverse flute), *gijak* (spike fiddle), and *tanbur* (plucked lute), as well as a fellow student of Malika opa, Bekzod Safarov, on the dutar. On the other side of the stage, musicians played a drum set, electric guitar, and synthesizer. For various numbers, dancers would come out to accompany Hudoinazarova as she sang, often in traditional garb, but occasionally in more modern costumes, including one estrada number that featured a Latin-style beat and featured female dancers in flamenco-like dresses.

In addition to the lighter estrada tunes accompanied by typical pulsating drumbeats and punctuated by synthesizer lines, Hudoinazarova's concert began and ended with patriotic estrada tunes, which are de rigueur in independence-era estrada concerts (and are often included on albums as well). Although I've never attended an estrada concert that does not include at least one patriotic song, most programs usually fit it in the middle, in between pieces that the artist is well known for. Hudoinazarova, her sponsor, or her manager clearly wanted to emphasize the Uzbek pride involved in her craft because she opened the program with "Assalomu O'zbek Halqi!" (Greetings to the Uzbek people!) and closed the concert with "Man O'zbek Qizaman" (I am an Uzbek girl), which features a synthesizer line that clearly mimics the nasal quality of the traditional shawm (surnay). Use of this timbre on synthesizer is common not only in patriotic tunes; wedding music ensembles that play estrada and other more traditional tunes for the entertainment of wedding parties and guests also often employ this sound on their synthesizers and recorded backing tracks. As a result, the performance of this tune clearly underscored Hudoinazarova's femininity and Uzbekness. As discussed in chapter 5, weddings are deeply significant cultural events as well as rites of passage from girlhood into womanhood. The inclusion of such surnay timbres in a song about being an Uzbek girl was clearly meant to highlight the interconnected nature of patriotism and femininity for Hudoinazarova's image.

Hudoinazarova is clearly trying to combine the popularity of estrada with her career and training in traditional music and maqom. After her debut concert, she went on to complete her master's degree in traditional music at the conservatory and began working with the maqom ensemble at the Uzbek state radio station, as well as performing concerts and weddings with a blend of traditional music and traditionally influenced estrada. When I spoke with her in 2009, she adamantly described herself as a traditional vocalist no longer interested in engaging with estrada except when singing patriotic songs (*vattan qo'shiqlari* [homeland songs]). This provides an interesting elaboration of estrada's purpose in concerts.

Although she is now a freelance vocalist, Hudoinazarova was a member of the maqom ensemble at the Uzbek State Radio and Television Company for one year before leaving to pursue other projects. However, like Malika opa and Komila opa, Hudoinazarova remembers her time in the maqom ensemble as extremely productive and helpful for her vocal abilities because she was singing maqom daily, practicing, and working with other talented musicians. She also mentioned a strong desire to learn the "classics" of other places, declaring, "If given the chance, I wouldn't sing estrada, provided my finances are okay. Now that I am comfortable, I can sing traditional songs and I also want to study other cultures' classics, like Turkey, France, and Russia" (Hudoinazarova 2009). This represents an interesting transnational direction for Hudoinazarova, one that somewhat mirrors Nazarkhan's role in the world music industry.

One major contrast with Nazarkhan that emerged in my conversation with Hudoinazarova was the conviction with which she pushed against the idea of continuing to sing estrada and against identifying as an estrada singer. Remembering her concert in 2005, she emphasized that there were plenty of traditional songs in addition to some high-quality estrada and patriotic songs (Hudoinazarova 2009). This passionate embrace of the identity of a traditional vocalist and her focus on singing only small amounts of high-quality estrada reveal how much cultural capital the label of *maqomist* or *traditional vocalist* carries with it. Hudoinazarova's passion for the music itself clearly drives her current focus on traditional music and maqom. However, clearly the situation is also complicated by the prestige afforded traditional singers that estrada vocalists struggle to access.

Hudoinazarova's transition back to traditional music and away from public spectacles was partly motivated by the fact that she had gotten married to her sponsor/manager. In our 2009 interview, she reported that she was no longer singing at weddings, only at concerts and recording sessions, per the desires of her husband, who continues as her sponsor and manager. Although this could be interpreted as highly controlling—and indeed the power differential is notable—Hudoinazarova was careful to express her great relief at not singing at weddings anymore.

The association of marriage with a withdrawal from (or less-severe change in) professional life is not unique to wedding music or Hudoinazarova's case. In Uzbek culture, it is generally seen as a masculine trait to provide for one's family, even though many women work outside the home and develop fulfilling careers. There is also the strong rhetorical link between marriage and impending motherhood that motivates newly married women from various musical disciplines to give up further education or the search for prestigious employment. Women who mentor talented students in every discipline at the conservatory mentioned the dilemma of coaching young women in their careers because they experienced so many who gave up the profession or focused on private teaching rather than performance after getting married. This results in some teachers focusing only on their most dedicated female students, those who show a strong desire for a successful career even after marriage.

This transition away from wedding performance and other public spectacles seems to occur for many newly married women who are trained in a variety of genres, even if they maintain strong ties to their careers in other genres. Wedding performance seems to have an especially strong association with unmarried women because the demands of home life can conflict with a grueling summer schedule of weddings. Some women go as far as to note that their husbands do not like them singing at weddings because they come in contact with too many strange men; however, that is not the explanation Hudoinazarova offered. She discussed her transition back to traditional music and away from estrada and wedding performances as a result of exhaustion. "Singing at weddings is very tough. You have to go every day during the season, in the summer after Ramadan. *Kelin salom* [bride-greeting ritual] in the morning, in the afternoon *challar* [celebration of the bride returning home], and *nikox* [marriage ceremony] in the evening . . . the voice gets tired" (Hudoinazarova 2009). After traveling the country to various cities to perform during one wedding season, she lost her voice and had to stop performing and avoid speaking for two months. This is one of the ways estrada is thought to be harmful to one's physical health, although in this case it is because of the strenuous schedule demanded of wedding singers rather than the nature of the music itself as pathogenic. Hudoinazarova's discussion of the huge demands placed on wedding performers rings true to the testimony of other musicians from a variety of backgrounds, all of whom describe the summer wedding season as a time of packed schedules and tired voices.

Balancing a career that involves traditional performance, large-scale pop music concerts, and wedding singing can be extremely demanding; it is not surprising that something needed to be given up. However, Hudoinazarova's situation also elucidates the power that husbands and sponsors have to shape women's careers. In this case, although it is framed as benevolence, Hudoinazarova's husband has the power and the means to shape her career in the manner he wishes. Indeed, the new system of sponsorship common in the independence era often puts the desires of rich men at the forefront, allowing them to wield their wealth to create or destroy successful careers. This may not be any more patriarchal than the Soviet system, which put government institutions and bureaucrats in charge of similar choices. It simply replaces one power structure with another.

Conclusions

The institutionalization of popular music in the conservatory highlights the complicated relationship this genre has with notions of prestige and credibility. Women's bodies and voices are the fertile ground on which many of these negotiations, conflicts, and adjustments occur. Pop stars, wedding singers, and even those like Hudoinazarova who eschew the label of pop singer all engage economies of prestige and acceptability in order to defend an appropriate image within estrada.

Ideas about talent are important within all the musical styles discussed in the book, but nowhere are they more hotly debated than in estrada, where musical ability is not taken as a given for a successful career. Thus women, with their already staunchly policed politics of dress and appearance, have to demonstrate and insist on their musical ability and virtuosity within this style more than any other.

This also has implications for how estrada is gendered within the larger national project. As female pop singers are often discussed more in terms of image than sound, artists like Usmanova and Nazarkhan have to carefully present their material as sufficiently national, but also internationally relevant and personally interesting. Pop music is consumed by an exceedingly wide audience and is especially important to young female listeners. As a result, it is the musical style with the largest and most complicated negotiation between official priorities and audience whims. That said, most audience members approve of a deep moral commitment in their pop singers, and national pride is viewed as a positive trait, as much as the required patriotic songs on albums and concerts are sometimes dismissed as de rigueur.

Songs in the Uzbek language, the visual cues provided by national instruments (even if their timbre is inaudible in the performance), and the inevitable use of national fabric in costumes implies that the performance of nationalism for women in estrada has a great deal to do with image. However, it is a locally specific vocal timbre, as well as training in maqom and Central Asian classics, that give pop singers the most credibility with discerning audience members. The visuals can be dismissed as stagecraft, but it is the quality of vocal line and the employment of Central Asian expressive ornaments that truly mark estrada as Uzbek, something women like Hudoinazarova, Nazarkhan, and Usmanova employ with great virtuosity.

5   Marrying Past, Present, and Future
The Essential Work of Wedding Music

It is a clear and bright summer morning in Tashkent in 2002. At 6:00 A.M. I step off the tram to walk a few blocks to Ro'za opa's apartment, where she and her entourage are gathering to drive across the city and perform at a kelin salom, the bride-greeting ritual that occurs the morning after a marriage ceremony. In the summer months they usually begin painfully early, as early as 6:00 A.M., so that they conclude before the heat becomes unbearable and so that those who need to get to work are not overly tardy. As I approach Ro'za opa's entryway, I see a flurry of activity: people packing up instruments and putting speakers and stereo equipment into the trunk of driver G'ulom aka's aging red Zhiguli (a Soviet-era automobile still common on the streets of Tashkent). With a dutar in its cloth case placed in the back window, we all pile in: Ro'za opa, her nephew G'ulomjon, her son Shahriyor, the driver G'ulom aka, and me. We wind our way through almost-empty Tashkent streets toward an address that leads us to a metal door set into a mud-brick facade. This door opens, welcoming us into a large and bustling courtyard with trees in the middle and a garden in the back, with doorways into adjacent rooms on three sides.

As the men begin setting up the stereo equipment, Ro'za opa and I are ushered into an upstairs room where ladies seated on cushions are enjoying a variety of treats set out on the *dastirhon* (tablecloth) on the floor. They welcome us, asking after our families and our health, then a typical argument over where to sit ensues. Ro'za opa eventually settles it, sitting near the head of the tablecloth while I sit directly below her. Women from the groom's family bustle around, rushing in and out of the room, serving us piping-hot tea and offering a range of dried fruits, nuts, chocolates, and other hors d'oeuvres. We participate in conversation as Ro'za opa asks for details about the families and the bride and groom that, while seeming like polite and innocuous small talk, is also important research for the proper execution of the ritual to come. Once everything downstairs is set up, Ro'za opa takes a seat near the area the hosts have set aside for dancing, with a table including her minidisc player, a microphone, a doyra (frame drum), and a teapot and set of tea bowls nearby. She takes out her reconstructed dutar, which has been modified with an electroacoustic pickup at its base, and plugs it into her system. After G'ulom aka runs the sound check for Ro'za opa and her nephew, he retreats to the car to wait. A woman approaches and asks for some music for dancing while they continue to get ready for the ritual and Ro'za selects a minidisc that includes the tune "Jonim" (My dear). She begins to sing while her nephew plays the doyra along with the synthesized backing that streams out of the speakers loudly and full of reverb.

Slowly the hustling relatives and mingling friends arrive at their chosen places and things begin to come to order. As women, including those from the groom's family as well as close friends and family of the bride, gather in the courtyard near the doorway of the bridal chamber, the groom's male relatives hang back around the edges or in other rooms. Someone signals to Ro'za opa and she takes up her dutar, angling a microphone stand, and begins to play the introduction to the tune "Kelin Salom." She starts with a fleet-fingered rapid introduction on the amplified dutar, giving extra rhythmic and melodic flourishes to the well-known melody she is about to provide as the basis for the ritual.

Ro'za opa provides musical undergirding for the procession of friends and relatives who come to ritually welcome the bride to her new home with her husband's family. The first to do so are always the grandmothers on the groom's side. They stand nearby, ready to approach the threshold of the bridal chamber, where the bride stands waiting in a dress made of traditional silk, with a silver embroidered sleeveless velvet robe (*chopon*) over the top and a thick veil covering her head. Two members of the bride's family, called *yangge* (aunties), flank the bride and help her as she prepares to bow to each of her new family members and any other friends and family in attendance who might want to give her a gift and welcome her.

As Ro'za opa's dutar introduction comes to a close, she begins singing "Kelin Salom" with semi-improvised verses using the information she gathered earlier. The tune is standard (nonimprovised) and used in all the kelin saloms I observed her perform, but the words change depending on the people present and their place in the familial hierarchy. Although there are standard couplets for the song text, Ro'za opa has to extemporize the material to match the guests as they approach to greet the bride. The song begins with a greeting for God (*hudo*) and then proceeds to a verse greeting the Prophet Muhammad. After this, the family members each get a verse in which they process to the threshold to greet the bride, give a wedding gift, and receive a token in return, such as a handkerchief.

> Yeru ko'kni nam qilgan
> Ikki gulni bir qilgan
> Salom salom kelin salom
> Avval hudoga salom
>
> Heaven and earth have become moist
> One flower has become two
> Greetings to the bride
> First give greetings (bow) to God
>
> Ummatli deb jon bergan
> Turnolarga don bergan
> Salom salom kelin salom
> Payg'ambarimizga salom
>
> She gave respect, called them her people
> She gave seeds to the birds
> Greetings to the bride
> Greetings (bow) to our Prophet
>
> Doka rumol boshlarida
> Parvonamiz qoshlariga
> Qabul ailang buvijonlar
> Sizga salom yor yor
>
> A fine silk scarf on her head
> Our butterfly lands on her eyebrows
> Receive the grandmothers
> Greetings to you (grandmothers)[1]

With her verses, Ro'za opa continues guiding all the family members and friends through the ritual. The bride bows elegantly to each one as her aunties organize the gifts in the room behind her and efficiently hand out party-favor-like tokens in return. All the women progress through the ritual, with Ro'za opa filling in any gaps or hitches with instrumental vamping. Then the men of the family take their turn, often bringing the biggest gifts—in this case, large rolled-up rugs and a television. Once the last male member of the groom's family has greeted their new family member, Ro'za opa transitions to celebratory estrada and a handful of women jump up to dance and celebrate. She and her nephew trade off singing a few more estrada selections, then one woman approaches them and asks if Ro'za opa knows any *tanovarlar* (folk dance tunes) so that the grandmothers can also dance and enjoy themselves.

After a pause in the music to allow a group of older ladies in loose dresses to express kind wishes and blessings for the new couple, Ro'za opa picks up her dutar and breaks into a version of "Farg'ona Tanovar." The older ladies (the grandmothers) make their way to the dance area and rhythmically move and bounce, waving their arms and circling their wrists to the syncopated duple rhythm of the tanovar. They get a raucously joyful reception from their relatives who are watching, and are given handfuls of paper money to dance with. Ro'za opa plays one more tanovar, "Ey Vo Sanam" (Hey, my beauty), and as she finishes and the grannies file off the dance floor, they lay the money they have been given on a handkerchief that has been laid out on Ro'za's table. Her son Shahriyor gathers it up and places it in a plastic shopping bag to be counted later. After the tanovars, Ro'za opa transitions back to her handheld microphone and minidisc-backed estrada tunes, singing a few more dance numbers with pauses for toasts/blessings for the new bride, and then (after an event lasting around ninety minutes) everyone is ready to pack up and get on with their morning. Ro'za and the musicians are offered more food before they leave—oily soup with large chunks of potatoes and garbanzo beans and more sweets—and at that time a member of the groom's family also slips her an envelope with her agreed-upon fee. After packing up, Ro'za and her entourage make their way back through the city, counting their tips in the car as Ro'za opa drops off the various members of her team and heads to the radio station, where she has a rehearsal with the folk orchestra there.

Weddings in Tashkent

Weddings in Uzbekistan are elaborate and deeply meaningful events; they are rites of passage and mark turning points, especially in women's lives. From the beginning of a child's life, people look forward to weddings, and every summer social calendars fill up with the various events involved in celebrating a new marriage.[2] In Uzbek culture there is a series of events that occur over multiple days connected to the marriage ceremony. Some are sex-segregated and require wedding musicians of the same sex, although many events are mixed and involve invited performers of all kinds. Most of the events I accompanied Ro'za opa to were the *bazm* parties/receptions after the nikox marriage ceremonies and kelin saloms, which usually occur the day after the nikox (marriage ceremony) and bazm (wedding reception). (The different events and specific aspects of wedding celebrations in Tashkent are outlined in detail later in this chapter.)

In Tashkent, the rituals surrounding the marriage ceremony evoke important symbols and social structures, even as they are reinforcing the social institution of marriage. They also enforce social norms and familial hierarchies, and provide a forum for varied musical performances. Wedding musicians perform with a great deal of flexibility in terms of repertoire and performance practice that positions in state ensembles and educational institutions do not tend to allow for. Ro'za opa thinks nothing of singing estrada, then turning to her reconstructed folk instrument and performing traditional dance tunes and ritual songs through a sound system that amplifies her voice and instrument with the addition of pulsing reverb. Her performance at this and many other kelin saloms demonstrates how, even when there is a firm disciplinary allegiance that is made official by important posts in the conservatory and state ensembles, Ro'za opa and many musicians like her traverse the boundaries of genre and discipline fluidly and without tension if the context demands it.

The successful performance of a bride-greeting ritual the morning after a marriage in cosmopolitan Tashkent demands a wide range of musical expertise to satisfy the needs of the ritual in combination with dance music tastes across the generations. The lived experience of Tashkenters celebrating the blending of families, the transition from girl to woman, and the relocating of the bride from her natal home to her married home is all wrapped up in the celebration of a kelin salom. Such a complex location, with complicated family dynamics, social expectations, hierarchies based on age, and gender norms, demands diverse musics that defy the rigid limitations of genre, but rather emphasize porous boundaries, unlikely combinations, and the joy of participating in all manner of musical activities. This manifestation of urban wedding festivities in the independence era involves a heady mix of pop music, traditional music, and even arranged folk and European classical elements.

The Importance of Wedding Music throughout Central Asia

Such a multilayered social event with various musics swirling together is unique to Tashkent's wedding season (the summer, except for the month of Ramadan, when [Muslim] weddings typically do not occur). However, there are distinct ties to similar celebrations, musical combinations, and social negotiations in other parts of Central Asia. Wedding music and its performance provides an excellent example of Anthony Seeger's assertion that "musical traditions often seem to be moving in two directions at once—backward in time toward their roots and toward the future to growing tips of innovation" (Seeger 1993, 500). At the same time that the timeworn practices of solidifying partnerships and reconstituting families are foregrounded, with special mind toward what are seen as precolonial practices, the modern condition is impossible to step out of. Even the most traditional dance tunes (tanovarlar) are piped through amplifiers with added reverb and, in this case, performed on a dutar that was reconstructed for concert performance with a folk orchestra and later modified with an electric pickup. On the other hand, the poppiest estrada tunes popular with youth on wedding dance floors are encoded with folk or traditional references and often include sounds meant to reference traditional instruments, such as a synthesizer programmed to mimic the sound of a traditional surnay (shawm). Such estrada tunes are essential to maintaining the tradition of music and dancing at celebrations, so the interaction with notions of tradition occurs even there at multiple levels. With this mélange of musical sources, wedding singers are actively doing the work of reaching toward both tradition and innovation.

The incorporation of popular music into wedding events that are construed as traditional is of course not unique to Uzbekistan (ethnomusicologist Federico Spinetti describes an almost-identical process in Tajikistan [2005]), or even to Central Asia. Ethnomusicologist Gregory D. Booth describes the phenomenon of brass-band-accompanied wedding processions in India and notes that the repertoire that such bands draw on most commonly is Hindi film music (Booth 1990, 247). Booth also notes a similar tipping economy in India as in Uzbekistan, in that tips for the musicians are waved over the dancers' heads (1990). However, in the case of Booth's research, the most popular dancers were young boys, whereas it was the dancing of elderly women in Tashkent that never failed to win Ro'za opa and her entourage the most tips. In the wedding celebrations I participated in that were not predominantly women's events, such as the bazm, young women were also lavishly rewarded for enthusiastic dancing, more so than their male counterparts. As with the brass band musicians in India with whom Booth worked, Ro'za opa's wedding repertoire was largely estrada; however, the most emotionally and ritually weighty moments still included music acknowledged as traditional (in the broader and noninstitutionalized sense of being connected to pre-Soviet folk traditions), such as the kelin salom bride-greeting ritual itself or the round of tanovar dances that motivated the grannies onto the dance floor. Although I never explicitly heard Western art music performed at any wedding events,

Figure 5.1. Faizila Shukurova dancing at a wedding celebration on the outskirts of Tashkent. Photo by author, 2009.

it does contribute some underlying material, including the solfège used to discuss a melodic line or the scalar warm-ups Ro'za sometimes would play during her sound checks. In this sense, carrying on the tradition of marriage for Uzbeks in Tashkent involves a great deal of hybrid musical performance.

Dancing is especially important to honor the new couple, and people of all different generations and musical tastes dance in order to mark their participation in the celebration of a new marriage.[3] Dance's important locus in the celebration means that musicians must be fluent in a wide range of genres and styles, even as they proudly announce their allegiance to a single discipline in other more institutionalized contexts. For an illustration of this blending, combining, and blurring of genres, practices, and identity markers, see figure 5.1, a photo of conservatory-trained conductor and folk orchestral hammer dulcimer (chang) performer Faizila Shukurova dancing at a wedding event on the outskirts of Tashkent in 2009. The music she is hearing as she dances in a largely all-female crowd is the traditional tune "Munojat" performed by Ro'za opa and the author. Although some traditional dances were performed at this event, the bulk of the dancing focused on estrada tunes that Ro'za opa either performed on her amplified, reconstructed dutar, or sang using karaoke-style backup tracks played on minidisc. The multigenerational nature of all the wedding events requires this range of performing ability for artists who perform for the entire event—as opposed to estrada singers who often show up to sing one set at a wedding, collect applause and tips before leaving, and continue on to appearances at other weddings, leaving the bulk of the event's music to a different performer.

Within Central Asia, musicians' multifaceted engagement with multiple genres, all of which interact with notions of tradition and the modern nation, is not unique to Tashkent or Uzbekistan. Although the details and the specific mix of musics, gender performance, and nationalist rhetoric is unique to Tashkent, there are similar processes and similar levels of cultural importance afforded to weddings throughout the Central Asian region. One of the earliest books to emphasize the importance of weddings as musical and cultural events is Veronica Doubleday's work focusing on Afghan women musicians titled *Three Women of Herat*. She notes that sex-segregated events necessitated professional female musicians for wedding parties and that although female wedding musicians had a shaky social status, their musical practices and the money they earned were highly valued within families and communities (1990).

Rachel Harris underlines the importance of wedding performances for Uyghur musicians in the Xinjiang region of northwest China, saying:

> Singers, even the most famous, earn their bread and butter from nightly performances in Ürümchi's up market Uyghur restaurants. . . . Wedding feasts in Ürümchi are an important part of an up market restaurateur's income. . . . No wedding is complete without a popular singer, a synthesizer, and perhaps a group of traditional instruments. (Harris 2002, 270–71)

This description of urban wedding celebrations in Ürümchi could describe a modern wedding celebration in Tashkent, albeit one that might not feature as much engagement with traditional music as the kelin salom described previously. For traditional and pop musicians alike, weddings are a vital source of income, especially when salaries at official institutions can fail to provide a living wage. For example, during my fieldwork period, it was normal for conservatory instructors to report making the equivalent of fifty to sixty dollars a month. A profitable performance at a wedding celebration could bring a performer that much in an evening. The result is that musicians from a range of disciplines perform at weddings for the profit and on the concert stage for prestige.

Performer's motives go beyond compensation and prestige—institutions establish disciplinary and generic boundaries, but musicians have much broader and more diverse musical lives than those mandated by their chosen discipline or style. Indeed, most musicians interact with the totality of the musical soundscape in Tashkent, rather than rigidly only making (and consuming) one kind of music. This allows for much more musical and rhetorical flexibility in how women use music to perform femininity and nationalism and to make their livings.

The Significance of Musical Performance at Weddings

Uzbek ethnomusicologist Razia Sultanova notes, "An Uzbek singer at a wedding has become an archetypal role" (2005, 141). Although she is speaking generally about both male and female traditional/folk singers, she does acknowledge the importance of estrada at weddings, especially during the reception/restaurant portion of the event (Sultanova 2005, 139–40). At the weddings I attended in Tashkent, estrada pervaded almost every part of the complex of events comprising a wedding celebration except for the *ertalabgi osh*, the serving of pilaf to the men of the neighborhood (and friends, coworkers, and relatives) on the morning of the wedding ceremony. That event was always accompanied by traditional music, usually performed by men, and I only had the opportunity to observe such events from the windows of my apartment. All the weddings that I was aware of in Tashkent between 2002 and 2009, even those discussed as embracing traditional values, involved some interaction with pop music. Most events involved pop music almost exclusively, especially the evening wedding receptions (bazm) held in restaurants or banquet halls.

In Tashkent at least, the attendance of various estrada singers was a highlight of the wedding. Most weddings I attended in Tashkent had coed nikox ceremonies after which male and female estrada singers would perform. People would often talk about which *artistlar* (artists/singers) showed up at recent events and brag about which famous singers their family was able to attract.[4] Having important pop stars attend one's wedding evoked a great deal of prestige, and singers of all types made a significant portion of their living from the practice.

Weddings are part of a larger category of life-cycle/rite-of-passage celebrations known as *to'ylar*. Both Sultanova (2005) and Levin (1996) discuss the importance of the to'y in Central Asian life—examples of these events include celebrations for the birth of a child (*beshik to'y*) and a celebration of a male child's circumcision (*sunnat to'y*). The nikox to'y (wedding celebration) includes a variety of rituals that can span many days, beginning with the serving of pilaf to men (ertalabgi osh), which is often accompanied by men performing maqom (women are reported to have been invited to perform maqom at these events occasionally, but they are never invited as guests). Later in the day, with men and women gathering separately, the bride is fetched from her natal home and proceeds to the house of her bridegroom, where the nikox, the wedding ceremony itself, is performed. The party that follows is often called bazm and involves food, music, and dancing for hours. The next morning, according to tradition, the bride is greeted by her new family (and other female guests—usually friends and relatives) in the kelin salom ceremony. Finally, what could be forty days later (forty-day periods, known as *chille*, are symbolically important lengths of time), but is now often the weekend after the wedding ceremony, the bride returns for the first time to her natal home to visit in the last ritual, the challar, which often includes the bride's family bestowing gold jewelry upon her to show how much she is valued and missed. The events at which I observed estrada featured included the gathering of women before proceeding to the groom's house (*qiz chaqiriq*), the bazm, the kelin salom, and the challar.

The prestige economy in weddings centers strongly on which musicians and singers one can attract to one's event. As a result, conversations about wedding receptions rarely focused on the food or the guests, usually not even on the bride and groom (although certainly people would offer opinions on whether the two made a good match or not). Instead, most people spoke about which artists showed up, what they sang, and how long their set was. There is also a range of popular songs with wedding themes that are commonly played, even though most estrada is in fact well-suited to weddings as most songs focus on love in one way or another—although the songs about unrequited love or loss are not popular on the wedding circuit. Wedding receptions connected to the nikox ceremony were usually mixed-gender events, although usually women and men would sit in separate groups, dancing in separate parts of the dance floor or at alternating times.

One of the times when the most mixing of men and women occurred was when men lined up to hand the guests money to dance with in their hands—the bills are shown off as they make broad sweeping gestures typical of this style of dancing. It was much more common for women dancers to be given money to hold and display while dancing. After the song came to an end, that money was collected as tips for the musicians, especially for the singer. As a result, wedding singers, even those just visiting for a set, acted like emcees of the event, calling on guests to come up and toast the bride and groom and bless them by dancing at their wedding. During these receptions, the bride and groom were usually seated behind a main table observing the dancing and eating; because they were not dancing themselves, watching others dance was crucially important entertainment. Most wedding singers are quite adept at picking catchy tunes for dancing and encouraging the crowd to dance.

Women generally dance with their arms and shoulders involved in the most movement, waving and snapping to accent certain beats. Dancing, even to estrada, does not involve much hip motion; usually there is a slight bouncing from foot to foot in a "step-ball-change" sort of move that does not involve covering much area on the dance floor. The most expressive and well-rewarded dancers at the weddings I attended usually had emphatic facial expressions, made graceful broad gestures with their arms and hands, and displayed a solid rhythmic sense. As a result, musical activity, both singing and dancing, is an important aspect of displaying femininity in Uzbek culture. Women, especially adolescent girls, are often pushed by their family to dance and enjoy themselves in this environment. Indeed, the wedding dance floor can be seen as an echo chamber of feminine performance, as a female pop star/artist presents a graceful, smiling, youthful embodiment of a feminine ideal, one that links up with national images as well, which is then reflected back and amplified by the young women on the dance floor all dressed in their finest, putting on the prettiest face they can and gesturing gracefully to the song in order to bless the rite of passage of their friend, relative, or classmate as she transitions from girlhood to womanhood.

It is worth noting that in this case gender performance is highly naturalized, and although there are certainly variances in the level of costuming, colors, fabrics, and cuts of skirts and dresses, the overarching gender expression is notably unified with very little range, although there is some diversity depending on a woman's age. At weddings, women of all ages wear dresses—occasionally skirts, but never pants. Their hair is carefully arranged, whether down, up, or covered with a *rumol* (scarf). Colors range through all the shades of the rainbow, from bright to dark to pastel; however, color is strongly favored by all female guests—black, white, and gray are rarely seen. This display of fashionable dress and jewelry is very important in one's participation in community events, as is the display of wealth that it implies. This is true in both the mixed-gender portions of the wedding event and those that are attended mostly or only by women. Indeed, this particular performance of femininity through festive clothes, smiling, and dancing is very much for the women in the community, rather than being oriented toward the male gaze, as some music videos or estrada concert performances may seem.

The sex-segregated nature of many events related to weddings makes them an important location for female singers to make a living and a name for themselves. This is not without risk, of course. Women who perform publicly on stage are a common sight in Uzbekistan, as they have been since the hujum liberation projects of the 1920s. However, the stigma of loose morals for women who take the stage is still present to a surprising degree. When I spent much of my 2002 trip attending weddings with musicians and singers, it surprised me how many people, usually middle-aged and older men, would click their tongues and tell me what a shame it was that these women were in an economic situation that necessitated performing on stage and coming into contact with strange men. So there is a difficult combination of prestige, profit, and stigma for women who sing at weddings. Clearly, profit and prestige win out for most, as pop singers, traditional musicians, and folk orchestra members all perform at weddings, most performing estrada (some in addition to traditional ritual songs), and many making the bulk of their living that way.

Such a stigma against women wedding singers is far from unique to Uzbekistan. Among other places, it certainly exists in Afghanistan, as Veronica Doubleday notes in *Three Women of Herat* (1990, 196, 210). Anthropologist Karin van Nieuwkerk addresses a similar situation for female performers in Egypt; she dedicates a large section to the discussion of shame, music making, and dancing (2010, 121–32). She notes specifically that female performers are associated with what are seen as the most shameful practices associated with nightclubs—"sexual excitement and prostitution" (2010, 132). Anthropologist Tiantian Zheng notes similar associations and processes occurring in karaoke bars in China, with singing hostesses being considered part of the courtesan lineage and also actively working to construct a submissive femininity (2013, 70–72). Ethnomusicologists Rachel Harris and Rowan Pease emphasize the fluid, transformational quality of gendered musical performance in China throughout history and its association with sex, sexuality, and morality (2013, 13–15).

In the introduction to her now-classic edited volume *Women and Music in Cross-Cultural Perspective*, ethnomusicologist Ellen Koskoff mentions this phenomenon of links between women's music, heightened sexuality, and loose morals across cultures. She provides a brief survey of early works that mention the perceived connection between female musicians and prostitution or courtesan traditions that range from Malta to Afghanistan (1989, 3). All these contexts emphasize the same notion of appropriate femininity as being located away from the professional sphere—public musical feminine performance is degrading, sexualized, and morally suspect. This notion has notable prevalence in Uzbekistan, especially outside official institutions and state-run venues. Even with such stigma, in gender-segregated or female-dominated wedding events, women's services as singers, musicians, and emcees are required for the functioning of the celebration, and, as mentioned previously, women from a variety of musical genres heed that call.

Thus, weddings are the great equalizer for musicians in urban Uzbekistan. Vocalists and instrumentalists from all corners of society and levels of prestige make wedding music, from the shawm (surnay) and doyra performers hired and picked up on the day of the ceremony from their usual waiting spot near the Chorsu Bazaar to pop stars like Rayhon who receive lucrative invitations and are treated as honored guests. Marriage ceremonies are generally culturally important rites of passage, but they take on an extra layer of relevance in Uzbekistan, providing an important separate economy, a musical arena separate from other institutions and patrons, and a unifying event across class, ethnic, and economic strata.

Conclusions

Wedding music is a vital part of the musical economy in Tashkent and is one that involves a wide range of musical styles, including most of those institutionalized in the conservatory that are discussed in this volume. In this sense, it is the great equalizer—everyone attends weddings for friends and family members and participates by dancing and sometimes singing and clapping. Furthermore, most musicians other than those primarily engaged with Western art music also perform at weddings, and the compensation received often makes up a significant percentage of any given musician's income. Wedding culture's prestige economy also hinges on musical performance, since the biggest and most important weddings are able to attract the largest number of the most famous singers to toast and contribute their songs to the evening's entertainment. However, it is not just the bazm reception following the nikox wedding ceremony itself that provides musicians with an important opportunity to be seen and to earn a living. The other events, many of which are more sex-segregated than the typical bazm in Tashkent, allow female wedding performers to provide important support for necessary ritual traditions. The kelin salom, especially, is an important event where women musicians are sought after and are able to participate in a larger, nationally significant performance of tradition that differentiates current weddings in Tashkent from the "red weddings" of the Soviet era. As a result, songs like "Kelin Salom" play an important role in the continued imagination of women's traditions and women's musical practices as they existed before Russian occupation and the rise of the Soviet Union.

Wedding performance for women, however, is not without its risks. The general stigma against performing in public, especially against performing in public in an entertainment context (rather than on the large and prestigious symphonic or operatic stage), is heightened in regard to performing at weddings. Many women continue to perform for weddings and in doing so provide a much-needed service, but they do so while facing down disapproval and social control, whether expressed directly or via sideways glances. Although some may express pity for those who "must" perform at weddings out of economic necessity, performers like Ro'za opa take pride in the prestige and the continuation of tradition that they are able to achieve through wedding music.

Wedding performance of all kinds of music—maqom, folk dances like the tanovars popular with the elder generations, and even the most saccharine estrada—allow female musicians an opportunity to build a career and make a name for themselves, gaining name recognition at the same time that they are negotiating the risks of wedding performance. A career singing or playing at weddings often runs parallel to one's career as a traditional maqomist, as a member of a state-sponsored folk orchestra, or even as a pop star with a significant following. Weddings provide important revenue at a time when salaries from state-run institutions do not always cover all of one's family's expenses, and they offer an opportunity to broaden one's repertoire and fan base. Women's wedding music fills a distinct social need, especially in sex-segregated events like the kelin salom, and has a more integrated repertoire that complicates the divisions so sharply defended in other institutions.

Conclusion

Women's Musical Communities Performing the Nation

It is a chilly day in early February 2005 and I signal for the *marshrutka* shuttle van to stop at the "Forty Years of Victory" neighborhood bus stop, then walk a few minutes in the cold into a cluster of Soviet-era cement block high-rises. I find the correct building and entrance and, like so many times before, I climb the metal staircase until I reach Malika opa's apartment. Instead of my normal greeting at the door accompanied by the mellow murmur of Ziyaev family life and musical activity, I am met at the door by Malika opa's daughter Farangiz and enter to the sound of chortling laughter. Today we celebrate Malika opa's birthday with a *gap* (talk/chat): a regular gathering of women that is part social club, part dinner party, part cyclical credit association. Women who meet for a gap often do so regularly for years, even decades. In Malika opa's case, she gets together monthly with a group of around a dozen women, most of whom studied at the conservatory together twenty years prior—most are traditional musicians, but women trained in Western art music and arranged folk music are also represented. They meet each month and eat, chat, and sometimes make music together. Every member contributes 10,000 sum (slightly less than ten dollars) to a pot that goes to a different woman each month; in this case, it goes to the woman who has a birthday during that month. This group is lucky enough to have appropriately spaced birthdays, establishing what would otherwise be an arbitrary system to distribute the lump sums of money during the course of a year.

After adding my shoes to an ever-growing pile and handing over the apple cobbler that I made as my contribution to the party, I wave hello to Malika opa's husband and sons, who are relaxing in a separate room. Farangiz ushers me into the brightly lit dining room, where I am pushed toward the "head" of the opulently laid table as an honored foreign guest. I try to argue my way down the table's hierarchy toward a spot more appropriate for one of Malika opa's students, but am unsuccessful. In the end I sit near the head of the table and am greeted in turn by each woman already present; we exchange niceties and inquire about one another's health and family. Salads and other small plates are already on the table; Malika opa plies me with various tasty treats—Russian salad made with potatoes, carrots, peas, and mayonnaise; a pickled beet salad; and some "Korean" carrot and noodle salad. I try my best to refuse the pickled beets and am rewarded for my efforts with a double scoop that Malika opa slaps on my plate, saying playfully, "You don't have to like it, it's good for your organism!" The ladies around me chuckle and make pleasant conversation as I try to politely eat my salads (and push the beets around on my plate). More women arrive for the festivities and the jockeying for table position and individual greetings occur again. Eventually all the women arrive and find their seats in the now-packed dining room. At this point, one lady near the head of the table leads welcoming blessings that we all murmur into our own open hands, then finally brush our palms down over our faces as we say "Allahu Akbar" (God is great). The event now begins in earnest.

Soon Malika opa's daughters and the youngest woman who recently joined the gap group (one of Malika opa's former students) are at the door with bowls of soup laden with lamb, potatoes, and garbanzo beans, and the eating and chatting begins. People reminisce about their time at the conservatory together, discuss their students and their work, and make a tally of who has contributed to the pool of money and who still needs to pay up. One common theme in the chatter is the high cost of weddings these days and what a challenge it is to afford them for all of one's children. After conversation and eating continues merrily for a while, a male friend of the family who is also a musician and was chatting in the other room with the other men enters with his saz (metal-stringed plucked lute) and hands it to one of the women seated around the table. Another woman picks up a doyra and they strike up a bouncy tune. Soon a prominent vocalist, Saida opa, begins to sing a lively song that she inflects with a great deal of expressive pulsating vibrato and microtonal glissandi. The piece includes choruses that a few others know and they join in enthusiastically. This musical interlude receives a passionate response as the women around the table clap and shout encouragement: "*Yashang!*" (Lively!). Although I do not recognize the song, it is clearly one of the lighter folk tunes that are often included in traditional music performances to add variety to programs that have a great deal of maqom in them. This piece had similarities to "Yallajonim" (My dear song) as heard on track 10 of Nazarkhan (2003) and "Omon Yor," a folk song from the city of Andijon, as heard on track 7 of Yulchieva (1997)—all include rousing choruses that invite participation by more than a single performer.

As the chorus begins and women sing along, Malika opa's student is pulled out of her seat and forcefully encouraged to dance. She finds the beat of Saida opa's song, shuffling her feet in tiny movements and waving her arms sinuously from shoulder to fingertip. Eventually more women, including myself, are pulled up and into the cluster of dancing women. Even Malika opa joins in, and someone shouts out that Malika opa and I dance alike. She responds, "Of course we dance alike, our bodies are alike!" Finally, the song and dancing comes to a close and people find their seats again. The man takes his saz back from the woman who accompanied Saida opa and asks another woman if she has anything to sing. She chooses a slower, more somber song from the maqom repertoire that slowly climbs up to the climax (*ouj*), which is loud, strident, and intense. It elicits whoops and cheers from the appreciative audience, but no one jumps up to dance.

After a few songs, the singing and clapping draws to a close and the main meal, the Uzbek national dish known as *osh* or *palov* is brought out on large family-style platters—it is a rice pilaf with lamb, carrots, raisins, and garbanzo beans and is commonly served at parties and weddings. Komila opa, who would normally sing a song while Malika opa accompanied her on the dutar at an occasion like this, and who is a core member of this gap, did not join in the singing as a result of a tired voice from traveling (Malika opa was also busy hosting, which may have influenced the choice of who performed and who comprised the audience in this particular gap). The women dig in to yet more food, some protesting that they are already full, but eating nonetheless. There is a pause in the conversation as well as the music as the women focus on their food, and then slowly the chatter returns. Eventually the palov is cleared away and some sweets are brought out—some slices of cake purchased from a well-known local store in the shopping center named for the Ganges River and my apple cobbler (Malika opa dubs it "American halva" for the occasion). Almost four hours have passed eating, chatting, singing, and dancing, so the already-stuffed women sample some sweets and begin making excuses about why they must leave. Singly and in pairs they say their good-byes (individually, to everyone, as with the greetings), find their shoes and coats in the hallway, and make their way back onto the chilly streets of Tashkent.

The Gap That Emphasizes a Musical Community of Practice

Social gatherings, like this gap, allow women to come together as a community (and a community of practice [Wenger 1998]).[1] It allows a subset of musicians to traverse the disciplinary borderlines set up by institutions like the conservatory. Although most of the women in Malika opa's gap trained in the Eastern Music Department during the Soviet era, not all did. It is the shared experience and friendship forged in the institution that allows for such strong bonds to form across disciplines, even between those whose departments compete for prestige and resources. As part of his "social theory of learning," educational theorist Etienne Wenger addresses learning as a community-centered as well as individual-focused activity that engages identity on multiple levels (1998, 3), and musical practice in the context of Tashkent works in similar multilayered and multicontextual ways. Like the more general framework of learning, music making, music teaching, and music learning allow groups to engage in complex meaning-making and identity-forming processes. In this case, the state conservatory, itself creating a larger community of practice, also engenders smaller groups that function as communities of practice. Wenger focuses on learning as a socially situated everyday practice that is central to processes of group and individual identity, as well as those of power and hierarchy in institutions (1998, 13). Music, for the women in this book, functions in the same way.

Music is a dynamic process at the center of institutional hierarchy, personal aesthetics and taste making, social occasions, and group dynamics of every size. It pervades the lives of its practitioners and traverses boundaries of all kinds. Wenger comments, "Learning . . . is not a separate activity. It is not something we do when we do nothing else or stop doing when we do something else" (1998, 7). Music is generally a more circumscribed activity that takes place within specific frameworks such as concerts or rehearsals. However, it can also take place spontaneously and provide a soundscape for other activities (as the radio in the kitchen does). Certainly if one broadens the idea of what music is into a larger sense of sonic experience, the application of Wenger's ideas about learning match up more easily. However, even with a relatively closed frame of purposefully musical activity, Wenger's emphasis on its interconnectedness with other practices is helpful. In Malika opa's gap, music facilitates a community of practice wherein women cross disciplinary and generic boundaries, engaging music as a joyful expression of group cohesion.

Notably, it is folk songs, similar to those that the elder women request to dance to at weddings, that bring women to their feet and to join in on the choruses in the context of a gap. This is music that is often performed as part of the traditional music repertoire in conservatory settings (with less raucous reception), but is afforded less prestige than either a complex symphonic work (performed by either a symphony orchestra or a folk orchestra) or a complicated piece of the Shashmaqom. In this sense, the more everyday context of a social gathering allows not only border crossing, but also an emphasis on the pleasure of music making and the joy of singing along.

Institutions Define Genres, Not Musical Experience

As the gap and the weddings described previously suggest, musicians' experiences rarely map neatly onto a single genre. However, alignment with disciplinary boundaries and genres has its benefits in terms of prestige—as well as a sense of comfort, belonging, and academic rigor. When musicians combine musical styles or shift from one to another, the resulting blur of disciplinary boundaries happens for a variety of reasons. Sometimes, it occurs simply because the larger public is not generally aware of the boundary, as is often the case between arranged folk music and traditional music. The two genres are certainly related and have similar instrumentaria, such that nonmusicians assume that all dutars are alike, whether the specific one being considered is large or small, has fixed metal frets or tied gut ones, or has nylon or silk strings. Public perception of different instruments' sameness seems to fuel the performance of difference by adherents of either musical style, at least when referencing one another and/or making claims of legitimacy in professional and institutional contexts. The result is an active discussion of difference that highlights tensions and nuances not perceived by average audience members.

Beyond the elision of disciplines through audience perception, musicians also actively cross generic boundaries for strategic reasons, sometimes attempting to co-opt another music's association with prestige. For example, arranged folk musicians perform Western art music, such as a movement of an orchestral suite by J. S. Bach, on their reconstructed Uzbek instruments. Another motivation for boundary crossing is to attain a link with Uzbekistan's perceived traditional past, such as when estrada performers incorporate folk tunes into their repertoire. Indeed, sometimes both prestige and nationalism come into play simultaneously, as when estrada musicians tout their extensive training in traditional music, like Nazarkhan and Hudoinazarova. This allows pop musicians to gird their reputation with credibility based on notions of tradition and academic rigor rather than the more common criteria of beautiful appearances, pleasant voices, appealing melody, and driving rhythm.

With such porous boundaries constantly traversed, the policing of styles and disciplines is often accompanied with tension and insistence by their most dedicated practitioners. The most dramatic example of this that I encountered occurred at a gathering where an aged and respected maqom performer turned to me at the dinner table and asked, "Do you hear how that Armenian [acoustician Ashot Petrosiants, who created the reconstructed Uzbek instruments used in folk orchestras] ruined our music?" The tension expressed here reflects an important dynamic at play, whereby rare criticism is focused on individuals rather than the system as a whole. There are tensions between enthusiasts and adherents to the different styles or disciplines, such that performers always posit the superiority of their chosen musical practice. Traditional music and arranged folk music had sufficient overlap in training and historical roots that tensions over shared resources arose. Although discussions and descriptions of such conflicts are often couched in terms of technical skill, musical literacy, preservation, or innovation, clearly the aesthetics of the resulting music and its associated prestige are at the heart of much of the tension.

There is also a range of terms that musicians from different disciplines use to describe the changes wrought upon their instruments as time progresses. Musicians and scholars sometimes react strongly against the term *reconstructed* as applied to their instrument and prefer the term *modernized*. Most traditional performers use the term *reconstructed* freely when describing any instrument involved in the performance of arranged folk music, even if that instrument is identical or nearly identical to the instrument used to play maqom and traditional music. The gijak (spike fiddle) and chang (hammer dulcimer) are prime examples of instruments that have undergone a well-acknowledged reconstruction over time, but those changes appeal to both performers of arranged folk music and traditional music, so they are adopted across the board.

The dutar, by contrast, is an example of an instrument that underwent significant changes that performers of traditional music rejected. As a result, I heard divisive terms from performers in both styles (such as the insistence on calling arranged folk music *academic* referenced in chapter 2). Performers of arranged folk music often highlight the differences by labeling their dutar the "narodnyy" (Russian: folk) dutar and by calling the dutar played by those in the traditional music department the "maqom" dutar. Traditional dutarists would highlight the difference even more strongly in casual conversation, occasionally going beyond the term *reconstructed* to label the dutars that they did not perform as "Petrosiants" dutars or, the most controversial, the "balalaikali" dutar (the balalaika-like dutar). These two labels specifically highlight both the sonic similarities between folk orchestras and the idea that many of the reconstruction projects caused the sound of traditional instruments to mimic the sound of the Russian balalaika. The employment of such pointed adjectives is divisive and meant to shore up the sense of prestige wrapped up with a notion of authenticity, regardless of the idea that all instruments undergo changes through time.

Even when these divisions invoke such passionate defense, the boundaries of musical styles create a convenient "social fiction." It is useful for music to have such categories for pedagogy and consumption, and to encourage appropriate behavior. This functions in much the same way that gender norms are also persuasive and convenient "social fictions" that police appropriate behavior.

Gender, Music, and Experience

The process of naturalizing gender norms (which underscores the understanding and performance of femininity in Tashkent) somewhat mimics the process of naturalizing musical styles in service of the nation. Butler refers to this process as "sedimentation":

> [T]here is a sedimentation of gender norms that produces the peculiar phenomenon of a natural sex, or a real woman, or any number of prevalent and compelling social fictions, and . . . this is a sedimentation that over time has produced a set of corporeal styles which, in reified form, appear as the natural configuration of bodies into sexes which exist in a binary relation to one another. (Butler 1988, 524)

Female bodies constantly reinscribe an Uzbek femininity that is smiling, young, beautiful, modest, traditionally rooted, and yet informed by cosmopolitanism. This gender performance combines with the constant institutional emphasis and repeated performance of behavior acknowledging and reifying disciplinary boundaries to give those boundaries (and the gendered performance of them) the effect of being completely natural and unquestionable, despite the constant transgression and combination of musics in the Tashkent soundscape. It is worth noting that while disciplinary boundaries are porous in musicians' lived experience, gender performance in Tashkent remains almost constantly normative, at least within the norms of a given group (for example, modern intelligentsia members perform femininity differently than those drawing on roles of traditional hearth-keepers for a sense of self-identity, but both types of femininity are naturalized within their given context).

These constantly reified boundaries between disciplines typify what Butler discusses as norms that can be simultaneously oppressive and liberating, depending on the person for whom the norm is applied and the context in which the norm is engaged (Butler 2004, 220). For Firuza Abdurahimova, arranged folk music represents an opportunity for innovation and for outreach to international audiences, while that same construction was deeply confusing for Malika opa as a young girl who was not yet fluent in those disciplinary boundaries. Indeed, both women's musical and professional choices serve to continually reestablish the norm that separates the two musical styles. Although similarities can be established musically, the discourse surrounding each constantly reifies difference. Indeed, that discourse allows Malika opa to trade on the prestige afforded to honoring ancient traditions in the independence era, whereas Firuza opa hinges the prestige of her work on ideas of innovation, modernity, and international relevance.

The femininity both display on stage also reflects the power of disciplinary norms. Both appear smiling and professional, Malika opa in a dress of traditional fabric and Firuza opa in a Western suit, both cut modestly to emphasize their age and seriousness in addition to their femininity. Men in both contexts are not expected to illustrate musical difference in the same way, as Western suits and ties are the norm for musical performances in both styles. Indeed, men seem to be able to engage with the norms for either discipline without wearing difference on their bodies. This highlights women's highly gendered role in what McClintock dubs "the intense emotive politics of dress" as she ties the performance of femininity through costumes and apparel together with nationalist projects (McClintock 1997, 97).

Clearly, women's lived experience is often more complicated than the feminine image that is so often performed publicly, whether it is one that favors an allegiance with the European intelligentsia as pianist Ofeliya Yusupova's does, or one that combines such notions of the cosmopolitan elite with reflective imagining of traditional women as both dutarist Malika opa's and Firuza opa's do, each to different extents and effects. Indeed, professional representations do not always neatly map onto one's internalized and personal ideals, although in the case of those women interviewed for this book, they do insist on deeply held emotional and moral attachments that connect their musical work to their self-perception and identity.

This complicated femininity is also important when considering the other aspect of many women's musical activities: pedagogy. Many students are dedicated to their teachers, but the language of motherhood is a powerful metaphor for describing how professional women fit into the historically male pedagogical apprenticeship system of musical transmission. It provides an important legibility for women who now participate in the close bond between teacher and student when studying maqom and traditional music. After spending many years with Malika opa's students and studying with her myself, it was not surprising to hear so many describe her as like their mother. They always reference her with terms of utmost respect, using the word *ustoz* (master) to refer to her and crediting every success to her patient instruction. Malika opa invests deeply in the progress and development of her students, giving freely of her time and knowledge. This creates a strong association as a maternal figure, which is not entirely unsurprising given the long historical ties between master-teacher and student-apprentice in the region (the ustoz-shog'ird system). Although women were not historically part of the master-apprentice oral transmission of maqom and traditional music, the intensity of the relationship maps easily onto associations with the mother-and-child relationship. That type of association led student Mehrihon Muminova to praise Malika opa's care and attention as a teacher.

> [Malika opa] looks after us like her own children. For example, during lessons, she gives a melody to us beat by beat, note by note, all the way until the end. "No, like this; no, like this," she'll say. She teaches us note by note until we master the entire piece. Some teachers don't do this [with such patience].... Because of this [patient teaching style] we are all so happy that we became Malika opa's students. (Muminova 2005)

One of Malika opa's star students, Ilyos Arabov, describes her in similar terms, saying that "students in the conservatory don't get to choose their instructors [for their primary instrument], but everyone in her studio is so happy they have Malika opa.... The kids look at her like a mother, with a very maternal quality... because if some kind of [personal] problem arises, Malika opa really tries to help us" (Arabov 2005).

Crossing Genre Boundaries

Returning to the issue of disciplinary alignment, the previously mentioned stark contrasts are often highlighted when discussing differences between arranged folk music and traditional music; however, crossings of those tension-ridden boundaries are an almost daily occurrence. Indeed, the palpable tensions between practitioners of these styles seem the strongest because of the permeability of the boundaries between them.

The differences between Western art music and traditional music are not infused with such emotion, primarily because they are not viewed as competing for the same pool of resources, students, or prestige. However, even here the boundaries blur and musicians engage with music of all kinds: Uzbek conservatory students who major in Western art music are required to take a course on the Shashmaqom, and when I sat in on this course in 2005, the students were enthusiastic and engaged with the material, acknowledging that Uzbek composers often write works inspired by traditional music. In the same vein, Malika opa and her students often emphasize their excellence in and deep knowledge of solfège and Western art music theory. As a result, in Tashkent there are permeable boundaries even between such divergent musics as European and Central Asian classics. Tensions are lessened because there is less competition. In this case, both types of musicians get to emphasize their well-rounded nature with their knowledge of one another's style.

The Precariousness of Public Performance as a Woman

In Tashkent's concert halls and wedding venues, women perform music publicly as a norm, rendering it unremarkable. Although Soviet-era liberation movements resulted in significant cultural change—it is now entirely ordinary for women to perform music in a public setting—notions of tradition and history persist in the social pressures felt by women musicians, many of whom give up or change careers after marriage. Despite such continued pressures, women play all kinds of music in a wide variety of settings and are often seen as unproblematic equals to their male counterparts, at least in professional contexts in the independence era. The ordinariness of it is only notable because so many remark on the rigors and challenges that women engage when musicking in public. Women themselves talk of the conflicts involved when balancing home and family with careers in music. Men often click their tongues and casually note what a shame it is that a woman would have to work for a living outside the home and be placed in front of so many strange pairs of eyes.

As with much cultural change, shades of old attitudes and mores remain, so that although women perform in public and gain significant prestige from it in some areas (especially those institutionalized and sanctioned by the state), venues like weddings and café performance[2] constitute a problematic and complicated space for women's music making. It is necessary and ordinary, but also still viewed by some as a pity and a potentially dangerous space. This may be the result of some renewed conservatism that has surfaced after independence in conversation with official Soviet and post-Soviet policy that emphasizes women's important role in professional life. Although not common across the board, certainly some of the nostalgia for a pre-Soviet past has involved the imagining of the appropriate role for woman being the homemaker and hearth-keeper, and viewing women's forays into professional life as an unfortunate economic necessity rather than a source of fulfillment and pride for working women, whether at the conservatory, in cafés, or at weddings. In this case, it is difficult to tease out which attitudes have persisted through history, which are newfound values that engage in imagining tradition, and which have roots in the Soviet-era phenomenon or resentment for the double burden or second shift that professional life creates.[3]

The result is that the binary created by the framing of the ichkari (inside/private) and tashkari (outside/public) is insufficient when viewing the moral nuances involved when women make music in Tashkent. Clearly the prestige afforded by a position in the Filharmonia orchestra, the conservatory, or the Alisher Navoiy Opera and Ballet Company mitigates some of the social tension that arises when women perform in public. Also, as noted previously, the large concert hall stage provides a significant physical and psychological barrier between women and the public observing them (often from a distance in a hall with dimmed lights). This poses less risk to the performer of harassment and unwanted contact by the strange men who populate the warnings and shamings I overheard about women musicians performing in public. Cafés and weddings rarely provide such buffer zones, as women performers have close and level contact with those listening and dancing to their music. This association of female musicians, especially wedding musicians, with immoral behavior, moral looseness, and (at the most extreme) prostitution is not unique to Uzbekistan. Certainly public music making has been considered a risk for women in a variety of cultures throughout history, including Croatia (Ceribasic 2003, 152) and Afghanistan (Doubleday 1990, 196).

This presents a constant challenge for female wedding musicians in Tashkent, who have the extra burden of appearing appropriately modest, professional, and moral while providing musical entertainment. Malika opa repeatedly expressed gratitude that her career was sufficiently successful that she never had to perform at weddings to supplement her family's income. Other musicians also expressed sorrow for Ro'za opa's status as a single mother who did need to supplement her income in order to provide the best opportunities for her son. Despite such social pressure, Ro'za opa repeatedly expressed pride about and enjoyment of her work at weddings. She would reject any notion of pity for her situation, even as she often described her hard work and the daunting schedule involved in raising a child, playing in a folk orchestra, teaching students at various institutions, and playing weddings. The added pressure of social stigma could not have made such undertakings any easier.

Even within such prestigious genres as traditional music and arranged folk music, women are still often discouraged from becoming musicians and singers, because of the perception of frivolity and immorality. Firuza opa mentioned in an interview that this sometimes makes it harder for female musicians to find husbands, and that those who marry are often pressured to leave the musical profession (Abdurahimova 2005b). In the post-hujum Soviet period, performing in a mostly male ensemble was still considered risky behavior that required marked professionalism. Malika opa addressed this aspect of her past, describing her behavior as the first female instrumentalist in the radio's maqom ensemble: "I always wore long sleeves, always dressed very modestly, wore duppi [traditional square hat], and was always very serious and didn't gossip" (Ziyaeva 2009). She went on to say that there were already quite a few women in the associated vocal ensemble, but that the public always noticed her as the one duppi-wearing serious young woman amid all the male instrumentalists. This emphasis on seriousness and professionalism belies the public assumption of female performers' loose morality or their effect on the desires and morality of the men in attendance, one that even the prestige of the radio maqom ensemble could not erase. A full two generations after the emancipatory efforts of the Soviet government thrust women into the public workplace, only markedly modest and serious behavior could firmly establish Malika opa's professionalism.

Conclusions: The Complex Relation of National Identity to Individual Feminine Experiences

Individuals such as Malika opa, Ro'za opa, Firuza opa, Faizila opa, Ofeliya Yusupova, Dilbara Abdurahmanova, Gulzoda Hudoinazarova, and their students are constantly and actively creating a space for women in the Uzbek academy and beyond. This space allows them to engage in meaningful musical work, as well as providing them access to a sense of clear participation in the Uzbek nation. National participation hinges on many varying identities all performing and internalizing national narratives in individualized ways. Performance of the Uzbek nation depends on these and other women's musical performances as much as women depend on national narratives to inform their diverse performances of femininity and music.

Although institutional boundaries and competitive tensions force perceived separations between traditional, arranged folk, Western art, and popular musics, in the wider view they unite as all are brought in service of the Uzbek national project. Regarding the notion of the nation as imagined community (Anderson 1991), all musics serve the same essential(izing) purpose:

to contribute to a national imaginary that is at once sophisticatedly modern and deeply rooted in authentic traditions, one whose existence can be taken for granted as natural, homogenous, and unquestionable. In this sense, all musical genres are engaging with universals when serving nationalism. Traditional and folk musics have a way of bringing the universal of music into a specific context, especially for those who perform them and dedicate their lives to ensuring that such musics continue to have meaning and relevance in an increasingly complex cosmopolitan Tashkent.

This individual interpretation and performance of gendered nationalism is relevant when considering not only how multilayered identity functions in a given context, but also how larger cultural movements gain credibility—individuals must support and subscribe to the identity markers that they perform on some level. Certainly many who criticize the artifice and somewhat forced nature of appreciation for government-run musical ensembles (Levin 1996, 2002; Frolova-Walker 2007; Zemstovsky and Kunanbaeva 1997) have a significant point to make. However, the issue becomes more complicated when one considers the individuals who find significant meaning in government-organized musical practices. How does their experience fit into larger narratives that alternately critique or support existing regimes and narratives?

Butler's notion of legibility and the sedimentation of norms (1988) becomes very relevant in this case because it allows us to see how any individual performance of a gendered and/or national selfhood may be relevant only to the individual performing it; but in the larger view, iterations of this performativity in turn solidify into norms that are endowed not only with a sense of meaning and group identity, but also with a sense of naturalness. Individuals mediating larger messages about self, nation, and gender are doing that work of naturalizing certain modes of femininity and imbuing them with a sense of being given. In this way, the performance of feminine gender and the performance of nationalism are inherently linked and lend themselves to being bolstered performatively by musicians who play a variety of instruments and a variety of styles. All are contributing to this sedimentation of the feminine Uzbek norm that can have stylistic diversity in terms of both sonic material and costume, but functions to contribute iterations of the ideal of a smiling woman at peace with a national identity and her position straddling modernity and tradition.

Scholars acknowledge that music and women's behavior, in turn, are of central importance when co-opted as representations of the nation (Buchanan 2002; Turino 2000; McClintock 1997). Ethnomusicologists document these processes, especially when women become important public figures who unify national sentiment around them, such as Umm Kulthūm in Egypt. Ethnomusicologist Virginia Danielson traces Kulthūm's biography and rise to fame, as well as her purposeful participation in Egyptian politics (1997). Musicologist Laura Lohman continues this project, focusing on the transformation of Kulthūm's image after Egypt's defeat in the 1967 Six-Day War. She focuses on Kulthūm's activism and continued performing career as a purposeful fashioning of image that supported national unity (2010). Certainly the clearest Uzbek analogue to Kulthūm's role in a national narrative is the prominence and fame that Yulduz Usmanova has consolidated in the past two decades. However, her stances are not always seen as supporting any given political regime; she has a more complicated relationship with her government than Kulthūm is remembered as having. Nonetheless, the discourse surrounding them has some similarities. The city of Tashkent does not stop for Usmanova's radio shows the way Cairo did for Kulthūm's, but both are admired for powerful voices that sing important words.

Similar processes linking female stars to political ideals and national symbolism also occur in Japan. Anthropologist Christine R. Yano traces female pop stars' similar trajectories in the Japanese genre of *enka*, linking the genre with nostalgia and images (and imaginings) of the past. She notes: "The enticement of enka is that it suggests a forum for collective nostalgia which actively appropriates and shapes the past, thereby binding the group together.... What is past becomes a kind of 'internal exotic'" (2002, 15). This notion of a multilayered "internal exotic" is helpful when thinking of the role of women as performers of tradition, regardless of how that tradition is transformed and reimagined through the various genres of professional musical performance. The notion of a common past that binds group identity is important, especially regarding Svetlana Boym's notion of "prospective nostalgia" (2001, xvi). In this sense the performance of national symbolism that represents an idea of the ancient past or tradition as it has always been is not just about the past; it is about a vision for the future. This vision of a unified and independent Uzbekistan includes a smiling femininity that embraces traditional roles and values.

Of course, women do not have to be huge stars and national figures to perform gendered nationalism. It is the constant reinscription of gendered images and sounds in everyday life that truly give weight to the idea of an Uzbek feminine norm. Humming along to the radio in the kitchen, singing lullabies, and dancing at weddings are vital aspects of the active musical construction of an Uzbek community that imagines a common musical practice among all. As important as Kulthūm and Usmanova are, it is the continued performance of national identity and gendered norms by audience members and ordinary citizens that provide the foundation for the larger mediated spectacles.

Even more important than the patriotic representations of national identity involving pop stars and national figures that viewers and audience members find on billboards, in television programs, and on the concert stage is how individuals internalize a meaningful experience from the performance of national identity. The musical, gendered, and specifically feminine performance of the Uzbek nation has levels and nuances that reach beyond its dismissal as a patriarchal bargain (Kandiyoti 1988). More than strategy, this multilevel internalization of national identity throughout one's complex self-identity reminds us that even the markers of identity that are pushed upon us by government campaigns and large institutions also carry the capacity to be expressed in an individualized manner that engages with existing tropes in liberating ways.

The clearest personal expression of national identity came in my 2005 conversation with dutarist Mehrihon Muminova (as discussed in chapter 1). Muminova emphasized that women carry a larger burden in the performance of the nation and posited this as something unique: "For us Uzbeks, we approach things differently." She continued, narrating a string of objects that were for her at once personal, national, and also inherently linked with musical performance and expressive culture: "Atlas fabric [brightly colored silk usually worn by women] is nationalism; duppi hats are nationalism . . . performing our ancient style of music is nationalism . . . braiding our hair in little braids [especially common in dance and musical performances] is nationalism" (Muminova 2005). In this litany of national activities, all of them are at least somewhat associated with women, especially atlas fabric and hair braiding. Wearing duppi hats and performing ancient traditional music is the purview of both sexes in Uzbekistan. Through this statement, a vision of the performance of national identity as something meaningful and individual becomes clear. For Muminova, a great deal hinges on traditional clothing and appearance: hats, fabrics, and braids are all visual. Music is the only practice on her list that engages other senses, one that is clearly very dear to her as a dedicated dutarist.[4] Music is also the practice given the clearest tie to the past, although other practices like atlas weaving could be considered equally historical. Perhaps it is music's naturally ephemeral quality that allows it to be so deeply immersed in notions of the past that are still attainable and expressible in the present.

Notes

Introduction. The Stories Women Tell about Their Music

1. Although I would not learn about this until the following year, when I traveled to Uzbekistan for the first time, such courteous inquiries about one's family, work, and health are the norm when greeting people in Uzbek culture.

2. In addition to spectacles with dancing boys, Western travelers noted what they often called "native music." Descriptions usually seem to correspond to either wedding music or the art music genres of *maqom*. In addition, some travelers note the presence of European-style military bands and Russian folk and dance music in the colonial areas of the cities.

3. Meakin does not acknowledge Skrine's coauthor, Edward Denison Ross, in her comments.

4. The *karnai* is a long trumpet that looks similar to the Tibetan *dungchen,* but rather than leaving the bell on the ground, the karnai is played lifted high in the air, often in acrobatic patterns with other karnai players. It is a common instrument heard at celebrations including weddings and other life-cycle festivities.

5. The connection of women's emancipatory projects and modern nationalism is not unique to the Soviet situation. Historian Charlotte Weber notes the same link in Middle Eastern nations, including Lebanon, Syria, and Palestine (2008, 84–85).

6. For further discussion of the Jadids and their role in early Soviet political spheres, see Khalid (2006, 239–42).

7. For further discussion of the reification of separate Uzbek and Tajik Shashmaqom repertoires, see Levin (1984).

8. Performance of pieces from the Shashmaqom and related repertoires from this era can be heard on *Uzbekistan: Great Voices of the Past (1940–1965),* a recording that Jean During compiled from Uzbek archival sources in 1999.

9. The process of creating folk orchestras, choirs, and dance troupes was not unique to Uzbekistan. For English-language material about this process in other Central

Asian republics, specifically Kazakhstan, see Mukhambetova (1995) and Rancier (2009a).

10. The use of the term *estrada* to refer to pop music comes to the Uzbek language from French via the Russian language and means "small stage," referring originally to entertainments that are performed outside the "large stage" that hosts symphony orchestras, ballet, and opera. For more information on estrada's Russian trajectory during the Soviet and post-Soviet era, see MacFadyen (2001; 2002); for a discussion of similar developments in Mongolia, see Chao (2010, 85–86).

11. A *kollej* is an educational institution that provides a pedagogical program focused in a specific field for students sixteen to nineteen years of age (corresponding to the last two years of high school in the US system). The current Uzbek term, *kollej*, replaced the Soviet-era Russian term *uchilish*.

12. Another repertoire related to the various regional maqom traditions is the *on ikki muqam* (twelve maqoms) performed by the Uyghurs in Xinjiang, China. For further explanation of the on ikki muqam and its performing contexts, see Wong (2006), Harris (2008), and Harris and Dawut (2002, 111–12).

13. As mentioned earlier, Abdurauf Fitrat was a well-known scholar in the colonial and early Soviet periods who was executed during the purge of the 1930s for his association with the Jadid pan-Turkic reform movement. Viktor Uspensky (1879–1949) was a Russian/Soviet musicologist who grew up in Central Asia, was educated at the St. Petersburg conservatory, and returned to Tashkent to help develop the state conservatory in the 1920s and 1930s (Levin 1996, 13). Both volumes are quite rare, even in local archives, and as a result I have not been able to personally locate Fitrat's work, although it is often mentioned by local scholars and cited in Djumaev (2005).

14. I was quite interested in the extensive ritual practices and various musical genres related to wedding music, perhaps because I was not too interested in the wedding practices of my Anglo-American Protestant heritage. My fascination with wedding music took shape in a similar fashion as Veronica Doubleday's interest in women's wedding music in Afghanistan (Doubleday 1990).

15. This monument in particular illustrates the purposeful representations of gender in the Soviet national project, one in which women are represented as strong and productive (nonveiled) members of society, but still protected by a yet stronger masculine figure. This differs significantly from the traditional femininity as remembered in the postindependence era, which contributes significantly to current national projects.

16. The state-run radio and television station in Tashkent is considered an important asset and possible target for attack; thus, it has a passport control stand and anyone not employed at the station must be listed as a guest and must present their passport as proof of identity.

17. My methodological approach, with its focus on musical learning and performance, is influenced especially by Mantle Hood's notion of "bi-musicality" (1960).

18. The Hamza Kollej is a music high school located on the former site of the Uzbek State Conservatory, which moved to a new building and location in 2002. The Hamza Kollej is one of a few music high schools throughout the country that provides specialized education for two years between school and conservatory.

19. This estimation of ethnicity is problematic on a number of levels because it does not allow for dual mixed ethnicities (neither does the Uzbek nationality listing on passports), and also because of the history of Soviet nationalities policy. Further, it is unsurprising that so many people would currently list Uzbek as their official nationality because many people of mixed ethnic backgrounds or of other Central Asian ethnicities believe that having Uzbek listed in their passport will make them better candidates for educational opportunities, jobs, and promotions.

20. Feminism is often discussed in terms of waves, with the first wave represented by the suffrage movement in the late nineteenth and early twentieth centuries, the second wave by the women's liberation movement of the 1960s and 1970s, and the third wave from the 1980s until the present. The term *third wave* is useful but also problematic because it is used to bring together diverse movements from a variety of groups, many of which criticize the exclusionary and privileged approach of the women's liberation movement. As a result, the third wave can alternatively be called "multicultural feminism(s)" or "plural feminisms."

21. In particular, many of these narratives focus on the veil and conditions for women in Afghanistan (a convenient monolith that is presented as important motivation for Western intervention) (Sirrs 2001; Shah 2001; Bumiller 2010).

22. I first observed this statue in a central location in the square during my fieldwork in 2008. It did not appear to be there when I visited the square in 2005 or during my earlier trips.

23. Applications of gender studies to musicological research are rare in current Uzbek scholarship. Unfortunately, there are no seminal works to cite from Uzbek authors, although recent conferences in Tashkent have encouraged research in that direction.

Chapter 1. Beyond the Canon

1. The following recordings provide solid examples of Shashmaqom performed in the manner described above: *At the Bazaar of Love: Timeless Central Asian Maqâm Music*, by the Ilyas Malayev Ensemble (1997), *Invisible Face of the Beloved: Classical Music of the Tajiks and Uzbeks* (2005), and *Tajikistan: Maqâm Navâ* (1997).

2. Theodore Levin traces some of the history and lineage in the Shashmaqom in many of his works, including his dissertation (1984) and the book *The Hundred Thousand Fools of God: Musical Travels in Central Asia (and Queens, New York)* (1996). Russian- and Uzbek-language sources that provide such a history include Matyoqubov (2004), Solomonova (1979), and Rajabov (1963).

3. Those who critique the work of the second wave often point out that women of color and of the lower classes were already in the workforce. As a result, the women whom second-wave feminists worked to add to the workplace and to heretofore masculine histories were usually white and upper-class. Second-wave feminism has its problems, but the project of including women in the stories that are told continues to be a worthwhile endeavor, especially in areas where their participation is commonly unremarked upon. In her introduction to *Feminism and History,* Joan Wallach Scott provides both an account of that period and the later critiques. The discussion includes

the problems that arise when visibility is equated with transparency and the problems of ideology and bias when presenting history, as well as the issue of essentializing groups of women without questioning "where the identities come from" (1996, 2–3, 7).

4. Theodore Levin (1996 and 1984) gives significantly more detail on the panethnic and panreligious histories and practices of the Shashmaqom.

5. There is a range of music that plays an important role in everyday life, especially in villages and rural areas. Although it is beyond the scope of this book, women are significant creators and performers of these music and song genres. Such genres include ceremonial music and music for life-cycle celebrations, as well as lullabies, work songs, and other songs that accompany everyday life. Some of this music is documented in Sultanova (2011) and Abdullayev (1994).

6. In 2008, UNESCO inscribed the Shashmaqom in its Representative List of the Intangible Cultural Heritage of Humanity, ascribing it to both Uzbekistan and Tajikistan. (See http://www.unesco.org/culture/ich/index.php?lg=en&pg=00011&RL=00089, accessed July 30, 2012.)

7. She is featured and named in the titles of two internationally released albums, which demonstrates her significant fame (1994; 1997).

8. Sodiqov's performing style on the dutar can be heard on During (1999), track 7.

9. I earned my bachelor's degree from the Peabody Conservatory in 2000, an accomplishment that gave me significantly more credibility with my Uzbek consultants than my PhD in ethnomusicology.

Chapter 2. Ancient Treasures, Modernized

1. For example, Soviet musicologist Tamara Vyzgo ties folk musicians to larger concert projects at the onset of the Soviet period. She remarks: "The first Uzbek concert brigade came about in 1918–1919, when Unions of art workers were created in the cities of the Turkrepublik, and they took on the purpose of organizing concerts. Many Uzbek folk musicians became members of these unions and took part.... In the performance style and repertoire, these ensembles continued the line of development of national professional music of oral tradition. But if before the revolution such ensembles performed in smaller circles of friends or readers, then now they have come to the wider concert stage. The folk musicians became participants in great mass-political measures" (Vyzgo 1972, 81). A. Odilov also confirms the overlap in repertoire and even personnel during that era (1995, 25, 48–49).

2. The balalaika's origins are very difficult to trace, and multiple theories exist as to its provenance. It is very similar to the *domra*, an instrument commonly used in minstrel (Russian: *skomorokhi*) performances, and is thus thought to be related. It is also possibly related to another minstrel instrument, the *gudok* (three-stringed bowed fiddle). The main difference between the two instruments is that the balalaika has a triangular body and the domra's is an oval. Both are considered to have come from the *dombra*, a long-necked lute from Central Asia. Other theories posit that it sprang forth in its triangular form with no ancestry whatsoever in the seventeenth century (Miszko 1995, 130–33). Andreev performed throughout Russia and also toured America with his folk ensembles that featured the instruments. This resulted in a

significant balalaika revival movement in the United States, as well as the creation of folk orchestras in Russia and later the Soviet Union.

3. Although no commercial recordings of Uzbek folk orchestras are currently available in the United States and Western Europe, recordings of folk orchestras that resulted from similar processes in Russia and Bulgaria are available. Although the modified folk instruments from each country and culture are different, the resulting sound is somewhat similar. See Hvorostovsky (1992) and Varimezova (2005) as reference recordings for Russian and Bulgarian folk orchestras.

4. "Backward" as a label for practices and peoples in need of transformation in order to conform to Marxist-Leninist ideals was common throughout the Soviet Union as well as China. Ethnomusicologist Helen Rees documents the phenomenon in China regarding attitudes toward local folk music, which people described as "backward" and "unscientific" as late as the 1980s (2009, 47). This connection is understandable, considering the overlap in cultural policy between the two countries, with Chairman Mao Tse-tung citing Lenin and Trotsky in his 1943 talks on the role of literature and the arts (McDougall 1980, 75–80).

Chapter 3. Like Tereshkova in the Cosmos

1. Similar processes occurred across the Soviet Union at the time; for example, in the Azerbaijan SSR, as discussed in Naroditskaya (2002, 97–99).

2. The preface to Yusupova's biography notes that 1987 was the first time that the Tashkent Conservatory had the freedom to choose its own director, as opposed to having one appointed from Moscow (Kalmykova 2001, 9). By choosing Yusupova, the community demonstrated the great confidence they placed in her during a time of difficult transition. It is noteworthy that they chose a woman to lead the institution during such a difficult time of transition and, indeed, have continued to select women for powerful roles there, including conservatory director Dildora Muradova, who held the position in 2004 and 2005.

Chapter 4. "Greetings to the Uzbek People!"

1. Usmanova continues to be highly regarded in Uzbekistan, but immigrated to Turkey in 2008, citing a need for artistic freedom. She currently has agents in both Tashkent and Istanbul. In fact, her agent's contact information for Tashkent specifically mentions that it welcomes inquiries from people interested in wedding performances (www.yulduz.uz/contact; Usmanova 2013).

2. For boys, companies offer school supplies with sports themes, including logos and pictures of the local soccer team Pakhtakor (Cotton workers) and images of international soccer stars such as David Beckham and Ronaldo.

3. Theodore Levin's account of his interview with Usmanova provides an excellent overview of her persona as it developed during the late Soviet era and immediately following independence (Levin 1996, 80–84).

4. For a full description of this concert and its relevance to estrada's place in Uzbekistan's national project, see Merchant (2009).

Chapter 5. Marrying Past, Present, and Future

1. The opening verses of a kelin salom as performed by Ro'zibi Hodjayeva, recorded August 17, 2002. Ro'za opa used a variant of these verses whenever I accompanied her to a kelin salom between 2002 and 2009. This version of the song/recitation has similarities with those listed in Uzbek scholarly collections of kelin salom recitations (including Mirzaeva and Mussaqulov 1992; Jo'raev and Ismonova 1999). However Ro'za opa's standard version is not identical to any that I have found.

2. This is similar to the cultural importance and anticipation given to weddings in many other cultures, including Prespa Albanian culture (Sugarman 1997, 1–2) and Afghan culture (Doubleday 1990).

3. Ethnomusicologist Inna Naroditskaya notes Azerbaijani women's important role in dancing at weddings at the same time she underscores the importance of female wedding performers in general in Azerbaijan (Naroditskaya 2002, 166–67).

4. Pop music's prevalence at weddings has been common in other former Soviet and Eastern Bloc countries since the Soviet/communist period as well, including estrada in Tajikistan (Spinetti 2005, 197–98), *disco polo* in Poland (Carr 2007, 273), and *svatbarska musika*, which involves incorporating rock and jazz elements into various Balkan folk musics, in Bulgaria (Rice 2002, 26–27; Buchanan 1996, 202–4, 225–26).

Conclusion. Women's Musical Communities Performing the Nation

1. They also allow men to come together; gaps are segregated along gender lines, but are practiced by both men and women. Levin describes a men's gap in his book, discussing it as primarily a male institution, which goes against my experience and probably emphasizes the gender limitations that shape the nature of our respective fieldwork experiences [1996, 35–38].)

2. Although not discussed in detail in this book, both women and men are often hired to perform estrada at cafés in the evenings for the entertainment of customers. The repertoire and performance practice overlaps a great deal with the estrada performed at weddings.

3. Slavic studies and women's studies scholar Beth Holmgren discusses the burden of the second shift for Soviet-era women in "Bug Inspectors and Beauty Queens: The Problems of Translating Feminism into Russian" (1995).

4. Many people expressed great pride in Uzbek food culture. Dishes such as pilaf (osh/Russian: plov) and dumplings (manti) were often labeled "national" by restaurants and home cooks alike. Clearly Uzbek food engages a sense of national identity on more than a visual level, but it was conspicuously absent from Muminova's discussion of how she defines nationalism. For further discussion of food and culture in Uzbekistan, see Rosenberger (2012).

Glossary

Aka—older brother, an honorific suffix often used when addressing a man who is older than oneself.

An'ana/An'anaviy—tradition/traditional, often used to refer to maqom and related repertoires within the framework of institutionalized professional musical performance.

Bazm—wedding reception, an event that can occur in either a private home or public banquet hall; it always follows the marriage ceremony (nikox).

Chang—hammer dulcimer.

Dekada (Russian)—decade, festivals celebrated during the Soviet era, usually focused on sports or the arts from a specific republic or region.

Doyra—a frame drum with steel rings lining the inside of the wood frame.

Dutar—a two-stringed, fretted, pear-shaped, long-necked lute common throughout Central Asia.

Estrada—popular music; the term comes to Uzbek from French via Russian where it refers to entertainments for the "small stage," such as music, juggling, and comedy.

Gap—chat, a gender-segregated group that meets regularly for conversation and entertainment. It also functions as a revolving credit organization, with members contributing money at each meeting that a different person takes home each time.

Gijak—spike fiddle; the current version has four strings and a spherical body and is played with the spike balanced on the knee. A violin is occasionally played in the same position (and is also called *gijak* in this context).

Halq cholg'u—people's performance, a term used to replace the Russian term *narodnyy* in reference to arranged folk music and reconstructed instruments.

Jonli ijro—live performance, used to emphasize that vocalists are not lip-synching.

Kashgar rubob—a fretted lute plucked with a plectrum that features a skin membrane over the body of the instrument. It has three double courses of metal strings and one gut or nylon string for timbral diversity in the performance of pitches in the lowest range of the instrument.

Kelin salom—bride-greeting ritual, one of the many to'ylar associated with marriage. This event occurs at the family home the morning after the marriage ceremony is complete and allows members of the groom's family to welcome the bride as a new member of their household. It is often segregated by gender, with the women of the family at the forefront of the ritual, and all other guests (such as the bride's family and friends) are female.

Maqom—melodic mode; in this case, it refers to specific scales as well as repertoires performed in court cities throughout Central Asia.

Millat/Millatchilik—nation/nationalism.

Mumtoz—classical, usually used to refer to Central Asian art music repertoires such as maqom rather than Western art music.

Nikox—wedding, specifically the event in the complex of wedding celebrations where the marriage ceremony is performed.

Opa—older sister, often used as an honorific suffix when referring to women older than oneself.

Shashmaqom—six maqoms, an art music repertoire with its roots in fifteenth-century Bukharan courts. It is usually played heterophonically by plucked and bowed lutes in small groups accompanied by frame drum.

Tanbur—fretted, long-necked, metal-stringed lute that is plucked with a plectrum called *nohun*. The same instrument is called *sato* when bowed.

To'y—a life-cycle celebration, usually held to mark important rites of passage such as the birth of a child (*beshik to'y*), circumcision (*sunnat to'y*), or marriage ceremony (*nikox to'y*).

Works Cited

Abazov, Rafis. 2006. *Culture and Customs of the Central Asian Republics*. Westport, CT: Greenwood Publishing Group.

Abdullayev, Rustam S. 1994. *Obryadovaya Muzyka Tsentralnoj Azii* [The ceremonial music of Central Asia]. Tashkent: Uzbek Republic Academic Press, Fan.

———. 2002. Personal interview with the author, July 30.

Abdurahimova, Firuza. 2005a. *O'zbekiston Taronalari: Sug'diyona O'zbek Xalq Cholg'ulari Kamer Orkestri Bisotidan* [Melodies of Uzbekistan: Selections from the repertoire of the Uzbek Folk Chamber Orchestra "Sogdiana"]. Tashkent: Turon-Iqbol.

———. 2005b. Personal interview with the author, July 24.

———. 2008. Personal interview with the author, August 11.

Abdurahmanova, Dilbara. 2008. Personal interview with the author, August 18.

Abu-Lughod, Lila, ed. 1998. "Preface" and "Feminist Longings and Postcolonial Conditions." In *Remaking Women: Feminism and Modernity in the Middle East*, vii–x, 3–31. Princeton, NJ: Princeton University Press.

Adams, Laura L. 2010. *The Spectacular State: Culture and National Identity in Uzbekistan*. Durham, NC: Duke University Press.

Akilova, Viloyat. 2008. Personal interview with the author, August 23.

———. 2009. Personal interview with the author, July 16.

Aminova, Komila. 2008. Personal interview with the author, August 21.

Anderson, Benedict. 1991. *Imagined Communities: Reflections on the Origin and Spread of Nationalism*, 2nd ed. London: Verso.

———. 2001. "To What Can Late Eighteenth-Century French, British, and American Anxieties Be Compared? Comment on Three Papers." *The American Historical Review* 106 (4): 1281–89.

Arabov, Ilyos. 2005. Personal interview with the author, February 13.

Ataboeva, Gulshod. 2003. Personal interview with the author, December 24.

Ayari, Mondher, and Stephen McAdams. 2003. "Aural Analysis of Arabic Improvised Instrumental Music (Taqsim)." *Music Perception: An Interdisciplinary Journal* 21 (2): 159–216.

Babaev, S. 1952. "O Rabote Soyuza Kompositorov Uzbekistana" [About the work of the Uzbek Composers' Union]. *Sovetskaya Muzyka* [Soviet music] 1: 41–45.

Baily, John. 1981. "Cross-Cultural Perspectives in Popular Music: The Case of Afghanistan." *Popular Music* 1: 105–21.

Balogun, Oluwakemi M. 2012. "Cultural and Cosmopolitan: Idealized Femininity and Embodied Nationalism in Nigerian Beauty Pageants." *Gender & Society* 26: 357–81.

Bayton, Mavis. 1997. "Women and the Electric Guitar." In *Sexing the Groove: Popular Music and Gender*, edited by Sheila Whiteley, 37–49. London: Routledge.

Begmatov, Soib. 2005. Class lecture to course "Uzbek Music before the 20th Century." Uzbek State Conservatory, March 2. Tashkent, Uzbekistan.

Begmatov, Soib, Qo'ldosh Mamirov, Avaz Mansurov, Dildora Karimova, and Ibrohim Ro'ziyev. 2001. *Musiqa: 6-Sinf Uchun Darslik* [Music: 6th-grade textbook]. Tashkent: G'afur G'ulom Nomidagi Adabiyot va San'at Nashriyoti.

Beliaev, Viktor. 1962. *Ocherki po Istorii Muzyky Narodov SSSR* [Excerpts of the music history of the peoples of the USSR]. Moscow: Gosudarstvenoe Muzykal'noe Izdatel'stvo.

Boelza, Igor. 1944. "1. From Moscow." *The Musical Quarterly* 30 (3): 356–58.

Bohlman, Philip V. 1992. "Epilogue: Musics and Canons." In *Disciplining Music: Musicology and Its Canons*, edited by Katherine Bergeron and Philip V. Bohlman, 197–210. Chicago: University of Chicago Press.

Booth, Gregory D. 1990. "Brass Bands: Tradition, Change, and the Mass Media in Indian Wedding Music." *Ethnomusicology* 34 (2): 245–62.

Bowers, Jane, and Judith Tick, eds. 1986. *Women Making Music: The Western Art Tradition, 1150–1950*. Urbana: University of Illinois Press.

Boym, Svetlana. 1994. *Common Places: Mythologies of Everyday Life in Russia*. Cambridge, MA: Harvard University Press.

———. 2001. *The Future of Nostalgia*. New York: Basic Books.

Brubaker, Rogers. 1996. *Nationalism Reframed: Nationhood and the National Question in the New Europe*. Cambridge: Cambridge University Press.

Buchanan, Donna A. 1996. "Wedding Musicians, Political Transition, and National Consciousness in Bulgaria." In *Retuning Culture: Musical Changes in Central and Eastern Europe*, edited by Mark Slobin, 200–230. Durham, NC: Duke University Press.

———. 2002. "Soccer, Popular Music, and National Consciousness in Post-State-Socialist Bulgaria 1994–96." *British Journal of Ethnomusicology* 11 (2): 1–27.

———. 2006. *Performing Democracy: Bulgarian Music and Musicians in Transition*. Chicago: University of Chicago Press.

Bumiller, Elisabeth. 2010. "In Camouflage of Veil, a Fragile Bond." *New York Times*, May 29. Accessed August 21, 2010. http://www.nytimes.com/2010/05/30/world/asia/30marines.html.

Burnaby, Frederick. (1874) 2001. *A Ride to Khiva: Travels and Adventures in Central Asia*. New Delhi: Asian Educational Services.
Butler, Judith. 1988. "Performative Acts of Gender Constitution: An Essay in Phenomenology and Feminist Theory." *Theatre Journal* 40 (4): 519–31.
———. 2004. *Undoing Gender*. New York: Routledge.
Carr, Daphne. 2007. "Dancing, Democracy, and Kitsch: Poland's Disco Polo." In *Listen Again: A Momentary History of Pop Music*, edited by Eric Weisbard, 272–85. Durham, NC: Duke University Press.
Ceribasic, Naila. 2003. "Social Canons Inherited from the Past: Women Players of Folk Music Instruments in Croatia." *Studia Musicologia Academiae Scientarum Hungaricae* 44 (1): 147–57.
Chao, David. 2010. "Urtiin Duu: The Mongolian Long Song in Mongolia and China." PhD diss., University of California, Los Angeles.
Chatterjee, Partha. 1993. *The Nation and Its Fragments: Colonial and Postcolonial Histories*. Princeton, NJ: Princeton University Press.
Cheah, Pheng. 1997. "Given Culture: Rethinking Cosmopolitical Freedom in Transnationalism." *Boundary 2* 24 (2): 157–97.
CIA World Fact Book. 2011. Accessed November 2. https://www.cia.gov/library/publications/the-world-factbook/geos/uz.html.
Citron, Marcia J. (1993) 2000. *Gender and the Musical Canon*. Urbana: University of Illinois Press.
Clifford, James. 1997. *Routes: Travel and Translation in the Late Twentieth Century*. Cambridge, MA: Harvard University Press.
Coates, Norma. 1997. "(R)evolution Now? Rock and the Political Potential of Gender." In *Sexing the Groove: Popular Music and Gender*, edited by Sheila Whiteley, 50–64. London: Routledge.
Cooley, Timothy J. 2005. *Making Music in the Polish Tatras: Tourists, Ethnographers, and Mountain Musicians*. Bloomington: Indiana University Press.
Danielson, Virginia. 1997. *The Voice of Egypt: Umm Kulthūm, Arabic Song, and Egyptian Society in the Twentieth Century*. Chicago: University of Chicago Press.
Daukeyeva, Saida, Elmira Köchümkulova, and Theodore Levin, eds. 2015. *The Music of Central Asia*. Bloomington: Indiana University Press.
Djumaev, Alexander. 1993. "Power Structures, Culture Policy, and Traditional Music in Soviet Central Asia." *Yearbook for Traditional Music* 25: 43–50.
———. 2005. "Musical Heritage and National Identity in Uzbekistan." *Ethnomusicology Forum* 14 (2): 165–84.
Doi, Mary Masayo. 2002. *Gesture, Gender, Nation: Dance and Social Change in Uzbekistan*. Westport, CT: Bergin and Garvey.
Doubleday, Veronica. 1990. *Three Women of Herat*. Austin: University of Texas Press.
———. 2008. "Sounds of Power: An Overview of Musical Instruments and Gender." *Ethnomusicology Forum* 17 (1): 3–39.
Eisenstein, Zillah. 2000. "Writing Bodies on the Nation for the Globe." In *Women, States, and Nationalism: At Home in the Nation?*, edited by Sita Ranchod-Nilsson and Mary Ann Tétreault, 35–53. New York: Routledge.

Ellingson, Ter. 1992. "Transcription." In *Ethnomusicology: An Introduction*, edited by Helen Myers, 110–52. London: MacMillan.

Ergashev, Kh., L. Scherbakova, and A. Inoyatov, eds. 1973. *Al'bom: Tamara Khanum* [Album: Tamara Khanum]. Tashkent: G'afur G'ulom.

Everett, Yayoi Uno. 2004. "Intercultural Synthesis in Postwar Western Art Music: Historical Contexts, Perspectives, and Taxonomy." In *Locating East Asia in Western Art Music*, edited by Yayoi Uno Everett and Frederick Lau, 1–21. Middletown, CT: Wesleyan University Press.

Everett, Yayoi Uno, and Frederick Lau, eds. 2004. *Locating East Asia in Western Art Music*. Middletown, CT: Wesleyan University Press.

Fayzullayev, Boboqul, Shokhnazar Sakhibov, and Fazliddin Shakhobov. 1957–67. *Shashmakom*, vols. 1–5, edited by Viktor Beliaev. Moscow: Izdatel'stvo "Muzyka."

Fisher, Paul. 2003. "Kazufumi Miyazawa: Such an Explorer." *fRoots* 238: 43–47.

Fitrat, Abdurauf. (1927) 1993. *O'zbek Klassik Musiqasi va Uning Tarixi* [Uzbek classical music and its history]. Tashkent: Fan.

Fitzgibbon, Kate. 2010. "Turn of the Century Art Photographer and Ethnographer S. M. Dudin." Accessed August 2. http://www.anahitaphotoarchive.com/Home/Essays/turn-of-the-century-art-photographer-and-ethnographer-sm-dudin.

Frith, Simon. 1996. *Performing Rites: On the Value of Popular Music*. Cambridge, MA: Harvard University Press.

Frolova-Walker, Marina. 2007. *Russian Music and Nationalism: From Glinka to Stalin*. New Haven, CT: Yale University Press.

G'anieva, Iroda. 2003. *Tanovarlar* [Tanovars]. Tashkent: Uzinkomsentr and Ozbekiston Respublik Madaniyat Ishlari Vazirligi.

G'anieva, Rayhon. 2013. Official website. Accessed June 18. http://www.rayhon.uz/.

Gelb, Michael. 1995. "An Early Society Ethnic Deportation: The Far-Eastern Koreans." *Russian Review* 53 (3): 389–412.

Giddings, Paula J. 2011. "Meridians Introduction, 11.2: Nationalism and Its Discontents." *Meridians* 11 (2): v–viii.

Goertzen, Chris. 1997. *Fiddling for Norway: Revival and Identity*. Chicago: University of Chicago Press.

Graham, Stephen. 1916. *Through Russian Central Asia*. New York: MacMillan.

Harris, Rachel. 2002. "Cassettes, Bazaars, and Saving the Nation: The Uyghur Music Industry in Xinjiang, China." In *Global Goes Local: Popular Culture in Asia*, edited by Timothy J. Craig and Richard King, 265–83. Honolulu: University of Hawaii Press.

———. 2008. *The Making of a Musical Canon in Chinese Central Asia: The Uyghur Twelve Muqam*. Aldershot, England: Ashgate Publishing.

Harris, Rachel, and Rahila Dawut. 2002. "Mazar Festivals of the Uyghurs: Music, Islam, and the Chinese State." *British Journal of Ethnomusicology* 11 (1): 101–18.

Harris, Rachel, and Rowan Pease. 2013. "Introduction." In *Gender in Chinese Music*, edited by Rachel Harris, Rowan Pease, and Shzr Ee Tan, 1–25. Rochester, NY: University of Rochester Press.

Hill, Juniper. 2009. "The Influence of Conservatory Folk Music Programmes: The Sibelius Academy in Comparative Context." *Ethnomusicology Forum* 18 (2): 207–41.
Hobsbawm, Eric. 1983. "Introduction: Inventing Traditions." In *The Invention of Tradition*, edited by Eric Hobsbawm and Terence Ranger, 1–14. Cambridge: Cambridge University Press.
Hodjayeva, Ro'zibi. 2007. *Dutar Taronalari* [Dutar melodies]. Tashkent: Musiqa.
———. 2008. Personal interview with the author, August 28.
———. 2009a. Personal interview with the author, July 17.
———. 2009b. Personal interview with the author, August 5.
Holmgren, Beth. 1995. "Bug Inspectors and Beauty Queens: The Problems of Translating Feminism into Russian." In *Genders 22: Post-Communism and the Body Politic*, edited by Ellen E. Berry, 15–31. New York: New York University Press.
Hood, Mantle. 1960. "The Challenge of Bi-Musicality." *Ethnomusicology* 4 (2): 55–59.
Hudoinazarova, Gulzoda. 2009. Personal interview with the author, August 4.
Iskandarova, Saida. 2009. "Ashrafi Museum Held Dialog of Arts." *Uzbekistan Today*, September 1. Accessed January 5, 2014. http://old.ut.uz/eng/culture/ashrafi_museum_held_dialog_of_arts.mgr.
Jarustovsky, Boris. 1974. "Soviet Musicology." *Acta Musicologica* 46 (1): 50–57.
Jo'raev, M., and O. Ismonova. 1999. *Qizil Gulning G'unchasi (Kelin Salom)* [The red flower's bud (bride greetings)]. Tashkent: G'afur G'ulom.
Kalmykova, Galina B. 2001. *Ofeliya Yusupova*. Tashkent: Ministry of Culture.
Kamp, Marianne. 2006. *The New Woman in Uzbekistan: Islam, Modernity, and Unveiling under Communism*. Seattle: University of Washington Press.
Kandiyoti, Deniz. 1988. "Bargaining with Patriarchy." *Gender & Society* 2 (3): 274–90.
———. 1998. "Afterword: Some Awkward Questions on Women and Modernity in Turkey." In *Remaking Women: Feminism and Modernity in the Middle East*, edited by Lila Abu-Lughod, 270–87. Princeton, NJ: Princeton University Press.
Karelova, I. 1952. "Noviy Uzbekskiy Balet" [A new Uzbek ballet]. *Sovetskaya Muzyka* [Soviet music] 10: 58–63.
Karimova, Roziya. 1979. *Tantsy Ansamblya "Bakhor"* [The dances of the Bahor Enemble]. Tashkent: G'afur G'ulom.
Karomatov, Faizulla. 1972. *Uzbekskaya Instrumental'naya Muzyka* [Uzbek instrumental music]. Tashkent: G'afur G'ulam.
———. 2005. Personal interview with the author, July 21.
Khalid, Adeeb. 2006. "Backwardness and the Quest for Civilization: Early Soviet Central Asia in Comparative Perspective." *Slavic Review* 65 (2): 231–51.
Kingsbury, Henry. 1988. *Music, Talent, and Performance: A Conservatory Cultural System*. Philadelphia: Temple University Press.
Koskoff, Ellen, ed. 1989. "An Introduction to Women, Music, and Culture." In *Women and Music in Cross-Cultural Perspective*, 1–23. Urbana: University of Illinois Press.
Kraus, Richard Curt. 1989. *Pianos and Politics in China: Middle-Class Ambitions and the Struggle over Western Music*. New York: Oxford University Press.

Kuznetsova, G., and Faruq Sadiqov. 1990. *Gosudarstvennyi Orkestr Narodnykh Instrumentov Uzbekistana imeni Tukhtasina Dzhalilova* [The State Orchestra of Folk Instruments named for Tuxtasin Jalilov]. Tashkent: O'zbekiston.

Lau, Frederick. 1996. "Forever Red: The Invention of Solo *Dizi* Music in Post-1949 China." *British Journal of Ethnomusicology* 5: 113–31.

Leaman, Oliver. 2004. *Islamic Aesthetics: An Introduction*. Edinburgh: Edinburgh University Press.

Lerner, Gerda. 1979. *The Majority Finds Its Past: Placing Women in History*. New York: Oxford University Press.

Levin, Theodore. 1980. "Music in Modern Uzbekistan: The Convergence of Marxist Aesthetics and Central Asian Tradition." *Asian Music* 12 (1): 149–58.

———. 1984. "The Music and Tradition of the Bukharan Shashmaqam in Soviet Uzbekistan." PhD diss., Princeton University.

———. 1993. "The Reterritorialization of Culture in the New Central Asian States: A Report from Uzbekistan." *Yearbook for Traditional Music* 25: 51–59.

———. 1996. *The Hundred Thousand Fools of God: Musical Travels in Central Asia (and Queens, New York)*. Bloomington: Indiana University Press.

———. 2002. "Making Marxist-Leninist Music in Uzbekistan." In *Music and Marx: Ideas, Practice, Politics*, edited by Regula Burckhardt Qureshi, 190–203. New York: Routledge.

Lohman, Laura. 2010. *Umm Kulthūm: Artistic Agency and the Shaping of an Arab Legend, 1967–2007*. Middletown, CT: Wesleyan University Press.

Lubin, Nancy. 1989. "Uzbekistan: The Challenges Ahead." *Middle East Journal* 43 (4): 619–34.

Luong, Pauline Jones. 2002. *Institutional Change and Political Continuity in Post-Soviet Central Asia: Power, Perceptions, and Pacts*. Cambridge: Cambridge University Press.

MacFadyen, David. 2001. *Red Stars: Personality and the Soviet Popular Song 1955–1991*. Montreal: McGill-Queen's University Press.

———. 2002. *Estrada?! Grand Narratives and the Philosophy of the Russian Popular Song since Perestroika*. Montreal: McGill-Queen's University Press.

———. 2006. *Russian Culture in Uzbekistan: One Language in the Middle of Nowhere*. New York: Routledge.

Magrini, Tullia, ed. 2003. "Introduction: Studying Gender in Mediterranean Musical Cultures." In *Music and Gender: Perspectives from the Mediterranean*, 1–32. Chicago: University of Chicago Press.

Mahmudov, Temur. 2006. *Ona Yurtim* [My motherland]. Tashkent: Ishonch.

Manuel, Peter. 1993. *Cassette Culture: Popular Music and Technology in North India*. Chicago: University of Chicago Press.

Marsh, Peter K. 2009. *The Horse-Head Fiddle and the Cosmopolitan Reimagination of Tradition in Mongolia*. London: Routledge.

Martin, Terry. 2001. *The Affirmative Action Empire: Nations and Nationalism in the Soviet Union, 1923–1939*. Ithaca, NY: Cornell University Press.

Matley, Ian Murray. 1994. "The Population and the Land." In *Central Asia: 130 Years of Russian Dominance, a Historical Overview*, 3rd ed., edited by Edward Allworth, 92–130. Durham, NC: Duke University Press.

Matyoqubov, Otanazar. 1990. "19th Century Khorezmian Tanbur Notation: Fixing Music in an Oral Tradition." *Yearbook for Traditional Music* 22: 29–35.

———. 2004. *Maqomot* [Maqoms]. Tashkent: Musiqa.

McClary, Susan. 1994. "Same as It Ever Was: Youth Culture and Music." In *Microphone Fiends: Youth Music and Youth Culture*, edited by Andrew Ross and Tricia Rose, 29–40. New York: Routledge.

McClintock, Anne. 1997. "'No Longer in a Future Heaven': Gender, Race, and Nationalism." In *Dangerous Liaisons: Gender, Nation, and Postcolonial Perspectives*, edited by Anne McClintock, Aamir Mufti, and Ella Shohat, 89–112. Minneapolis: University of Minnesota Press.

McDougall, Bonnie S. 1980. *Mao Zedong's "Talks at the Yan'an Conference on Literature and Art": A Translation of the 1943 Text with Commentary*. Michigan Monographs in Chinese Studies No. 39. Ann Arbor: Center for Chinese Studies, University of Michigan.

Meakin, Annette M. B. 1903. *In Russian Turkestan: A Garden of Asia and Its People*. London: Ballantyne, Hanson.

———. 1907. *Woman in Transition*. London: Methuen.

Merchant, Tanya. 2005. "Identity and Exoticism in Sevara Nazarkhan's *Yol Bolsin*." *Image and Narrative* 11. Accessed May 20, 2013. http://www.imageandnarrative.be/inarchive/worldmusicb_advertising/tanyamerchant.htm.

———. 2006. "Constructing Musical Tradition in Uzbek Institutions." PhD diss., University of California, Los Angeles.

———. 2009. "Popping Tradition: Institutionalizing, Performing, and Consuming Uzbek 'National' Estrada in the 21st Century." *Popular Music and Society* 32 (3): 371–86.

Mirzaeva, Muazzam, and Asqar Musaqulov. 1992. *Ostonasi Tillodan (To'y Qo'shiqlari)* [From the gold of the threshold (wedding songs)]. Tashkent: Fan.

Miszko, Martin. 1995. "The Balalaika—A Reappraisal." *Galpin Society Journal* 48: 130–55.

Mohanty, Chandra Talpade. 1991. "Introduction: Cartographies of Struggle," and "Under Western Eyes: Feminist Scholarship and Colonial Discourses." In *Third World Women and the Politics of Feminism*, edited by Chandra Talpade Mohanty, Ann Russo, and Lourdes Torres, 1–50, 51–80. Bloomington: Indiana University Press.

———. 1997. "Women Workers and Capitalist Scripts: Ideologies of Domination, Common Interests, and the Politics of Solidarity." In *Feminist Genealogies, Colonial Legacies, Democratic Futures*, edited by M. Jacqui Alexander and Chandra Talpade Mohanty, 3–29. New York: Routledge.

———. 1998. "Crafting Feminist Genealogies: On the Geography and Politics of Home, Nation, and Community." In *Talking Visions: Multicultural Feminism in a Transnational Age*, edited by Ella Shohat, 485–500. Cambridge, MA: MIT Press.

Morgan, Robin, ed. 1970. "Introduction." In *Sisterhood Is Powerful: An Anthology of Writings from the Women's Liberation Movement*, xiii–xl. New York: Vintage Books.

Mukhambetova, Asiya. 1995. "The Traditional Musical Culture of Kazakhs in the Social Context of the 20th Century." *The World of Music* 37 (3): 66–83.
Muminova, Mehrihon. 2005. Personal interview with the author, Feburary 13.
Murav'ev, Nikolay Nikolayevich. (1824) 1871. *Muraviev's Journey to Khiva through the Turcoman Country, 1819–1820*. Translated by W. S. A. Lockhart. Calcutta: Foreign Department Press.
Naroditskaya, Inna. 2002. *Song from the Land of Fire: Continuity and Change in the Azerbaijanian Mugham*. New York: Routledge.
Nettl, Bruno. 1995. *Heartland Excursions: Ethnomusicological Reflections on Schools of Music*. Urbana: University of Illinois Press.
Northrop, Douglas. 2004. *Veiled Empire: Gender and Power in Stalinist Central Asia*. Ithaca, NY: Cornell University Press.
Odilov, A. 1995. *O'zbek Xalq Cholg'ularida Ijrochilik Tarixi* [The history of Uzbek folk orchestral performance]. Tashkent: O'qituvchi.
Olson, Laura J. 2004. *Performing Russia: Folk Revival and Russian Identity*. London: RoutledgeCurzon.
Pekker, Yan Borisovich. 1963. *Uzbekskaya Opera* [Uzbek opera]. Moscow: Gosudarstvennoe Muzykal'noe Izdatel'stvo.
Pendle, Karin, ed. 1991. *Women and Music*. Bloomington: Indiana University Press.
Petrosiants, Ashot. (1951) 1990. *Instrumentovedenie: Uzbekskie Narodnye Instrumenty* [Instrumentation: Uzbek folk instruments]. Tashkent: G'afur G'ulom.
Prinsloo, Jeanne. 1999. "Cheer the Beloved Country? Some Thoughts on Gendered Representations, Nationalism, and the Media." *Agenda* 40: 45–53.
Racy, A. J. 2003. *Making Music in the Arab World: The Culture and Artistry of Tarab*. Cambridge: Cambridge University Press.
Rajabi, Yunus. 1970–76. *Shashmaqom*, vols. 1–6. Tashkent: G'afur G'ulom Nashriyoti.
Rajabov, Ishoq. 1963. *Maqomlar Masalasiga Doir* [Concerning the issue of maqoms]. Tashkent: Fan.
Rancier, Megan. 2009a. "The Kazakh Qyl-Qobyz: Biography of an Instrument, Story of a Nation." PhD diss., University of California, Los Angeles.
———. 2009b. "Cultural Speedbumps along the Silk Road, or the Problem of Musical Institutions in Kazakhstan." *SEM Newsletter* 43 (1): 6–7.
Rapport, Evan. 2014. *Greeted with Smiles: Bukharian Jewish Music and Musicians in New York*. New York: Oxford University Press.
Rees, Helen. 2000. *Echoes of History: Naxi Music in Modern China*. New York: Oxford University Press.
———. 2009. "Use and Ownership: Folk Music in the People's Republic of China." In *Music and Cultural Rights*, edited by Andrew N. Weintraub and Bell Yung, 42–85. Urbana: University of Illinois Press.
Rice, Timothy. 1994. *May It Fill Your Soul: Experiencing Bulgarian Music*. Chicago: University of Chicago Press.
———. 2002. "Bulgaria or Chalgaria: The Attenuation of Bulgarian Nationalism in a Mass-Mediated Popular Music." *Yearbook for Traditional Music* 34: 25–46.

———. 2003. "Time, Place, and Metaphor in Musical Experience and Ethnography." *Ethnomusicology* 47 (2): 151–79.
Riley, Denise. 1988. *"Am I That Name?": Feminism and the Category of "Women" in History*. London: Macmillan.
Rosenberger, Nancy. 2012. *Seeking Food Rights: Nation, Inequality and Repression in Uzbekistan*. South Melbourne, Australia: Cengage Learning.
Schuyler, Eugene. 1877. *Turkistan: Notes of a Journey in Russian Turkistan, Khokand, Bukhara, and Kuldja*, vol. 1. New York: Scribner, Armstrong.
Scott, Joan Wallach, ed. 1996. "Introduction." In *Feminism and History*, 1–13. Oxford: Oxford University Press.
Seeger, Anthony. 1993. "Politics and Musical Performance: A Cross-Cultural Examination." *Revista de Musicologia* 16 (1): 499–504.
Shah, Saira. 2001. "Inside Afghanistan: Behind the Veil." Interview with *BBC News*, June 27. Accessed August 21, 2010. http://news.bbc.co.uk/2/hi/south_asia/1410061.stm.
Sharipova, Fatima. 2006. *Ty—Moya Melodiya* [You—my melody]. Tashkent: Sharq.
Shukurova, Faizila. 2008. Personal interview with the author, August 18.
Sirrs, Julie. 2001. "Lifting the Veil on Afghanistan." *The National Interest*, November 1. Accessed August 21, 2010. http://nationalinterest.org/article/lifting-the-veil-on-afghanistan-793.
Skrine, Francis Henry, and Edward Denison Ross. 1899. *The Heart of Asia: A History of Russian Turkestan and Central Asian Khanates from the Earliest Times*. London: Methuen.
Slobin, Mark. 1971. "Conversations in Tashkent." *Asian Music* 2 (2): 7–13.
Sobirova, Sofiya, and Firuza Abdurahimova. 1994. *Ashot Petrosiants*. Tashkent: Murabbiy.
Solomonova, Tamara E., ed. 1979. *Istoria Uzbekskoy Muzyki* [The history of Uzbek music]. Moscow: Muzyka.
Spinetti, Federico. 2005. "Open Borders: Tradition and Tajik Popular Music: Questions of Aesthetics, Identity and Political Economy." *Ethnomusicology Forum* 14 (2): 185–211.
Spruhan, Paul. 2006. "A Legal History of Blood Quantum in Federal Indian Law to 1935." *South Dakota Law Review* 51 (1): 1–51.
Steinholt, Yngvar B., and David-Emil Wickström. 2009. "Introduction." *Popular Music and Society* 32 (3): 307–11.
Stock, Jonathan. 1996. *Musical Creativity in Twentieth-Century China: Abing, His Music, and Its Changing Meanings*. Rochester, NY: University of Rochester Press.
———. 2001. "Toward an Ethnomusicology of the Individual, or Biographical Writing in Ethnomusicology." *The World of Music* 43 (1): 5–19.
Strong, Anna Louise. 1929. *Red Star in Samarkand*. New York: Coward-McCann.
Stronski, Paul. 2010. *Tashkent: Forging a Soviet City, 1930–1966*. Pittsburgh: University of Pittsburgh Press.
Sugarman, Jane C. 1997. *Engendering Song: Singing and Subjectivity at Prespa Albanian Weddings*. Chicago: University of Chicago Press.

Sultanova, Razia. 2005. "Music and Identity in Central Asia: Introduction." *Ethnomusicology Forum* 14 (2): 131–42.

———. 2011. *From Shamanism to Sufism: Women, Islam and Culture in Central Asia*. London: I. B. Tauris.

Suny, Ronald Grigor. 2000. "Nationalities in the Russian Empire." *Russian Review* 59 (4): 487–92.

———. 2001. "Constructing Primordialism: Old Histories for New Nations." *Journal of Modern History* 73 (4): 862–96.

Tomoff, Kiril. 2004. "Uzbek Music's Separate Path: Interpreting 'Anticosmopolitanism' in Stalinist Central Asia, 1949–52." *Russian Review* 63: 212–40.

Turino, Thomas. 2000. *Nationalists, Cosmopolitans, and Popular Music in Zimbabwe*. Chicago: University of Chicago Press.

UNESCO. 2013. "Cultural Space of Boysun District." Accessed December 16. http://www.unesco.org/culture/ich/en/RL/00019.

Usmanova, Yulduz. 2013. Official website. Accessed June 20. http://www.yulduz.uz.

Uspensky, Viktor A. 1924. *Shest' Muzykal'nykh Poem (Makom)* [Six musical poems (maqom)]. Bukhara: Izdanie Narodnogo Nazarata Prosvesheniya Bukhrespubliki.

van Nieuwkerk, Karin. 2010. *"A Trade Like Any Other": Female Singers and Dancers in Egypt*. Austin: University of Texas Press.

Vyzgo, Tamara. 1972. "Uzbekskaya Kontserno-Etnograficheskaya Truppa" [The Uzbek concert-ethnographic troupe], "Muzykal'naya Kul'tura Uzbekistana v 1933–1941 Godakh" [The musical culture of Uzbekistan from 1933–1941], "Pervye Muzykal'nye Uchebnye Zavedeniya" [The first musical educational institutions], and "Sozdaniye Opery" [The creation of opera]. In *Istoria Uzbekskoy Sovetskoy Muzyki*, tom 1 [The history of Uzbek Soviet music, vol. 1], edited by Tamara Vyzgo, I. N. Karelova, and Faizulla Karomatov, 81–85, 103–12, 129–43, and 168–90. Tashkent: G'afur G'ulom.

Weber, Charlotte. 2008. "Between Nationalism and Feminism: The Eastern Women's Congresses of 1930 and 1932." *Journal of Middle East Women's Studies* 4 (1): 83–106.

Wenger, Etienne. 1998. *Communities of Practice: Learning, Meaning and Identity*. Cambridge: Cambridge University Press.

Whiteley, Sheila, ed. 1997. "Introduction." In *Sexing the Groove: Popular Music and Gender*, xiii–xxxvi. London: Routledge.

Wong, Chuen-Fung. 2006. "The Future of the Uyghur Musical Past: Reconstructing Uyghur Muqam in Chinese Central Asia." *Asian Musicology* 9: 7–62.

Wong, Deborah. 2001. *Sounding the Center: History and Aesthetics in Thai Buddhist Performance*. Chicago: University of Chicago Press.

Yano, Christine R. 2002. *Tears of Longing: Nostalgia and the Nation in Japanese Popular Song*. Cambridge, MA: Harvard University Asia Center.

Yusupova, Ofeliya. 2008. Personal interview with the author, August 28.

Zakrzhevskaya, S. 1968. "K Voprosu o Stanovlenii i Kharaktere Garmonii v Uzbekskoi Professional'noy Muzyke" [To the question of the creation and character of harmony in Uzbek professional music]. In *Ocherki Istorii Muzykal'noy Kul'tury*

Uzbekistana [Excerpts of the history of Uzbekistan's musical culture], edited by I. Rusanova and I. Akhmedova, 212–23. Tashkent: Uqituvchi.

Zemtsovsky, Izaly, and Alma Kunanbaeva. 1997. "Communism and Folklore." In *Folklore and Traditional Music in the Former Soviet Union and Eastern Europe*, edited by James Porter, 3–23. Los Angeles: UCLA Department of Ethnomusicology.

Zeranska-Kominek, Slawomira, Beniamin Kostrubiec, and Joanna Wierzejewska. 1982. "Universal Symbols in the Bukharan Shashmaqam." *Asian Music* 14 (1): 74–93.

Zhang, Zhen. 2000. "Mediating Time: The 'Rice Bowl of Youth' in Fin de Siècle China." *Public Culture* 12 (1): 93–113.

Zheng, Tiantian. 2013. "From Courtesans to Modern Hostesses: Music and Construction of Gender in the Entertainment Industry in China." In *Gender in Chinese Music*, edited by Rachel Harris, Rowan Pease, and Shzr Ee Tan, 66–81. Rochester, NY: University of Rochester Press.

Ziyaeva, Malika. 2004. Personal interview with the author, October 25.

———. 2005a. Personal interview with the author, March 22.

———. 2005b. Personal interview with the author, June 15.

———. 2005c. Personal interview with the author, January 5.

———. 2005d. Personal interview with the author, January 7.

———. 2008. *Dutar: F. Sodiqov Ijro Uslubi* [Dutar: F. Sodiqov's performing style]. Tashkent: Uzbek State Conservatory Publishing Department.

———. 2009. Personal interview with the author, July 29.

———. 2014. Personal interview with the author, July 9.

Discography

During, Jean. 1999. *Uzbekistan: Great Voices of the Past (1940–1965)*. Ocora C 560142.

G'anieva, Rayhon. 2004. *Sevgilim* [My love]. Pan Terra Studio.

———. 2005. *Faqat Muhabbat* [Only love]. Pan Terra Studio.

———. 2007. *Sog'indim* [I missed you]. Pan Terra Studio.

———. 2009. *Orzuinga Ishon* [Believe in your dreams]. Pan Terra Studio.

Hvorostovsky, Dmitri, and the Ossipov Russian Folk Orchestra. 1992. *Dark Eyes: Russian Folk Songs*. Philips 434 080-2.

The Ilyas Malayev Ensemble. 1997. *At the Bazaar of Love: Timeless Central Asian Maqâm Music*. Shanachie B000000E43.

Invisible Face of the Beloved: Classical Music of the Tajiks and Uzbeks. 2005. Music of Central Asia, vol. 2. Smithsonian Folkways SFW40521.

Nazarkhan, Sevara. 2002. *Otmagay Tong* [Don't let the dawn come]. Yitco Entertainment DA 0097.

———. 2003. *Yol Bolsin* [Where are you going?]. Real World Records 7243 543206 2 0.

———. 2007. *Sen* [You]. Real World Records W145 884108 2 8.

———. 2011. *Tortadur* [Stretching/pulling/melting]. Sevaramusic.com.

Pirmatova, Nodira. 2010. *Popular Classics from Bukhara and Beyond*. Music of Central Asia, vol. 7. Smithsonian Folkways SFW40526.

Shashmaqam. 1991. *Music of the Bukharan Jewish Ensemble Shashmaqam.* Smithsonian Folkways SFW40054.

Tajikistan: Maqâm Navâ. 1997. Ocora PID6541.

Varimezova, Tzvetanka. 2005. *Tzvetanka's Magic: Bulgarian Traditional Songs.* Varimezova 4978.

Yulchieva, Munâjât. 1994. *Ouzbekistan: Munâjât Yulchieva.* Ocora B001DETD7S.

Yulchieva, Munadjat, and Ensemble Shavkat Mirzaev. 1997. *Munadjat Yulchieva and Ensemble Shavkat Mirzaev: A Haunting Voice,* vol. 38: Uzbekistan. WDR World Network 28.297.

Index

Abdullayev, Rustam (composer), 115, 121–22, 124
Abdullayev, Rustam S. (musicologist), 97
Abdullayeva, Nasiba, 146
Abdurahimova, Firuza, 80, 91–95, 116, 181; director of Sogdiana Folk Orchestra, 28, 40, 102–4; international outreach, 98–99, 107–8, 177; remembers Soviet era, 12, 38, 89, 116
Abdurahmanova, Dilbara, 12, 116–20, 122–24, 128, 181; director of Alisher Navoiy Opera, 17, 28, 41, 92; international outreach, 115–16, 130
Abdurasulov, Hoja Abulaziz, 53
Agrenev-Slavianskiy, Dmitri, 84–85
Akilova, Viloyat, 22–23
Al Farabi, 47–48
Alimatov, Turgun, 60–61, 65
Alisher Navoiy State Opera and Ballet, 124, 180; directed by Dilbara Abdurahmanova, 17, 28, 41, 92, 117–20; state-run institution, 32, 111
Aminova, Komila, 40, 172; member of maqom ensemble, 72–73, 152; student of Faxriddin Sodiqov, 66, 76; voice teacher, 27, 59–63
Andreev, Vasiliy, 84
Arabov, Ilyos, 178
arranged folk music (halq cholg'u musiqasi), 16, 24, 30, 64–65, 78–108, 160; conservatory department, 33, 51, 138, 170, contrast with traditional music, 50, 177–78, 181; and dance, 20–21, 44; ensembles, 40, 55, 73–75; pedagogy, 26–27, 54, 73; in state institutions, 36, 140, 174–75
Ashrafiy, Muxtor: composer, 111, 116, 127; directory of Alisher Navoiy Opera, 113, 116–18; director of conservatory, 56, 87, 90
Ataboeva, Gulshod, 22–23
atlas (national fabric), 42, 70, 146, 184

backwardness, 84, 86, 101, 126
Balasanyan, Sergei, 112
bazm (wedding reception), 159–61, 165, 168
Begmatov, Soib, 51–52, 54, 100
Beliaev, Viktor, 10, 50, 52
Bojalar, 142
Bukhara, viii, 23, 54, 151; city of Shashmaqom 10, 12–13, 19, 47, 49–50; history, ix, 5, 29, 31
Bukharan Jewish musicians and communities, 12, 17, 23
Buran (the storm), 111–12, 116, 119

canonization: of male masters, 45–48, 63–66, 66–67; of maqom, 19, 51–53, 71, 128
challar (bride's return home), 153, 165
chang (hammer dulcimer): performing contexts, 42, 55, 75, 175; played by Faizila Shukurova, 40, 87, 89–91, 162
code switching, vii, ix, 33–35, 123, 145
community of practice, 41, 173–74
Composers' Union, 111, 113, 115, 124–25
cosmopolitanism, 33, 40, 120, 176–77; historical, 12, 123; in Tashkent, 29–30, 33, 106–8, 160, 182

dance, 49, 55, 90, 113, 184; concertized folk dance, 20–24, 44, 80, 84–85; in educational institutions, 100, 121; in estrada concerts, 131, 133–35, 146, 151; at a gap 172, 174; at weddings, 159–62, 165–66, 169. *See also* tanovar

dancing boys, 5–6

doyra (frame drum): in estrada, 144–45, 147–48; played by women, 20, 81, 89; in traditional music, 42, 171, at weddings, 17, 157, 168

Dudin, S. M., 6–8

duppi (national dress), 42, 44, 58, 70, 181, 184

dutar (plucked lute), viii, 3–4; associations with femininity, 89, 177; contrasting styles, 35, 40, 97–99, 174–76; in estrada, 148, 151; Hodjayeva lessons, 26–28, 96; memories of, 90, 92, 94; and nationalism, 39, 59, 77, 82, 184; performance of maqom, 42–44, 56, 58–59, 69, 172; at weddings, 156–57, 159, 161–62; women's history playing, 6–7, 20, 55, 65; Ziyaeva lessons, 13, 24–26, 67. *See also* dutar ensembles, Uzbek State TeleRadio Company: Young Women's Dutar Ensemble; women's dutar ensembles

dutar ensembles, 45, 73–76, 104–7, 109. *See also* dutar; Uzbek State TeleRadio Company: Young Women's Dutar Ensemble; women's dutar ensembles

estrada, 16, 41, 131–55, 174; pedagogy, 12, 14, 54, 65, 97, 100; at weddings, 27, 96, 159–67, 169

Fayzullayev, Boboqul, 10–11, 50, 52, 64
Fitrat, Abdurauf, 9, 19, 50, 52–53
Fizuli, 112
Friendship of Nations Concert Hall (Bunyodkor Concert Hall): estrada concerts, 131, 135, 142, 146–47, 151; renaming, 16, 41

G'anieva, Rayhon, 16, 41, 131–34, 142–45, 168
Garayev, Gara, 112
gender norms: enforcement of, 38, 139, 142, 160, 176–77, 182; in musical performance, 74, 89, 137, 179
gender performance, 3, 163, 166, 176
gijak (bowed lute), 42, 74, 191
Glière, Reinhold, 112
Glière Music School, 15, 117

Hajibeyov, Uzeyir, 112
Hodjayeva, Ro'zibi (Ro'za), 40, 94–96, 181; dutar teacher, 26–27, 78–81, 99, 104–8; remembers the Soviet era, 46, 74, 89; wedding performer, 156–59, 160–62, 169, 180
Hudoinazarova, Gulzoda: and estrada, 41, 135, 150–55; traditional training, 139, 144–45, 174, 181
hujum: and education, 12–13, 21; effect on music, 55, 65–67, 87, 90, 107, 167, 181; as emancipatory project, 8–9, 22, 89

Ibn Sino/Avicenna, 47
ichkari (interior/private sphere): musical performance in, 13, 20, 40, 75, 77; as women's domain, 55, 180
international standard (for music): for arranged folk music, 40, 86, 101, 106–7; for Western art music, 112, 114, 118, 122, 129–30
Ishakova, Barno, 17, 66
Izrailova, Zulfiya, 71

Jadids, 9, 19, 50
Jalilov, Tuxtasin (composer), 53, 78–79. *See also* Tuxtasin Jalilov Folk Orchestra
juries/performance exams, 28, 110, 138, 149

karaoke, 16, 41, 133, 137, 163, 167
Kari Yaqubov, Muxitdin, 21
karnay (long trumpet), 16–17
Karomatov, Faizulla: founder of conservatory's traditional music department, 33, 56; musicologist, 19, 48, 64, 86–88, 127
kelin salom (bride greeting ritual), 153, 156–61, 163, 165, 168–69
Khanum, Tamara, 21, 113
Khiva: history, ix, 5, 29, 31; maqom in, 19, 47, 49, 51
kollej (music high school), 57, 69, 73, 87–89, 92, 97
koryo saram (Korean diaspora), 33
Kulthûm, Umm, 28, 183

Leila and Majnun (Leili i Majnun), 111–12, 119
Leningrad Conservatory, 124, 127
Lola, 16, 142

Mahmudov, Temur, 53, 69
maqom, 15, 18–19, 42–76, 150–52; and dance, 20, 22; on dutar, 25–26, 175; as foundation

for arranged folk music, 93–94, 99–100; pedagogy, 33, 127, 178; three repertoires, 12–13, 40, 172; at to'ylar, 165, 169. *See also* maqom ensemble at the Uzbek State Tele-Radio Company; Shashmaqom; Tashkent-Feghana maqom; Xorazm maqom; Yunus Rajabi Maqom Competition

maqom ensemble at the Uzbek State Tele-Radio Company, 16, 63, 148–49; women's roles in, 56–58, 60, 62, 72–73, 152, 181

master-apprentice system. *See* ustozshog'ird system

Meakin, Annette, 6–8, 55

Melodiya record company, 134

Mirzaev, Shavkat, 59, 62, 65, 66–67

modesty/modest attire: in arranged folk music, 103–4, 176–77; in estrada, 134, 139, 180; in traditional music, 103–4, 176–77

Moiseyev, Igor, 22, 85

morality, 5, 39, 103–4, 177; and estrada, 133, 140–41, 144, 146, 154; and wedding performance, 137, 180; and women on stage, 62, 87, 90, 167, 181

Moscow Conservatory, 121

motherhood, 37–38, 153, 177–78

Muminova, Mehrihon, 39, 70, 77, 178, 184

Murav'ev, Nikolay, 5

Mushel, G., 113

musical literacy: in arranged folk music, 40, 85, 93, 95, 97; and prestige, 15, 56, 110, 129, 139–40, 175

musical notation/scores, 8, 118, 125; in arranged folk music, 78, 91, 98–99; and musical literacy, 56, 97, 129; in traditional music, 51, 52, 64, 109–10

music lessons, 15, 123; dutar lessons, 3, 24–27, 67, 70, 178; voice lessons, 59–61, 110

music schools: classes, lessons, and rehearsals at, 15, 27, 58, 69, 89; curriculum, 53, 100, 137; ensembles in, 73–74, 78; women's early education in, 11, 44, 56, 93, 95, 121. *See also* Glière Music School; kollej; Uspensky Music School

music videos (kliplar): estrada in, 44, 132, 145, 166; watching of, 27, 44, 143

Nancy Ajram, 144

national dress, 38, 82, 104; in estrada, 138–39, 144, 154–55; in traditional music, 42, 44, 72. *See also* atlas; duppi

Navoiy, Alisher, 48, 71

nay (transverse flute), 151

Nazarkhan, Sevara, 41, 144–45, 147–50, 152, 154–55; recordings, 148–49, 172; traditional training, 135, 139, 150, 174

Nihol (sprout) Award, 151

nikox to'y (marriage ceremony), 153, 159–60, 164–65, 168

nola (vibrato-like vocal ornamentation), 43, 59, 61

nostalgia, 36, 179, 183

Oltin Meros television program, 42–43

osh (pilaf), 164, 172

Ota Jalol/Ata Jalal-Eddin-Nazirov, 52–53

Oybek va Nigora, 142

patriotic songs, 101, 138, 144, 147, 151–52, 155

Petrosiants, Ashot, 94, 95, 108; creator of reconstructed instruments, 11, 49, 84–87, 106, 175–85; students of, 91, 93

Piatnitskiy, Mitrofan, 84–85

Pirmatova, Nodira, 17

Primkulov, Bahrom, 149

Rajabi, Yunus: as member of canon, 53, 63–65; transcriptions of Shashmaqom, 10–11, 47, 52–53, 56–57, 67, 71. *See also* Yunus Rajabi Maqom Competition

Real World Records, 145, 148, 150

rubob (plucked lute), 15, 90, 147; played by women and girls, 75, 89, 92, 95, 99; in traditional music, 42, 48, 55–56

Russian Association of Proletarian Musicians (RAPM), 84

Russian Turkistan, 4–9, 19, 29

Safarov, Bekzod, 151

Samarqand, 87, 90, 92, 115, 117, 120; history, 8, 12, 19, 54, 92; regional link to Bukhara, 12, 19, 54

Sart, 6–8

Schuyler, Eugene, 5, 8

shared repertoire between Jewish and Muslim musicians, 17, 48, 50

Sharq Taronalari (Eastern Melodies, a festival sponsored by UNESCO), 151

Shashmaqom, 16, 36, 174; learning of, 70, 179; as men's repertoire, 13, 17, 55; multiethnic and multireligious, 9–12, 50–51, 71, 125; recordings of, 23, 147–48; as regional repertoire, 18–19, 40, 60–61, transcriptions, 52–54, 63–65

Shukrona Ensemble, 59, 73

Shukurova, Faizila, 40, 80, 108, 162, 181; remembers the Soviet era, 87–88, 89–91, 103–4
Skrine, Francis Henry, 5–6
Sodiqov, Faruq, 93
Sodiqov, Faxriddin, 53, 59, 62, 66, 69
Sogdiana Folk Orchestra (full name: Sogdiana Uzbek Chamber Folk Orchestra), 28, 40, 92, 101–4, 107
sponsorship/private sponsors, 137, 139, 141–42, 150–53
Strong, Anna Louise, 87–88, 89
Sultanova, Razia, 1–4, 24–25, 36, 66, 164
surnay (shawm), 16–17, 144–45, 151, 161, 168

Taghiev, Alakbar, 132
talent, 46, 85, 125, 152; debate over, 135, 137–42, 154; as hereditary, 13, 68; and youth, 56–58, 87, 117, 144–45, 153
tanbur (plucked lute), 42, 48, 51, 74–75, 151
tanovar, 12, 21, 95–96, 159, 161, 169
Tashkent Conservatory. *See* Uzbek State Conservatory
Tashkent-Ferghana maqom, 12, 19, 40, 51, 60–61
Tereshkova, Valentina, 116
Toshmuhamedov, Mulla To'ychi, 53
to'ylar (life cycle celebrations), 16–17, 75, 156–59, 164. *See also* bazm; challar; kelin salom; nikox toy; wedding music; wedding musicians
transcription, 57, 64–65, 67, 71, 110
travelers' tales, 4–8, 55, 71–72, 87–89
Turgunbaeva, Mukkaram, 21
Tuxtasin Jalilov State Folk Orchestra, 92, 85, 101

UNESCO, 17, 48, 65–66, 108, 151. *See also* Sharq Taronalari
Usmanova, Yulduz, 41, 142, 145–48, 154–55, 183; traditional training, 135, 139, 150
Uspensky, Viktor, 19, 50, 52, 64, 110, 113
Uspensky Music School, 15, 121
ustoz-shog'ird system (master-apprentice system), 48, 65–66, 76, 83, 107, 113
Uzbek State Conservatory, 16–17, 26–28, 130, 153; arranged folk music department, 85, 97, 102; curriculum, 51–52, 69, 110, 116; directors, 41, 56, 90, 117, 120–22; estrada department, 134–35, 137–41, 154; faculty, 65–67, 86–87, 92, 163, 170–71; Leningrad Conservatory evacuation to, 124–25, 127; lessons and rehearsals at, 60–62, 78, 80, 92, 109; new building, 14, 78; prestige, 128, 173, 180; as state-run institution, 9, 11–12, 31–32, 107–11, 160, 168; students, 70, 73–74, 89–91, 97–100, 108, 115, 123, 178–79; Tashkent Conservatory, 12, 24, 33, 56–58, 62, 93–95, 116, 121; traditional music department, 15, 19, 36, 44–45, 48–49, 146–47, 149–52
Uzbek State Philharmonic, 86, 91, 121, 125, 180
Uzbek State TeleRadio Company: ensembles housed there, 16, 26, 28, 32, as primary media outlet, 14, 49; as state-run institution, 9, 65, 137; Young Women's Dutar Ensemble, 74, 80–81, 95 (*see also* maqom ensemble at the State TeleRadio Company)

vachcha. *See* dancing boys
vocal ornaments. *See* nola

wedding music. *See also* wedding musicians
wedding musicians, 26, 41, 151, 156–69, 180. *See also* wedding music
women's dutar ensembles (dutorchi qizlar ansembli), 27–28, 73–74, 77–78, 80–83, 95. *See also* dutar; dutar ensembles; Uzbek State TeleRadio Company: Young Women's Dutar Ensemble

Xatamov, Orifxon, 53
Xorazm maqom, 12, 19, 40, 51

Yoshlar television channel, 42
Yulchieva, Munojat: as Mirzaev's student, 59, 61–62, 66–67; vocalist, 17, 40, 65, 76, 96
Yunus Rajabi Maqom Competition, 27, 63, 151
Yusupova, Ofeliya, 41, 120–22, 181; pianist, 28, 124, 177; publicizing Uzbek compositions, 115–16, 128, 130

Zazou, Hector, 148–49
Ziyaeva, Malika, viii, 40, 53, 55–64, 151, 170–73; dutarist, 68–76, 97–98; lessons with, ix, 24–27; radio maqom ensemble member, 13, 42–44, 152; remembers the Soviet era, 38, 89, 95, 99, 177; student of Faxriddin Sodiqov, 66–67; teacher/ensemble director, 103, 109, 178–81

TANYA MERCHANT is an assistant professor of ethnomusicology at the University of California, Santa Cruz.

New Perspectives on Gender in Music

In Her Own Words: Conversations with Composers
    in the United States   *Jennifer Kelly*
Roll Over Tchaikovsky! Russian Popular Music
    and Post-Soviet Homosexuality   *Stephen Amico*
A Feminist Ethnomusicology: Writings on Music
    and Gender   *Ellen Koskoff*
Stunning Males and Powerful Females: Gender
    and Tradition in East Javanese Dance   *Christina Sunardi*
Women Musicians of Uzbekistan: From Courtyard
    to Conservatory   *Tanya Merchant*

The University of Illinois Press
is a founding member of the
Association of American University Presses.

Composed in 10.5/13 Adobe Minion Pro
at the University of Illinois Press
Manufactured by Cushing-Malloy, Inc.

University of Illinois Press
1325 South Oak Street
Champaign, IL 61820-6903
www.press.uillinois.edu